Opting Out

The Politics of Marriage and Gender:
Global Issues in Local Contexts

Series Editor: Péter Berta

The Politics of Marriage and Gender: Global Issues in Local Context series from Rutgers University Press fills a gap in research by examining the politics of marriage and related practices, ideologies, and interpretations, and addresses the key question of how the politics of marriage has affected social, cultural, and political processes, relations, and boundaries. The series looks at the complex relationships between the politics of marriage and gender, ethnic, national, religious, racial, and class identities, and analyzes how these relationships contribute to the development and management of social and political differences, inequalities, and conflicts.

For a list of all the titles in the series, please see the last page of the book.

Opting Out

Women Messing with Marriage around the World

EDITED BY JOANNA DAVIDSON AND
DINAH HANNAFORD

RUTGERS UNIVERSITY PRESS

NEW BRUNSWICK, CAMDEN, AND NEWARK, NEW JERSEY, AND LONDON

LIBRARY OF CONGRESS CATALOGING-IN-PUBLICATION DATA

Names: Davidson, Joanna, 1969– editor. | Hannaford, Dinah, editor.
Title: Opting out : women messing with marriage around the world /
    edited by Joanna Davidson and Dinah Hannaford.
Description: New Brunswick, New Jersey : Rutgers University Press, [2023] |
    Series: Politics of marriage and gender: global issues in local contexts |
    Includes bibliographical references and index.
Identifiers: LCCN 2022009275 | ISBN 9781978830103 (paperback) |
    ISBN 9781978830110 (hardback) | ISBN 9781978830127 (epub) |
    ISBN 9781978830134 (pdf)
Subjects: LCSH: Single women—Cross-cultural studies. |
    Marriage—Cross-cultural studies.
Classification: LCC HQ800.2 .O68 2023 | DDC 306.81/53—dc23/eng/20220303
LC record available at https://lccn.loc.gov/2022009275

A British Cataloging-in-Publication record for this book is
available from the British Library.

∞ The paper used in this publication meets the requirements of the American
National Standard for Information Sciences—Permanence of Paper for
Printed Library Materials, ANSI Z39.48-1992.

www.rutgersuniversitypress.org

Manufactured in the United States of America

To Our Husbands

CONTENTS

PART THREE
Within Marriage

SERIES FOREWORD

The politics of marriage (and divorce) is an often-used strategic tool in various social, cultural, economic, and political identity projects as well as in symbolic conflicts between ethnic, national, or religious communities. Despite having multiple strategic applicabilities, pervasiveness in everyday life, and huge significance in performing and managing identities, the politics of marriage is surprisingly underrepresented both in the international book publishing market and in the social sciences.

The Politics of Marriage and Gender: Global Issues in Local Contexts is a series from Rutgers University Press examining the politics of marriage as a phenomenon embedded into and intensely interacting with much broader social, cultural, economic, and political processes and practices such as globalization; transnationalization; international migration; human trafficking; vertical social mobility; the creation of symbolic boundaries between ethnic populations, nations, religious denominations, or classes; family formation; and struggles for women's and children's rights. The series primarily aims to analyze practices, ideologies, and interpretations related to the politics of marriage, and to outline the dynamics and diversity of relatedness—interplay and interdependence, for instance—between the politics of marriage and the broader processes and practices mentioned above. In other words, most books in the series devote special attention to how the politics of marriage and these processes and practices mutually shape and explain each other.

The series concentrates on, among other things, the complex relationships between the politics of marriage and gender, ethnic, national, religious, racial, and class identities globally and examines how these relationships contribute to the development and management of social, cultural, and political differences, inequalities, and conflicts.

The series seeks to publish single-authored books and edited volumes that develop a gap-filling and thought-provoking critical perspective, that are well balanced between a high degree of theoretical sophistication and empirical richness, and that cross or rethink disciplinary, methodological, or theoretical boundaries. The thematic scope of the series is intentionally left broad to encourage creative submissions that fit within the perspectives outlined above.

Among the potential topics closely connected with the problem sensitivity of the series are "honor"-based violence; arranged (forced, child, etc.) marriage; transnational marriage markets, migration, and brokerage; intersections of marriage and religion/class/race; the politics of agency and power within marriage; reconfiguration of family; same-sex marriage/union; the politics of love, intimacy, and desire; marriage and multicultural families; the (religious, legal, etc.) politics of divorce; the causes, forms, and consequences of polygamy in contemporary societies; sport marriage; refusing marriage; and so forth.

Opting Out: Women Messing with Marriage around the World offers a fascinating new perspective on studying the dynamics of marriage. Instead of focusing on often researched topics such as why and on the basis of which preferences marriage is established in various sociocultural contexts or how it functions, the authors propose a refreshing analytical lens that concentrates on why and how women try to avoid or reject marriage in places where it has long been obligatory. The ethnographically informed chapters in this volume not only analyze the most frequent causes, forms, and consequences of gendered resistance within the context of and to the institution of marriage but also shed light on complex cases where women reject entering into marriage (or into remarriage). By meticulously examining ethnographic contexts where marriage becomes disappointing for more and more women, the authors convincingly outline how and why the steadily growing individual need to reconceptualize the value, significance, and meaning of marriage emerges, and they also demonstrate the limits and risks of this effort. A detailed analysis of the global tendency of decreasing popularity of marriage not only can contribute to a better understanding of the most important local, transnational, or global·transformations that are behind this tendency but also draws attention to the need to concentrate the analytical gaze more and more consistently on how marriage as a social institution itself is undergoing significant transformations.

Péter Berta
University College London, School of Slavonic and
East European Studies / Budapest Business School,
Department of Communication

Opting Out

Introduction

Messing with Marriage

JOANNA DAVIDSON AND DINAH HANNAFORD

> The most incomprehensible thing in the world to a man, is a woman who rejects his offer of marriage!
>
> –Jane Austen, *Emma*

Women around the world, it seems, are opting out of marriage. Unprecedented divorce proceedings initiated by women in Japan, "singles day" celebrations in China, increasing numbers of single women in India, widows and divorcées who sidestep remarriage in Guinea-Bissau and Brazil, women who "forget" to marry in South Korea, Senegalese women who marry absent migrant men, white women in Barbados who no longer put up with unsatisfying marriages for the sake of respectability, and Southern African women who would not consider forgoing motherhood but increasingly do not bother with marriage. These examples from across the globe intimate a new combination of the accessibility and desirability of alternatives to marriage for women in diverse geographic contexts. This volume examines the conditions that make this widespread—although locally variable—phenomenon possible and considers what the implications of opting out might be, both for marriage itself and for the anthropological study of it.

Opting out does not mean outright rejection of marriage but signifies a range of novel practices both within and outside of marriage that reflect changing economic, legal, demographic, and ideological circumstances for women and suggests that a reworking of marriage is in motion. This is not, as we elaborate below, a crisis of marriage or masculinity. It is, rather, an unorchestrated but widespread transformative process that may have some common causes and outcomes but is also as varied and improvisational as the "messy, often contradictory activities at the heart of women's everyday lives" (Takeyama, this volume; see also Abu-Lughod 1998, 25).[1]

This volume is not an attempt to redefine marriage, nor is it a collective effort that points to its demise. Rather, it is an assemblage of nuanced ethnographic analyses that show us a wide array of ways that women are confronting unanticipated conjugal challenges, reckoning with long-standing inequities inherent in wifehood, and carving out fulfilling lives within and outside of marriage. Many of these life paths have existed under the radar, invisible to researchers and, in some cases, to those in close proximity—relatives, neighbors, friends—to these very women. This absence of recognition (Davidson, this volume) or willful erasure (Nelson, this volume) has its own logic; the very silence and lack of a lexicon to name these phenomena, novel relationships, or even the women themselves speaks (albeit in quiet and coded ways) to deeper fissures and more profound realignments in social relations more generally.

Not only are we qualifying our use of "opting out" in terms of its more subtle and multidimensional relationship to transformations within and outside marriage, but we also want to add a note of caution with regard to the agentive assumptions such a phrase implies. Many of the chapters in this volume emphasize the very mixed emotions that women have about marrying or not marrying, and most—if not all—of these women find themselves in unanticipated circumstances wrought by forces beyond their own control. Opting out is not only tempered by various constraints, and often enacted within an already limiting set of choices, but also not necessarily experienced as unequivocally liberating or celebratory. Carla Freeman captures this ambiguity well when a Bajan woman, in telling her story, vacillates from "stoic and confident to emotionally vulnerable and a little sad." Likewise, Jacqueline Solway accentuates women's increased ambivalence toward marriage, rather than their explicit decisions or ability to dictate their marital status. Laura Nelson reveals how unmarried women in South Korea "slip into spinsterhood" as an unplanned outcome, often resulting from taking care of their parents, although they somewhat sheepishly admit to Nelson that "it's good not to be married." Both Sarah Lamb and Julia Pauli are even more pointed when they insist that choice simply does not accurately represent what is going on in Bengali or Namibian women's experiences of singledom, in terms of either their desires or their realistic possibilities regarding marriage. As these examples suggest, opting out of marriage is usually not fully by design. By continuing to use the term, however, we want to strike a balance between calling attention to the ways in which women are working to shape new marital dynamics, without exaggerating their autonomy or romanticizing their agency in doing so.[2] There are contrasting shades of choice and constraint, autonomy and ambivalence that texture these women's marital and unmarried experiences, and the chapters in this volume consider each of these facets as they sharpen our collective understanding of contemporary conjugal change. In this way, this book heeds the call for a more inclusive version of feminist scholarship that attends to the paradoxes often definitive of women's lives, both within and outside the bounds of marriage, or somewhere in between.

But why are we just talking about women? Haven't men been opting out of marriage for much longer, in much greater numbers, and perhaps with even better success and validation? By choosing to focus exclusively on women we are not suggesting that men do not opt out, nor are we denying the importance of studying their reasons for doing so (although we do note that much attention has already been brought to bear on these dynamics for men, especially in terms of their decreasing economic capacity to "earn" a wife, which leads to their extended and often embittered "waithood" [Singerman 2007; Inhorn and Smith-Hefner 2020]). Nonetheless, we intentionally choose to place women at center stage on this unfolding drama for a number of intertwined reasons. First, we want to highlight how many of the dynamics pertaining to opting out are also, in overlapping ways, shaped by and shaping new possibilities—financial, sexual, social, professional— for women's personhood. This, in turn, is not only influencing marital outcomes but also coming head to head with long-standing patriarchal prerogatives. By focusing squarely on how women are operating outside the normative boundaries of marriage—even when they are doing so as wives—we hope to shine an even brighter light on the inequities and absurdities often swept under the rug of assumed marital compliance and resignation.

There is actually nothing new or surprising in the fact that women are the transformative agents here. Parkin and Nyamwaya's (1987, 16) edited volume, *Transformations of African Marriage*, predicted decades ago that "it will not be strange if it is . . . women who will bring about the greatest transformations in ideas and practices relating to marriage in Africa. For, though women have often been depicted as the backbone of the agricultural economy and as subordinate producers of men's children, they have also been shown . . . as the primary agents of change in marriage and the family. The ambivalence in women's status . . . is perhaps the pivot on which society turns, often in unexpected ways." Even with our caveats regarding agentive choice, we stand by our claim that women are the worthy protagonists of this volume.

Relatedly, although we are focusing on what seem like contemporary phenomena, we are not suggesting that they are *entirely* new. In fact, what we would like to encourage is a revisiting and rereading of marriages in the past. Whether in the form of ghost marriages, Nandi women marrying their parents' house post (Oboler 1985), "rounding up spinsters" in colonial Asante (Allman 1996), "marriage resistance" in nineteenth-century China (Topley 1978), "wicked" women and runaway wives in twentieth-century Africa (Hodgson and McCurdy 2001), the dominance of matrifocality and "visiting unions" in much of the postcolonial African diaspora, or the "wayward lives and beautiful experiments" of young Black women in the ghettos of Philadelphia and Harlem at the turn of the twentieth century (Hartman 2019), it seems that there are hints of women opting out in the cracks and crevices of the historical and anthropological record. Laura Nelson's chapter in this volume is an excellent example of what we might find when we read between the lines of demographic reports, archival records, and family memories. She uncovers the existence of otherwise forgotten single women in South Korea's first decades, thereby debunking the country's claim to universal marriage. Although the rest of the chapters attend to more recent experiences, collectively they open up a series of questions about what the dynamics of opting out might have been in different historical moments, how women might have found ways to buck conventions or even move the needle on marital normativity, and how—like Nelson's demographers—anthropologists and historians might have been blind to these not-quite-marital arrangements given what Setume calls "methodological nuptialism" (Solway, this volume), among other obstacles. We are especially inspired by Saidiya Hartman's groundbreaking effort to write a "fugitive text of the wayward . . . [and] craft a counter-narrative liberated from . . . judgment and classification" (Hartman 2019, xiv). Our own efforts to take seriously the lives of women who do not fit neatly into familiar conjugal categories consistently push back against attempts to pathologize them, characterize them as aberrant, or simply ignore their existence. Rather, we are interested in how these women pave new pathways for intimacy, sociality, and fulfillment as they rearrange marriage in various ways. Their experiences might very well teach us to recognize heretofore unimagined possibilities and a continuum of relational forms for women, both past and present.

Finally, we acknowledge that this volume is limited by its broad focus on heterosexual marriage. Queer romantic partnerships do appear in several chapters (see especially Lamb's chapter), and gender categories are meaningfully troubled when women operate outside of heteronormative conjugal pathways. Women sex workers in India "move like men" (Walters), widows in Guinea-Bissau proclaim they are "both mother and father" (Davidson), and breadwinning, bar-going Southern African women disrupt reigning gender norms (Solway). Still, in all of these settings, heterosexual marriage remains the expected norm with which women must contend. We hasten to add, however, that the legal and public battles for the right to opt in that queer couples continue to wage across the globe have undoubtedly shaped the landscape of possibilities for marital and family formations that all women encounter in the twenty-first century.

Framing Intentions

For the past few years, at annual conferences convened by the American Anthropological Association, the African Studies Association, the American Ethnological Society, and other anthropological watering holes, we noticed that many of our colleagues spoke of women in the places where they conducted research—places where marriage had long been obligatory—who were avoiding or outright rejecting marriage. New coinages like "come-we-stay" partnerships in Kenya, "waithood" across the Middle East, and "white marriage" in Iran spoke to this phenomenon. It seemed like something must be in the water, as Carla Freeman's interlocutor put it, and we wanted to see if we could connect some of these otherwise disparate dots.

Our intention in putting together this volume is threefold: First, we see value in simply gathering these diffuse ethnographic narratives into a collection of case studies that speak to each other from different contexts. Second, as curators and editors of this collection, we probe them for patterns and insights into issues of broader anthropological concern, such as changing relationships between production and reproduction, economy and affect, and natal and affinal ties. Finally, by focusing squarely on shifts in marriage practices that suggest a rejection or avoidance of marriage itself, we ask what the implications of such widespread but heretofore muted or barely visible phenomena might be for anthropology's epistemological and methodological approaches to marriage.

When we began this exploration into the ways in which women were opting out of marriage in various parts of the world, we initially emphasized this last point, framing it as a way that anthropology might think through the decentering of marriage in its own continued focus on conjugality as a central and universal social institution. But as we continued our conversations, and as the ethnographically rich contributions in the form of conference papers and chapters began to accumulate, we found that we had to rethink our initial—and perhaps overzealous—emphasis on the decentering of marriage. Opting out does not require a wholesale rejection of marriage, nor is it a bellwether that marriage itself is on the wane, even though marriage rates have certainly declined in many of the places in which these chapters take place. Instead, by opting out of certain conventional forms and approaches to marriage, these women's experiences opened up the possibility for themselves and for anthropology to think through the reorganization and recalibration of certain aspects of marriage, the continually upheld aspirations for a certain kind of marriage, and the refusal of women to settle for anything less than that, or to be consigned and resigned to the disappointments of marriage. But marriage was still very much at the center, often the forefront, of the imaginations, preoccupations, and practices of the women who were the protagonists of this opting out phenomenon. And in our own reckoning, marriage is still the fulcrum for understanding other forces and changes that work to radically shift the meanings and practices of conjugality itself.

So rather than decentering marriage, either in women's lives or in anthropology's analysis of what was in the proverbial water, we instead ask what the seemingly widespread trend of opting out tells us *about* marriage. Each chapter invites us into the lives of particular women and the changing circumstances in which these lives unfold—sometimes painfully, sometimes humorously, and always unexpectedly. We see some similar dynamics, such as the increasing capacity of women to economically support themselves and the decreasing possibility of men to support women; the concomitant shifting dynamics of dependence and independence within marital and family structures; and changing notions of intimacy, fidelity, and emotional and sexual fulfillment. As these are changing, marriage is rethought, but it does not quite go away. Even when it is not taken up in typical legal and customary frameworks, it cleaves very firmly to the imaginations and aspirations of the women we are chronicling.

The Anthropology of Marriage: A Protracted Engagement

Before elaborating on some of these patterns and dynamics, we briefly consider anthropology's engagement with marriage as both subject and object of inquiry. Anthropologists have been preoccupied with marriage since their first forays into fieldwork. They have charted marriage's emergence, evolution, transformation, and variation. They have debated its definition, function, value, and eventual obsolescence. Kinship and marriage—more often than not appearing together— have served as anthropology's bread and butter since the discipline's earliest days, feeding our field's foundational hunger for human practices and social institutions that seemed at once universal and highly diverse; that is, they could speak to anthropology's animating impetus to grapple with both our shared humanity and our infinitely varied ways of being human. Debates about marriage systems often served as fodder for grand anthropological theory-building projects posited on either/or framings of marriage: Descent or alliance? Monogamous or polygamous? Endogamous or exogamous? Traditional or modern? Marriage has also served as a productive lens through which anthropologists have explored often-elusive concepts and practices such as power, exchange, structure, agency, gender, affect, intimacy, and of course sexuality. As our discipline moved away from paradigms that emphasized structural integrity and continuity, and as the ethnographic weight of rapidly transforming conjugal beliefs and practices pushed against long-dominant analyses of marriage, anthropologists opened up their inquiries to look at, among other phenomena, "companionate marriage" and "affective circuits" (Hirsch and Wardlow 2006; Cole and Groes 2016). The ways in which contemporary marriage—as a social, political, and legal institution—is being simultaneously shored up, torn down, and reimagined have provided fertile ground for anthro-pological inquiry, whether focused on the expansion of same-sex marriage rights, the reshaping of marriage in the context of transnationalism and globalization, or the changing emphases and understandings of affect and intimacy in conjugal aspirations.

This recent boom of social scientific and humanistic scholarship on marriage around the world has been especially attentive to the ways in which new economic and social formations are reshaping it, whether because of migration and transnationalism (Cole and Groes 2016; Derks 2008; Elliot 2016; Hannaford 2017; Kibria 2012; Kringelbach 2016), delayed marriage or "waithood" (Dhillon and Yousef 2009; Hasso 2010; Singerman 2007; Inhorn and Smith-Hefner 2020), the impact of new media (Agrawal 2015; Gershon 2011; Sotoudeh, Friedland, and Afary 2017), the broadening scope of alternative sexualities (Blackwood and Wieringa 1999; Boellstorff 2005; Najmabadi 2013; Stout 2014), shifts in gendered political and economic power (Alexy 2010; Jean-Baptiste 2014; Lynch 2007; Nelson 2000; Osborn 2011), or many other forces that impact marriage both as a social and legal institution (Bunting, Lawrance, and Roberts 2016; Burrill 2015; Nolte 2017; Pauli and van Dijk 2016) and as one of the most fraught forms of human relations (Cole and Thomas 2009; Davis and Friedman 2014; Zelizer 2005).

Beyond this highly condensed snapshot, we are not concerned to rehearse the very long and robust interrogation into marriage in its many forms over the history of our discipline—that would be a book in and of itself. Nonetheless, we would like to harken back for a moment to one of our field's earliest theoretical touchstones on the question of marriage: Friedrich Engels's effort to understand its origin as the outcome of the exigencies of private property regimes and the state. Embedded within Engels's flawed evolutionary account is a still-resonant question about marriage: what's in it for women?

Engels, like Marx, believed that marriage was a tool of women's oppression in classed society, "the world historic defeat of the female sex." Because of the passage of private property and thus the need to make certain of the paternity of children, a wife is "delivered over unconditionally into the power of the husband; if he kills her, he is only exercising his rights" (1884, 120–122). Further, he argued that the "modern individual family is founded on the open or concealed domestic slavery of the wife" (137).

Responding to Henry Louis Morgan's prediction that monogamy in its Victorian form would not necessarily last forever, Engels predicted that the end of capitalism would mean the end of marriage in its contemporary form. What would emerge, he posited, would be something much more flexible, based not on women's economic dependence or concerns about private property but on individual desire and "real love."

> Thus, what we can conjecture at present about the regulation of sex-relationships after the impending downfall of capitalist production is, in the main, of a negative character, limited mostly to what will vanish. But what will be added? That will be settled after a new generation has grown up; a generation of men who never in all their lives had occasion to purchase a woman's surrender either with money or with any other means of social power; and a race of women who have never been obliged to surrender to any man out of any consideration other than that of real love, or to refrain from giving themselves to their lovers for fear of the economic consequences. Once such people appear, they will not care a rap about what we think they should do. They will establish their own practice and their own public opinion, conformable therewith, of the practice of each individual—and that's the end of it. (68)

Feminist anthropologists have recurrently returned to Engels's essay on the origin of the family, finding its questions continually germane even if their answers require repeated reframing and revision. Perhaps more to the point, the first decade of the new millennium saw an especially lively flourishing of scholarship on shifting practices around love, marriage, sexuality, and gender, which seemed to corroborate Engels's prophecy regarding love-based marriages, if not the end of capitalism (Ahearn 2001; Constable 2004; Hirsch and Wardlow 2006; Padilla et al. 2007; Cole and Thomas 2009; Smith-Hefner 2005). Anthropologists and historians in that moment focused on the ways in which couples were claiming the centrality of "emotional intimacy" in their conception—and hoped-for practice—of "modern love." But if this bubbling up of love and affection was brought front and center in that moment, a decade later we have begun to sense the disappointment and often dissolution of those very bonds, some of which was predicted by the authors in those early 2000s volumes (see Smith 2006; Hunter 2009b). Women, especially, are fed up. Or perhaps they have been fed up for much longer and are newly able to *do* something, like opt out of at least some—if not all—of marriage's more distasteful and dissatisfying dimensions.

A Crisis of Masculinity?

The trope of a "crisis of masculinity" has permeated both social science and popular culture in many of the countries featured in these chapters. It is generally used to capture the idea that shifting work patterns and new family demands put pressure on men who feel uncertainty and distress about their changing role in family and society. Changes in the labor market such as the rise of the service economy and the automation of manufacturing, the increase in flexible working practices, and the feminization of the workforce make steady and remunerative employment for men harder to come by. Meanwhile, the rise of feminism challenges many received understandings of the duties of men and women. Such conditions are said to push marriage, independent household formation, and other avenues to successful adulthood out of reach for many men.

This "crisis of masculinity" is used as an explanation for high rates of male suicide (Jordan and Chandler 2019), but also for all kinds of troubling male behavior such as alcoholism (Hinote and Webber 2012; Utrata 2019), risky sexual behavior (Walker 2005; Hunter 2010; Hirsch 2015), intimate partner violence (Chowdhry 2005; Frosh, Phoenix, and Pattman 2002), and larger-scale forms of violence and aggression such as terrorism and mass murder. The inability to provide is seemingly a hallmark of what it means to be an African man today (see Lindsay and Miescher 2003) or a Black man in general (see Matlon 2016). Men in Nigeria are in crisis, unable to provide for families and thus vulnerable to being deemed useless as men (Cornwall 2002). Urban Ivoirian men struggle to stake their claim over urban space in the wake of their social and financial impotence (Matlon 2014). South African men and their grappling with masculine identity are the focus of numerous scholarly articles (Decoteau 2013; Gibbs, Sikweyiya, and Jewkes 2014; Morrell 2001; Leopeng and Langa 2017). Male marginality has become a global trope—used to explain everything from the dreadful incel movement to Modi's Hindu supremacism in India.

We wish here to undermine the idea of a crisis in masculinity. We do so partly to show that it ignores men's continued privilege and power even in the face of so-called crisis (see Wyrod 2016, 85), but also to draw attention to the way that such talk of crisis is deployed as a critique of feminism and a rejection of gender equality (see Dupuis-Déri 2012 for a historical argument on this point). What do we miss when we see nonmarriage as aberrant or a temporary lull on the road to marriage? When we engage in "methodological nuptialism," are we reducing what might be a more transformative movement into a picture of, say, "delaying marriage" or "waithood," seeing this as a temporary "crisis" in masculinity rather than a larger reordering of gendered norms under late capitalism?

Rather than a crisis, we can perhaps speak of these changes as adjustments toward a new status quo. Crisis, as Janet Roitman notes, "implies a certain *telos*—that is, it is inevitably though most often implicitly directed toward a norm. Evoking crisis entails reference to a norm because it requires a comparative state for judgment: crisis compared to what?" (2017, 25). Crisis, she says, points to an axiological problem—a rupture in the normative order of things. A crisis implies negativity, a disaster, a change for the worse. Whose crisis is this?

Embedded throughout this volume is the seeming ubiquity of generally disappointing men. Carla Freeman's interlocutor, Lillianna, cogertly sums up women's exasperation with men's errant behavior when she proclaims, "[We] just don't want to put up with that shit." That shit, and no longer putting up with it, reverberates across almost all chapters, whether manifested in Bajan "outside families," Brazilian women's dashed dreams for fidelity, Indian husbands who—at worst—sell their wives into sexual slavery or, perhaps more mundanely and lamely, are drunkard layabouts, Indonesian philanderers, Japanese husbands' cold disinterest, Namibian husbands' broken promises, or absentee South African fathers. Brady G'Sell's chapter title says it all: "What's wrong with these mens?" Of course, infidelity and disappointing or abusive husbands are nothing new, as the authors themselves point out. That these behaviors prompt some women to opt out might be new, sometimes facilitated by women's economic independence, sometimes by shifts in expectations for marriage, sometimes by other factors. Taken together, the chapters prompt unavoidable questions: Why is marriage so consistently disappointing for women? When the singular rewards of economic stability and the social status that marriage confers are troubled, does marriage offer women anything compelling at all?

In nearly all of the cases presented in this book, a shifting political economic background generates new sources of income and increased financial autonomy for women. We learn about the neoliberal emergence of entrepreneurial women in Barbados, the new (albeit low-wage and precarious) employment opportunities for women in northeastern Brazil's ecotourism industry, increasing professional opportunities for middle-class women in Indonesia, rising urbanization in Namibia, Botswana, and South Africa that often leads to new forms of salaried employment for women, Indian development schemes that promote education for girls and work for women, and even a shifting agricultural economy in Guinea-Bissau that tips the scale ever so slightly toward women's self-reliance. The particular contexts vary widely, but the implications seem to harmonize across them: these relatively new sources of income for women decrease their dependence on men (who, in many cases, were already struggling to hold up their end of the provisioning bargain). This, in turn, opens up new possibilities for gender relations and nonmarital—or, at least, differently configured marital—formations.

Examples like these echo around the world. Women are now able to bypass marriages that no longer guarantee financial and social stability, finding alternative pathways to both of those things on their own. As Gloria Steinem put it, women are becoming the men they wanted to marry. With financial stability no longer being a significant or readily available draw into marriages for women, they can afford to be more selective. No longer culturally or legally kneecapped into a forced dependence on male partners, they can evaluate what value a marriage might bring to their lives against the sacrifices it requires.

We can see the outcome of these evaluations in the numbers. Although there is a great degree of heterogeneity across and within regions, the past decades (from 1980 to 2010) have been characterized by delays in women's age at first marriage as well as increases in cohabitation, separation or divorce, and nonmarriage (UN Women 2020, 50). These trends are already seen as quite commonplace in Europe, Australia, the United States, and Canada. Scandinavian countries in particular are even caricatured as postmarriage societies. In the United States, the median age of first marriage has risen from a 1956 low of 20.1 for women and 22.5 for men to 27.1 for women and 29.2 for men in 2016 (Fry 2016). But even in regions where marriage is generally considered compulsory, unprecedented change is afoot. Currently, 89 percent of the world's population lives in a country with falling marriage rates. As marriage rates have decreased globally since the 1980s, the share of never-married women ages forty-five to forty-nine increased from 3.1 percent circa 1990 to 4.3 percent circa 2010. This confirms that women are gradually opting out of marriage and other formal unions and not just postponing them, at least in some regions and countries (UN Women 2020, 53). Based on data circa 2010, a significant share of women in their late forties had never married in Australia and New Zealand (14.1 percent), Latin America and the Caribbean (13.4 percent), and Europe and North America (10.8 percent), followed by sub-Saharan Africa (6.1 percent) (UN Women 2020, 53–54). Between the 1970s and the 2000s, the number of countries where at least 10 percent of women had never married by age fifty increased from 33 to 41, and from 31 to 49 with respect to men who had not yet married by age fifty.[3] Even in contexts where marriage continues to be the dominant form of partnership, there is evidence of greater autonomy for women in spousal selection (UN Women 2020, 50). In a nutshell, around the globe the average age at first marriage is climbing, the number of divorced or separated women has risen steadily, and the number of never-married women has increased in all regions of the world in the past thirty years (UN Women 2019).

In this volume, we examine these changes without assuming that they constitute a "crisis" in the normative, correct, gendered distribution of power in relationships. Rather, we argue for a more protracted negotiation of what makes for a successful and fulfilling life for women and show how new economic and social opportunities are shaping the imagined possibilities of women's lives within and outside marriage.

News-in-Brief

Anthropologists and demographers are not the only ones paying attention to these recent developments. As marriage rates continue to drop and marital age increases across the world, journalists have taken note. Headlines from mainstream press announce "Craving Freedom, Japan's Women Opt Out of Marriage," "Nearly Half of Canadians Feel 'Marriage Is Simply Not Necessary," "Chileans Are Marrying Less and Later," "'You Don't Have to Settle': The Joy of Living (and Dying) Alone," and, bluntly, "Marriage Rates Are Plummeting."[4] Reports and policy papers decry "The Middle Eastern Marriage Crisis" and pose the question "A Half-Century of Fewer People Marrying: What Explains It?"[5] Other sources attempt to explain "Why More Women Are Choosing to Stay Single Now," "Why We Don't Marry," "Why China's Millennials Are Saying No to Marriage," "Why More Women Are Seeking Divorce in West Africa," "Why Women Are Choosing to Marry Themselves," and "Why Opting Out Is the New Leaning In."[6] Essayists ponder "What You Lose When You Gain a Spouse."[7] Cleverly coined new words and phrases—such as "untying the knot," "I don't," "spinster revolution," "single minded," "leftover women," "sologamy," and "single positive"—pepper these articles, as journalists track and develop a new vocabulary and lingo to represent these trends.

Joining the chorus, a number of top-selling popular books have taken on the subject of contemporary alternatives to marriage, particularly in North America. Hannah Rosin's *End of Men* (2012) makes a compelling, if largely anecdotal, argument that women are outpacing men academically, financially, and emotionally and thus are better off without them. Rebecca Traister's *All the Single Ladies* (2016) argues that the growing number of single women in their thirties and beyond is the most important new economic and voting bloc in the United States. Recent pop feminist books with cheeky, provocative angles on the liberating power of breakups and singledom for women have found tremendous success and attention (Bolick 2015; Korducki 2018). Mavis Hetherington and John Kelly's popular *For Better or Worse: Divorce Reconsidered* emphasizes the positive aspects of divorce, arguing that particularly for women, divorce can be a pathway to "life-transforming personal growth" (2003, 5).

A plethora of popular books make the case that contemporary marriage is broken. Andrew Cherlin's (2010) *The Marriage-Go-Round* posits a contradiction in the very idea of marriage for Americans. The individualistic ethos that characterizes American identity confronts the collective ideal of marriage and keeps Americans in a perpetual loop of marriage, divorce, and remarriage. Stephanie Coontz's (2006) historically focused survey of marriage says that its recent iteration as a vehicle for romantic love has destabilized and collapsed the institution. Marilyn Yalom's *A History of the Wife* (2001) comes to a similar conclusion and emphasizes that marriage has always been a better deal for men than women. Of course, we can look back to Arlie Hochschild's seminal study, *The Second Shift* (1989), for an earlier illustration of the way marriages can be a raw deal, especially for working women. Even "pro-marriage" books like Eli Finkel's *The All-or-Nothing Marriage* (2017) that tout the possibility for optimizing marriage to allow both partners to flourish or Lori Gottlieb's grim *Marry Him: The Case for Settling for Mr. Good Enough* (2010) acknowledge the reality that the majority of marriages are unsatisfying. Couples therapist Esther Perel's wildly popular duo of books about marriage, *Mating in Captivity* (2006) and *The State of Affairs* (2018), suggests that contemporary marriages fall into predictable patterns of disenchantment, miscommunication, and infidelity.[8]

Along with many of our peers we gobbled up these books, winking (and sometimes smirking) to ourselves that the evidence was clearly mounting. But as we started to focus more carefully on the dynamics of women opting out of marriage in our own and our colleagues' ethnographic research in non-Euro-American contexts, our antennae become more finely tuned to the ways in which these transformations were being chronicled in the Western popular press. The profusion of journalistic and popular coverage about women rejecting or evading marriage seemed, on the one hand, to confirm our hunch that *something* was going on. On the other hand, although we found many of these accounts tantalizing, the popular books largely limited their lens to the United States, and most of the journalistic accounts relied on superficial and unsatisfying explanations for this phenomenon, and often rested on hackneyed portrayals of cultural beliefs and practices. Nonetheless, their very popularity, as well as their presence on the pages of such publications as the *New York Times*, the *Guardian*, CNN, the *Los Angeles Times*, and other bastions of mainstream journalism, piqued our interest, and, as "news-in-brief" snapshots (de Botton 1997), they prompted our Proustian impulse to slow down, dig deeper, and imagine the range of possibilities that might broaden our understanding of what on earth was going on. So we turned to ethnography. A more multifaceted understanding of the stories and statistics capturing the attention of journalists, popular book authors, and even conference-going anthropologists intimates not that women are eschewing marriage all over the world—as the headlines and book titles would have it—but they are engaged in a range of improvisations and negotiations—within and without marriage—to escape or reshape it into a more rewarding arrangement.

Chapter Summaries

Each chapter in this volume takes an ethnographic deep dive into a context in which women are pushing against the normative bounds of marriage, or sometimes avoiding it altogether. We have organized the chapters into three sections. The chapters in part I focus on women who have never married. Part II attends to the dynamics of opting out for women who find themselves—whether because of divorce, loss of virtue, or spousal death—outside the anticipated or normative bounds of married life. Part III considers what opting out means from within seemingly intact marriages.

We start with Julia Pauli's exploration of why so many Namibian women remain unmarried. Pauli adds nuance to the central notion of opting out by pointing to the various constraints and conflicting desires of her interlocutors regarding marriage. Pauli demonstrates that opting out framed as choice does not quite capture what is going on in Namibia, where motherhood remains compulsory for female status and belonging, but men routinely fail to measure up to women's expectations for partnership. Her chapter is simultaneously an argument about complexity regarding choice (e.g., not fully opting out, but instead opting out to a certain extent) and generational dynamics.

On this second point, Pauli offers some original insights into the generational accretion of knowledge and attitudes about marriage; that is, how daughters learn from, as one of her respondents puts it so well, their mothers' "indignities." The mother/daughter pairing of the two life stories she presents is a powerful narrative and analytic strategy to convey this point. This suggests that the decrease or dissolution of marriage (or, at least, its increasing optional status) can be understood not just through a changing backdrop (political economy, labor migration, etc.) but through the most intimate domain of a kind of osmosis—of experiences, attitudes, models, mistakes, and lessons—between mothers and daughters. Pauli's story of Silvia and Mara illustrates the intergenerational solidarity between the two women and seems to further deemphasize the importance of a romantic or domestic partnership with a husband.

We stay in Southern Africa with Jacqueline Solway, who starts her chapter by informing us that because marriage rates have long been low in Southern Africa, "the rest of the world appears to be catching up to Botswana." Given the long-standing phenomenon of "marriage in the abstract" in Botswana, Solway focuses on different forms of conjugality and residence. The fact that the majority of Tswana are "officially single" does not tell us much about the multiple sorts of relationships and residential circumstances, not to mention the highly variable factors and calculations women make regarding conjugality. Solway's cogent elaboration of the cascading effects of political economic transformation, shifts in residence patterns, and other dramatic (but seemingly backdrop) changes helps contextualize and complicate the too broad and simplified notion of opting out. In doing so, she pluralizes possibilities for singlehood and conjugality, opening up these categories, statuses, and ways of being. Solway moves beyond a cause-and-effect framing to show how massive political economic changes and shifts in control over resources have unlocked new economic and residential possibilities for women, which in turn subtly but persistently move the needle on social regulation by affines and ritual inculcation.

Sarah Lamb's discussion of Bengali women who have never married also pushes back on opting out as a matter of choice and as primarily motivated by a quest for self-actualization. She highlights an array of other motivations that led her interlocutors—often unwittingly—to a never-married position and delineates the range of constraints and opportunities that textured the lives of these unmarried women. As she probes the intersection of class and gender for Bengali women, she emphasizes the precarity of never-married women as they navigate the "out-of-placeness" of their position in society. The challenges of finding housing, ensuring familial support, avoiding harassment, and performing a nonthreatening muted sexuality all shape these women's choices and constrain their freedom. Nevertheless, by operating from their position outside of the norm of marriage, these women open up a broader vision for Bengali womanhood—performing new kinds of gendered roles as caretaker daughters who never leave their natal kin, as wage-earning wives to other women, and even as single mothers.

Similarly, Laura Nelson deepens our understanding of singledom, in her case never married women of a certain age in South Korea. These women remain conspicuously invisible in official records, demographic studies, and family histories. Nelson connects this erasure to the biopolitics of a state focused on increased fertility and population and therefore a strong and promising national future. Her focus on the ambivalent feelings of unmarried women, who are able to retain close connections to their natal kin and in many cases see themselves as having avoided an undesirable fate as wives, suggests another latent threat to the universality of marriage in Korea, namely the comforts and pleasures of opting out. Like the never married women in the chapters above, the single Korean women in Nelson's chapter discreetly enjoy what she calls "the underappreciated rewards of marriage resistance in a culture of compulsory heteronormative marriage."

Part II begins in South India, where Kimberly Walters provides a chilling account of the "algebraic inevitability" of sex work for women whose husbands (dead or alive) have failed them. Her analysis hinges on the fiction of the Parthivratha woman—the chaste, cocooned wife under the magical protection of *Lakshmana rekha*. From the mythological Shiva to contemporary women in Hyderabad, Walters shines a light on the problematic precarity of this idealized version of womanhood, as well as the opportunities for mobility, self-reliance, recognition, and respect (*gurtimpu*) they realize once they leave the highly contingent protection of the Lakshmana rekha. Walters shows how sex work not only crosses the boundary of Lakshmana rekha, but—if successful—also traverses normative bounds of gender, class, and caste. It becomes, in some cases, an "unexpected means of redefining one's own purview and possibilities." Her chapter demonstrates how sex work feels like an inevitable destination for women in South India whose more traditional domestic situation has failed them due to either the death or delinquency of a husband or father. Outside the bounds of normative marriage, this is uncharted and ambiguous territory.

Moving to Latin America, Melanie Medeiros also considers how men's failures push women toward unanticipated singlehood and independence. Her chapter centers on young, Black, working-class women in northeastern Brazil who opt to end their unfulfilling and disappointing marriages in order to maintain self-respect and respectability. That they also choose not to remarry underlines how these women are shaping and being shaped by changing gendered understandings of respectability and personal value. Medeiros moves beyond a simple idea of the shift to companionate values in marriage and toward a more nuanced discussion of how the racialized history of Brazil combines with economic shifts that have opened up new possibilities for financial independence for women through jobs in the ecotourism industry to reframe perceptions of respectability surrounding marriage for women in contemporary Brogodó. Like many of the other cases, there is a great deal of mixed emotion regarding these always-fraught choices. One way that women have addressed the disappointing outcomes of marriage is to shift—or, really, reduce—their expectations through the creation of a new, hybrid category—the *namorido* (boyfriend/husband), who fulfills some of the sexual and companionate aspirations for such partnerships but cannot assume the possessive role of a husband because he is "only a boyfriend." Medeiros highlights how women in Brazil do, in fact, seek companionship and intimacy from men, and if they can have that without the risk and suffering of marriage, they can find real contentment.

Race and respectability are also key features in Carla Freeman's chapter on marriage choices in Barbados. After decades of fieldwork focused on Black Barbadian women, Freeman now turns her keen ethnographic eye toward the minority white, middle-class women she has known for many years. This largely invisible group of women has long stood for respectability and the idealized "definitional norm" of marriage in a context where formal marriage has never been the norm. Recently, they have pursued marriage as a form of romantic intimacy and self-actualization, only to confront disappointment and ultimately divorce. Their circumstances are now more similar to the island's majority-Black Bajan matrifocal women who have previously served as their alter. White Bajan women have moved, then, from occupying the place of an idealized exception (that is, formally married) to more closely resembling an island-wide norm (matrifocality). In so doing, they expose the simultaneity of "threat and possibility, shame and freedom" that characterizes so many women around the world living their lives outside the bounds of marriage. One of the most intriguing aspects about this case is the way in which these very women may be upending the long-standing "crab antics" dynamics that have characterized women's relationships with each other. *Opting out* of marriage has, in some ways, led to *opting for* new forms of female sociality—matrifocality and friendship—that, as Freeman invitingly concludes, "suggests a rich new frontier"—which we take to mean both for these women and for ethnographic inquiry into nonconjugal forms of intimacy.

The final chapter in this section highlights the invisible and unspeakable dimensions of opting out of marital conformity. Joanna Davidson introduces us to a category of unnamable women in the Jola society in Guinea Bissau, West Africa, to demonstrate how certain forms of opting out are so threatening to the patriarchal status quo as to prohibit their very mention. There is no Jola word for widow, although their houses have a name and are commonplace across the village landscape. Davidson explores this paradox and suggests that widows pose a problem to the social order in a society where women are meant to play a particular role in sustaining the domestic and agricultural lives of men. The very presence of Jola widows haunts the institution of marriage because it provokes the dangerous suggestion that women might very well manage a life outside of it.

Part III comprises four chapters about women who, on the face of it, seem to be married, some of them quite contentedly. But a deeper look into their marriages reveals yet more insights into how, even as wives, women can opt out of marital norms and expectations and open up possibilities for transforming marriage from *within* the very bounds of marriage itself. These novel practices and inventive strategies regarding marriage seem to corroborate Basu's assertion that "marriage's resilience seems to lie in creative and fluid variations to the form" (2020, 185).

Akiko Takeyama's chapter provides an intriguing portrait of married Japanese women who pursue commercial sexual relationships with professional "hosts." Takeyama shows how women look to these boyfriends for hire to provide them not only with romantic and sexual companionship but with the means to a new self-fashioning. In a culture that prizes youth as a woman's primary virtue, these aging women look to intimate relations with paid companions to reinvigorate their self-worth. The financial and social rewards of marriage are still compelling enough for the women featured in her chapter to remain in sexless marriages; indeed, the "bounded authenticity" (Bernstein 2007) of this extramarital activity in fact allows women to stay in sexless or otherwise disappointing marriages without demanding that they transform. Women make a distinction between these commodified encounters and extramarital affairs, claiming that far from threatening the institution of marriage, their liaisons with hosts enhance their marriages and their abilities to be good wives. Although it may seem counterintuitive to call attention to these women—who are devoted to and benefitting from their marriages—as opting out of marriage, a more penetrating scrutiny of their subtle performances exposes otherwise invisible fissures, and maybe even transformations, in hegemonic forms of marriage and gender, by decoupling sex and marriage, and finding satisfaction in each on their own terms.

Brady G'Sell offers another portrait of a group of Black Southern African women who are dissatisfied with the status quo of marriage in their society. Instead of eschewing marriage altogether, her interlocuters in Durban, South Africa, have opted for socially risky unions with foreign men as a means to getting what they deem valuable out of marriage. While there is status to be gained from a formalized marriage complete with *ilobolo* payment, marriage to a foreign man means a threat to social status in a xenophobic climate in which migrants are not only scorned and marginalized, but seen to be opportunists in their marriages to South African women. Foreign men, however, seem to make good (or, at least, better) husbands: they are more likely to be employed than their South African counterparts, more likely to stay on and care for their children financially and affectively, and less likely to subject their wives to the will of their own mothers. We take the double-entendre of her chapter's title—"What's wrong with these mens?"—to refer to both the deadbeat South African men and the lurking suspicion about foreign husbands. Either way, it is the women's creative and courageous responses to the question that constitute the heartbeat of G'Sell's account.

Similarly, Dinah Hannaford's chapter on Senegalese women who marry migrants offers another view of what both *opting out* and *opting for* might entail. Marriage is still the only viable path to adult status and respectability for women, but its more onerous dimensions are increasingly seen as a nuisance better evaded. Rather than abjuring marriage itself, some Senegalese women do the next best thing: by marrying husbands who, because they live abroad, remain largely absent from day-to-day affairs, they gain wifely status but evade the over-bearing obligations (sexual, domestic, affective) of quotidian catering to a husband and his kin, especially his mother. Within the still somewhat constricted options available to them, they have refashioned marriage to better fit their otherwise incompatible goals of financial and social security, relative freedom and autonomy, and primarily female sociality. This enables them to achieve the adult status and respectability that comes with marriage and to opt in for other kinds of relationships, such as friendship with other women and closeness with natal kin.

Finally, Carla Jones's chapter tells us the story of Dita, a successful middle-class professional woman in Indonesia who, after the heartbreaking failure of her first marriage, eschewed remarriage for fifteen years. But on the brink of middle age and to everyone's surprise, Dita marries again. Although her family members are quick to comment that Dita is not a "normal wife," Jones's detailed account of Dita's life choices as a mother, activist, daughter, sister, colleague, and socially fulfilled adult exposes the "potentially pathological" aspects of Indonesians' heretofore normative framing of conjugality. Dita's life, improvised and unexpected as its various twists and turns might be, reflects profound changes in the topography of contemporary Indonesian family and gender relations and shows how some middle-class women are, in Jones's felicitous phrasing, "reconfiguring marriage . . . in ways that refuse choosing between servitude and solitude." Jones reveals that opting out and opting back into marriage each contain their own logics and transformative potential—as "quiet but radical expression[s] of hope"—by prying open the presumed inflexible bars of normativity and paving the way toward newly recognized and appreciated forms of care, domesticity, and intimacy.

What's in a Name?

Even with the positive and expansive framing of Dita's marriage as a "political act of optimism," Jones acknowledges the "paucity of terminology to capture what [Dita and her new husband] found in each other." Developing a language for these nonnormative innovations is a preoccupation for the authors of these chapters as well as their interlocutors, and this concern even manifests in our own linguistic gymnastics in composing—and then qualifying—a fitting title for this volume. Multiple chapters call attention to the ambiguous search for terminology to capture innovations within and outside of marriage. It is clear that language, too, struggles to see outside of marriage as a hegemonic norm and thus new forms of partnering or nonpartnering are sometimes elegantly, sometimes awkwardly named, borrowing from the language of marriage to find their place in the collective understanding.

Perhaps most successfully, Melanie Medeiros tells us about the *namorido*—a new name for a new category of relationship that speaks to the wonderful flexibility of Brazilian Portuguese and to the ways these women—who do not have a husband and hence "don't have a name" in the reputational sense—reclaim their respectability by creating a new relationship category, as well as shifting the expectations projected upon this relationship. The obligations of a namorido are "intentionally slightly obscure." The namorido does not have the "weight of expectations" placed on marriage, so what might seem disadvantageous on the surface (lack of financial support) is experienced by Brogodó women as empowering and autonomy saving, and less subject to the disappointments of unmet expectations.

Carla Freeman's chapter also points to new names for reimagined statuses and categories, flagging Sasha Cagen's website in which the pejorative "spinster" becomes the whimsical "quirkyalone," and in her own case of Barbados, "visiting unions" straightforwardly encapsulating those in-between, not-quite-marital arrangements. In a different vein, Kimberly Walters's chapter offers at least two examples of transformed terms: the protective "aunty," which otherwise politely refers to a generic and caring older woman, has come to mean, for sex workers in South India, a madam who introduces women into sex work and often manages (and takes a cut of) the payments for their sexual labor. Also, the Hindi word *randi* and the Telegu word *munda*" slide from their literal meaning—"widow"—to their now-understood meaning—"prostitute"—indexing, in this slippage, anxieties around widows' unleashed, potent, but taboo sexuality.

Finally, two of the chapters highlight not the proliferation of new or differently construed terms but the unspeakability and unknowability of unmarried women. Laura Nelson reads between the lines of historical accounts that (mis)represent marriage universality in South Korea and finds in them hints of "marriage-divergent life trajectories" otherwise invisible to demographers who myopically focus on fertility and are thus blinded to evidence of unmarried women in their own data. Not only do South Koreans not see these women, they literally cannot even speak of them. Given widespread teknonymic practices, "marriage [was] not just expected, but *definitional* of being a Korean woman. A woman without a husband and child was in a real sense almost unnamable."[9] Similarly, albeit in a very different context, Joanna Davidson tries to understand not a neologism but the lack of a name for Jola widows who opt out of remarriage. This seeming omission of the invention of new terminology to account for transformations in marital practices, by its silence, acknowledges a related dynamic: by not naming widows, the social fiction of marriage is preserved, if only rhetorically.

All of these terms (or lack thereof) reveal the creative linguistic and cultural work being undertaken to account for (or deny) new dynamics and categories, not to mention the sensitivity of these ethnographers to be attuned to them. But they might also remind us of the legitimating power of a name or term and the inventive work we all could do in thinking through the phenomena, experiences, and life possibilities encountered through ethnographic research that are not quite encapsulated by either local or anthropological terms. The Schneiderian turn away from kinship did not include a similar analytical discomfort with marriage. After a long hiatus, studying kinship came back into anthropology with the more expansive purview—and terminology—of *relatedness* and *sociality* (Carsten 2000, 2003; Franklin and McKinnon 2002; Strathern 2020). One of the implicit provocations of this book is that the term "marriage" may be (and perhaps always was) too limited and limiting a container to hold the many forms of relationships currently assumed to be inside and outside its normative bounds.

Natal Kin and Inheritance

But anthropology's original coupling of both the terms and processes of kinship and marriage seems to find resonance in many of these chapters, although the stakes and outcomes have shifted in significant ways. A very compelling insight from these chapters involves the connection between opting out of marriage and opting for other affective relationships, especially natal kin. Sisters, brothers, parents, and other kin come through as vitally important and are often seen as more reliable and safer sources of support and care than affines. As Freeman demonstrates for matrifocal Barbados, "one's extended kin has been women's time-honored survival strategy." This is reinforced even in mythic form: Walters relates contemporary marital precarity in South India to the story of the goddess Sita, whose eventual rejection of Lord Rama's plea to return and "be his queen" is followed by her homecoming, instead, to her mother, who happens to be the goddess Bhudevi, the very earth mother herself. In Indonesia, it is Dita's parents and brothers who come to her rescue after her first marriage fails, filing her divorce papers and helping to raise her daughter as Dita pursues far-flung educational and professional opportunities. Even beyond her immediate kin, Jones explains how generations of activist families in Indonesia continue to "expand the boundaries of normal" that make it possible for Dita to be "not a normal wife." Nelson, Hannaford, and G'Sell each reveal, respectively, that South Korean single women, Senegalese migrants' wives, and South African women married to foreigners avoid the arduous work of living with and catering to in-laws. But they are quick to point out that the most fortunate among these women remain in the homes of their own parents, providing domestic labor to their own kin and enjoying more security in those relations. As Nelson shows in her account of forgotten unmarried women in South Korea, some of them "slip into spinsterhood" because of the more pressing needs—or their own desire—to stay with their natal family, even though this family seems to willfully erase their existence.

In Solway's story of waning marriage in Botswana, strong loyalties to natal kin pull on both men and women and thus affect marital outcomes for both husbands and wives, although for different—even opposing—reasons. Although patrilocal residence is no longer universally assumed, marriage in Botswana still "usually entails a shift in affiliation and authority for the wife . . . [and] many women do not desire to have such a rupture with their natal kin who provide them with love, security and support." From a different angle, increased divorce is seen as an outcome of strained relations between a wife and her in-laws, especially because of the "powerful bonds between mothers and sons and the great deference shown to mothers on the part of sons . . . [which] can be jarring and feel oppressive to wives." So, in Botswana, the wellspring for both the decrease in marriage and increase in divorce finds its source in close natal ties, whether in the form of a daughter reluctant to reduce her primary affiliation with her natal family or a son disinclined to favor his wife over his mother, and thereby irritating his spouse to the point of no return.

Most powerfully and poignantly, though, it is the relationship between mothers and daughters in many of these chapters that captures our attention, especially in terms of how the experiences and lessons passed from mother to daughter texture expectations and decisions about marriage. This is most clearly evident in Pauli's chapter, in which she makes a solid case for the sedimentation of sentiment about marriage across generations of women. More specifically, daughters learn from their mothers' "indignities," and mothers—through their words and life experiences—pass down admonitions to their daughters about remaining independent and not settling for Mr. Wrong. Likewise, Bajan Grans tell their children, "Always have your own house; he can visit but he cannot stay." In Botswana, bridal advice (*go laya*) becomes hoist with its own petard for would-be brides.

These examples suggest a new way to understand inheritance as it pertains to marriage. Anthropological attention to inheritance in the context of marriage has conventionally focused on the legalistic and genealogical dimensions of heredity, especially in terms of entitlements over resources. But an alternate way to think about inheritance emerges through many subtle ethnographic cues in these chapters; namely, what insights do young women receive from their mothers and grandmothers that inform their ideas (and, if possible, their choices) about marriage? Indeed, if Engels located the origin of marriage alongside the advent of private property and the need for paternity certainty for the sake of its inheritance, perhaps we can point to the emergence (or at least increase) of women opting out of marriage as part and parcel with a very different kind of inheritance—an intimate and immaterial inheritance passed along the matriline. Less private property than intangible wisdom, this shows up in whispered phrases, catchy quips, and observed inequities and shapes, so it seems, subsequent generations of women regarding their marital expectations and strategies. We can discern a circular dynamic here, in which the increasing incidence of women opting out of marriage not only is prompted by but brings about stronger and more enduring ties (and often proximity) to natal kin—especially mothers—which, in turn, provides greater opportunity for the transmission of this distinctly maternal inheritance, perhaps coming full circle to influence young women's marital trajectories.

Many of the chapters give us glimpses into these generational dynamics, sometimes emphasizing subtle or radical shifts, sometimes demonstrating continuity. And here we want to signal that although in some instances such maternal bequests can transform marital norms, we also see the inverse. Often, patriarchal norms of marriage are most strictly enforced by women themselves. Even though the matrilineal transmission of conjugal acumen might provide more impetus for opting out, we should remain cognizant of the fact that marriage of younger women can give older women power, and older women may stand to lose the most when the traditional structures of marriage bend to give younger women more autonomy.

Ethnographic Engagements

By way of conclusion, we want to spotlight another facet regarding the transmission of knowledge among women, although this one pertains to the authors themselves as long-term field workers in each of these settings. The stories in many of these chapters happen over the course of decades, during which their authors come back and forth between their university homes (in North America and Europe) and their fieldwork homes (in Africa, Asia, Latin America, and the Caribbean). It is striking to us how enmeshed many of the authors are in their interlocutors' lives and how the relationship between anthropologist and research subject blurs into friendship, and sometimes family. The sustained commitment to a particular place and the people who populate it is key here: several of the chapters chart the changes in women's lives from youthful romantic adolescents to wives, mothers, divorcées, widows, and hopeful romantics again (or throughout). Freeman sums this up when she points out that "as sometimes happens in fieldwork that stretches from years to decades, patterns I described as novel and transformative in the early 2000s began to show visible fault lines if not out-right rupture." The stories in these chapters are not just memories recounted by research subjects; they are lived in real time alongside the ethnographer, who sometimes serves as chronicler, other times as confidante, and more often than not as both. It is these very bonds, in their depth and sincerity, that make for exemplary ethnography because "our knowledge of others and of their lifeworlds is contingent on the ways we engage and interact with them" (Jackson 2012, 66).

It is neither an accident nor a coincidence that these rich, sensitive, and humane portrayals are authored by anthropologists devoted to both long-term fieldwork and genuine relationships with their interlocutors. Even more, many of the authors experienced their own marital ups and downs alongside those of their interlocutors. Their research and writing were undoubtedly shaped and enriched by their own experiences. This volume is a testament to the fact that women anthropologists at various stages in their life cycles, their own romantic and family lives, and their careers are able to ask different questions and make different observations about patriarchal bargains and the limits of what is possible for women's lives. We do not view this as tangential to the production of ethnographic knowledge that informs this book. Rather, what is on vivid display here is how ethnographic knowledge is built up relationally (Bank 2016), and how good fieldwork actually depends on the kind and quality of labor we do on ourselves and in relation to others.

Each chapter, then, exemplifies the kind of engagement that lies at the heart of sound, ethical, and illuminating ethnographic research. The combination of long and often intimate fieldwork, a robust and reflexive orientation to anthropological research, and an up-close-and-personal perspective on the "messy, often contradictory activities at the heart of women's everyday lives" informs every aspect of these accounts. It enables the authors of these chapters to see and understand marital dynamics that are—for a range of reasons explicated throughout—more often than not kept under the radar. As such, the ability of each author to recognize and represent what *opting out* entails for their interlocutors is predicated on a commitment and capacity to *opt in* to the kind of fieldwork—sustained, socially sensitive, and intersubjective—that holds the most promise for feminist anthropology.

NOTES

1. We are also indebted in this framing to Mollett and Faria's (2013) invitation to "mess with gender."
2. We are grateful to Marcia Inhorn for helping us develop this point.
3. UN Department of Economic and Social Affairs. 2011. Population Facts. World Marriage Patterns 2011. https://www.un.org/en/development/desa/population/publications /pdf/popfacts/PopFacts_2011-1.pdf
4. See https://www.nytimes.com/2019/08/03/world/asia/japan-single-women-marriage.html; https://globalnews.ca/news/4191139/canadian-attitudes-marriage/; http://www.ipsnews.net /2001/03/population-chileans-are-marrying-less-and-later/; https://www.theguardian.com /commentisfree/2019/oct/13/you-dont-have-to-settle-the-joy-of-living-and-dying-alone; https://www.bentley.edu/news/nowuknow-why-millennials-refuse-get-married.
5. See https://www.brookings.edu/on-the-record/the-middle-eastern-marriage-crisis/; https:// www.psychologytoday.com/us/blog/living-single/201805/half-century-fewer-people -marrying-what-explains-it.
6. See https://www.happysinglehood.com/single-post/2019/07/21/Why-more-women-are -choosing-to-stay-single-now; https://www.city-journal.org/html/why-we-don't-marry

-12215.html; https://www.todayonline.com/world/i-dont-why-chinas-millennials-are
-saying-no-marriage; https://www.independent.co.uk/world/africa-divorce-womens
-rights-niger-marriage-a8729491.html; https://www.vogue.com/article/women-marrying
-themselves-sologamy; https://www.harpersbazaar.com/culture/features/advice/a17317
/opting-out-the-new-leaning-in/.

7. See https://www.theatlantic.com/family/archive/2019/07/case-against-marriage/591973/.

8. The richest exploration of changes in marital practices is to be found, of course, in novels. We have found much enjoyment and inspiration in recent novels that resonate with our efforts in this volume, including Fatou Diome (2010), Jokha Alharthi (2019), Soniah Kamal (2019), Ayobami Adebayo (2017), and Peace Adzo Medie (2020).

9. See also Jesook Song's work on single women and the creation and circulation of "a new category of single women: *pihon yôsông*, meaning literally 'unmarried' but with the added connotation of being 'unassociated with marriage'" (Song 2015, 21).

PART ONE

Never Married

1

Almost Married

Two Generations of Single Mothers in Namibia

JULIA PAULI

Up until the late 1960s most Namibians were married, but marriage rates have declined since the 1970s (Pauli 2010, 2019). This decline was triggered by multiple causes. Apartheid and the male labor system forced many couples to separate, resulting in a strong increase in so-called female-headed households. Apartheid also deepened existing social and economic inequalities and led to accelerated processes of class formation. Small "modernising elites" (Pauli 2011) in the newly established ethnic "homelands" heavily invested in their prestige and status. Unlike the simple format that weddings had up to the middle of the century, the weddings of this new elite in the 1970s and 1980s were increasingly conspicuous and costly. As a result, practices and meanings of marriage were fundamentally reconfigured. Today, most Namibians are unable to afford weddings. Marriage has changed from a widespread rite of passage into an exclusive celebration of wealth and distinction. Comparable dynamics have been described for other regions of Southern Africa (Claassens and Smythe 2013; Hunter 2016; Mupotsa 2015; Pauli and van Dijk 2016; Posel and Rudwick 2013; Reece 2019; Solway 2016, this volume; van Dijk 2017). Yet, despite the decline in marriage, most men and women in Southern Africa still want to marry: "Rather than a reduction in the *value* attached to marriage, circumstances brought about by prevailing socioeconomic and demographic changes are making it difficult to realize marriage in contemporary South Africa" (Mohlabane, Gumede, and Mokomane 2019, 158, emphasis added; see also Hosegood, McGrath, and Moultrie 2009; Sennott, Madhavan, and Nam 2021).

Against the background of these historical trajectories, to what extent do women "opt out of marriage"? Marriage is no longer a social norm or expectation in present-day Namibia and does not carry the same moral force as, for example, in Nigeria (Smith 2020), Senegal (Hannaford 2017), India (Lamb 2018), or Pakistan (Maqsood 2017). Still, historically speaking the decline in marriage has also been linked to women "opting out" of marriage. Since approximately the 1960s, women have increasingly participated in the labor force. These economically independent women did not opt out of marriage per se but opted out of marriage with what they considered "problematic" men: deciding against marrying unemployed, violent, or impoverished men (Mohlabane, Gumede, and Mokomane 2019, 158; G'Sell, this volume; Solway, this volume; van der Vliet 1984). Building on this line of research, I focus on the biographical narratives of two single women, a mother and her daughter. I will call them Silvia and Mara. They are both mothers.

I met Silvia and Mara in 2003 when we were all living in the village of Fransfontein in northwest Namibia.[1] I revisited them in 2015 and 2016, catching up with them on what had happened during my absence. Silvia, the mother, now in her sixties, was still living in Fransfontein while her daughter Mara, now in her thirties, had moved to Namibia's capital Windhoek in 2004. In addition to my participation in their everyday lives as their neighbor (2003–2004) and later a friend, and the stories they were willing to share with me, I collected biographical narratives of another eighteen women in Fransfontein while doing fieldwork there from 2003 until 2006 together with my colleague and husband Michael Schnegg (Pauli 2019). In 2015 and 2016, I extended my field site to the urban setting of Windhoek, where I interviewed nineteen married couples and twenty-one single women and men on marriage, love, and sexuality. Thus, although I focus here on the narratives of two women, the experiences and expectations gathered from a range of other women also inform my interpretations. I focus on the narratives and experiences of single women, realizing that studying men "opting out of marriage" and/or remaining single is also important (Bourdieu 2008; Davidson and Hannaford, this volume; Lahad 2012). While I did collect some narratives from men, most of my data come from women.

In the first section I discuss the emergence of economically independent and unmarried women in Southern Africa and Namibia. I suggest that the lifestyle of these women is indeed an important trope and role model for women more generally, especially younger women. However, to understand why women in Namibia remain unmarried I argue that it is necessary to go beyond this powerful narrative of female agency. Many women I talked with described how they had almost married. In at least one situation these women had wanted to engage in, or had at least hoped for, a more permanent and institutionalized conjugal relationship, very often a marriage. None had made a categorical decision to opt out of marriage or remain single. In her research on single women in India, Sarah Lamb argues along the same line: "The popular notion of 'choice'—based as it tends to be on an image of a freely acting agent—does not well capture the sense of ambivalence and constraint in single women's representations of their life paths" (2018, 59). In Namibia, I encountered a general willingness to marry (see also Solway, this volume). However, having a plan of when one wants to marry was something many perceived as almost impossible. Too many factors were unpredictable and contingent (see also Bledsoe 2002; Johnson-Hanks 2006; Whyte 1997). Similarly, Jennifer Johnson-Hanks shows that Cameroonian women's marital and reproductive histories should not be understood as the result of a series of rationally planned choices but rather as what she terms "judicious opportunism" (2005, 370). She argues that for the Cameroonian women "the challenge is not to formulate a plan and implement it regardless of what comes but to adapt to the moment, to be calm and supple, recognizing the difference between a promising and an unpromising offer" (2005, 370; also 2006). By taking an in-depth look at the biographical narratives of two single Namibian women from different generations, I unravel some of the specific and situational aspects of "opting out" of potential marriages and consider some of the wider political and economic implications.

Women Staying Single in Southern Africa

Throughout the twentieth century, Southern African women's lives were framed and constrained by colonialism and apartheid. Within the boundaries of these severe limitations, women struggled hard to maintain their families. From the midcentury onward, they increasingly had to take care of families and children on their own. For most women this was not a "choice" but the outcome of the racist political structures imbued in the male labor system. But women were not simply passive victims. Ethnographic accounts from South Africa, Botswana, and Namibia show how women actively shaped their constraining life circumstances, including the decision to opt out of certain marriages and stay single (Chimere-Dan 1997; G'Sell, this volume; Gulbrandsen 1986; Iken 1999; McKittrick 1997; Preston-Whyte 1978; Shemeikka, Notkola, and Siiskonen 2005; Solway, this volume; van der Vliet 1984).

Virginia van der Vliet observes that several Xhosa women in a township of Grahamstown (present-day Makhanda), South Africa, in the 1970s decided against marriage: "The women who were opting to remain single were by no means necessarily rejected—all were wage earners, often educated and keen to have children and with eligible suitors lined up" (1984, 4). Similarly, Zulu women who had migrated to a township in the Durban area in the 1960s stressed the importance of independent economic decision making outside of marriage: "Some of them would prefer to be married, but others regard marriage with mixed feelings, predominant amongst which is a fear of losing the independence and freedom they experience as wage earners in town" (Preston-Whyte 1978, 58).

Parkin and Nyamwaya (1987) argue that educated, urban women were primary agents of change in marriage and the family throughout Africa. Unmarried, financially independent women also served as role models for younger women in Namibia (Chimere-Dan 1997) and Botswana: "Legitimization of the status of the unmarried mother may stem from the fact that high-status women are often in this category" (Gulbrandsen 1986, 21).

Yet, even in the 1970s and 1980s unmarried women were not a new phenomenon in Southern Africa (Gulbrandsen 1986; Hunter 2002; Mayer 1961; van der Vliet 1991, 235). Philip Mayer, for instance, describes so-called *amankazana* or "free women," unmarried women living at their fathers' homesteads and bearing their children there (1961, 85). He suggests that these women may have provided a model for the independent unmarried mothers of South Africa's townships and some rural areas. However, the single women whom van der Vliet and others interviewed in the 1970s were not confined to their father's compound like the amankazana. They often lived on their own and raised their children by themselves: "Like so many women, from the elite to the humblest hawker or domestic worker, this option [to stay single] had become possible with the chance the towns offered for financial independence" (van der Vliet 1991, 236–237).

Importantly, the women's unmarried status did not lead to social isolation. Quite the opposite, single women were in most cases the center of complex female family networks and households (Hellman 1974; Preston-Whyte 1978). The family households of these wage-earning women represented new forms of female cooperation, including both wage-earning and non-wage-earning women, in general connected through kin ties. Eleanor Preston-Whyte calls these families "female linked" (1978, 59). Men often participated in these households only temporarily as lovers, fathers of children, sons, or brothers. Preston-Whyte (1978, 55–58) underscores the similarities of these units to matrifocal families that have been described for the Caribbean (see also Kuper 1987, 147). Matrifocality, however, emphasizes the link between mothers and daughters. Other significant female relations, especially between sisters, are often overlooked in studies on matrifocal households (Pauli 2013). Concepts like "femifocality" (Pauli 2013) and "female linked" families (Preston-Whyte 1978) resolve this bias, enabling more nuanced insights into the specific kinds of female kin relations in these households. Understanding these female relations outside of marriage on their own terms helps overcome the misrecognition of "other forms of relatedness as less than or weaker than heteronormative marriage" (Blackwood 2005, 3; see also Allerton 2007; Davidson 2020).

In Namibia, the phenomenon of the economically independent and unmarried woman emerged in the 1970s and 1980s (Pauli 2019; for parallel dynamics in Botswana, see Solway, this volume). As a role model, it continues to be important today. In a study in the early 2000s of eight congregations in the Omusati and Oshikoto administrative regions in north-central Namibia, many young women said that they were trying to protect their independence by remaining unmarried (Shemeikka, Notkola, and Siiskonen 2005, 103). Women at the head of some Nama households from southern Namibia also emphasized a preference to remain unmarried, as Adelheid Iken found (1999, 179–183). These women had definite views about the requirements of a marriage partner—not all men were perceived as equally suitable (see also G'Sell, this volume, for South Africa). Iken emphasizes that such opinions "point to the potential for conflicting gender roles and new directions in gender relations" (181). Situating these developments in historical perspective, she explains, "Single motherhood reportedly became a more common feature among the Nama and other communities in Namibia and southern Africa after 1918, and went hand in hand with a declining marriage rate" (Iken 1999, 172). However, until the 1960s marriage remained a common and normative event in the life course of most Nama women (180), and an accelerating increase of the percentage of never-married women and men became visible only from the 1980s.

In research on Tswana migrant communities in Botswana in the 1970s, Ørnulf Gulbrandsen (1986) analyzes how the rise of economically independent women is also connected to the spread of more and more impoverished men. From the 1960s onward male migrants gained in agency and prestige through the incomes they made working in South African mines. The young men married, albeit later in life and not on their fathers' terms but their own. This meant that it was no longer the lineage or family of the groom that was responsible for providing bridewealth but the grooms themselves. The migrants' cash incomes led to a strong increase in the levels of bridewealth. They also thoroughly transformed male identities. By linking economic success and independent spending power to masculinity, impoverished and unemployed men began to be marginalized and excluded from marriage. Comparable transformations occurred in Mandeni, KwaZulu-Natal (Hunter 2009a). Mark Hunter argues that the economic crisis of the past decades has deprived most South African men of the means to fulfill the male provider role, meaning that they remain unmarried (Hunter 2007, 2016; G'Sell, this volume). Similarly, poor men in Namibia's northern regions "without resources, without a job, and without a house" cannot marry: "The basic building stones of male identity and masculinity are unavailable to men" (Tersbøl 2002, 367). A comparable marginalization of increasing numbers of impoverished men has also been noted more widely in Africa (Cole 2004; Hannaford 2017; Masquelier 2005; Parkin and Nyamwaya 1987, 15; Smith 2020).

To understand the contingencies of marriage and nonmarriage, these wider structures of the political economy are crucial. In the next section I introduce the life stories of Silvia and Mara and discuss their singlehood against the background of the wider transformations of marriage, gender, and class.

A Mother and Her Daughter:
Two Generations of Namibian Single Women

Silvia Had Enough of Men

Fransfontein is a remote village located in Kunene South in northwest Namibia. During apartheid times the village was part of the "Damaraland homeland," the supposed "home" of the Damara. In reality, Damaraland and Fransfontein were multilingual and multiethnic, including Khoekhoegowab speakers ("Damara" and "Nama," the majority of the population) as well as Oshiwambo and Otjiherero speakers (Pauli 2019). Fransfontein is a quiet, dusty, and dry place. Many households keep livestock on the surrounding cattle post. In addition to the income acquired through pastoralism, most people live from pension money, petty economic activities like collecting firewood, and remittances sent by kin working in one of the urban regions and at the coast (Greiner 2011; Pauli 2019). Food sharing through a local institution called *augu* is crucial for the survival of many households (Schnegg 2016).

When I met Silvia, born in 1950, in 2003, she was an influential woman in the village. Although she had retired a while ago, she was still very active. She was a church elder and kept herself busy with various religious and educational projects. She lived in a part of the village where one finds many households headed by unmarried mothers in their fifties and sixties. The women and their kin lived in brick houses constructed during the apartheid period. In the 1970s and 1980s, when the infrastructure of the so-called homelands was built, these women found employment as domestic workers in the newly opened government institutions. They became a local middle class (Pauli 2019, 113). If not still working, they received state pensions much higher than the standard pensions that Namibians sixty years and older received. These women were in between the small rural elite—made up of a handful of wealthy pastoralists, teachers, and local administrators—and the large majority of impoverished households that had very few resources. Almost all of these women were unmarried mothers and now also grandmothers. It was very common that they raised their grandchildren while their children worked in the city or at the coast. When I met Silvia, she was living together with one of her grandsons, an alert and active four-year old boy.

When chatting with Silvia, she often expressed her disappointment with men, saying that she had enough of them. During a morning chat in May 2004, she laughingly told me that if she should ever consider marrying again, he would have to be a very, very rich man! Otherwise it would not be worth the struggle. To make me understand why she thought so, she told me the story of her "almost marriage," as she called it. This was a story embedded in other stories about coming of age, pregnancy, and migration.

Together with four siblings, Silvia was born in the south of Namibia. Because of her father's occupation in the Protestant church, the family moved frequently. Silvia described her father as a friendly but also dominant, even authoritarian person. She feared and respected him very much.

Silvia did well in school and completed tenth grade. This was rare in the late 1960s, especially for girls. She wanted to continue her schooling but became pregnant in 1970 while attending eleventh grade. Silvia claimed that she had no clue what was happening to her and was very scared. Only after the birth of her second daughter a few years later did she learn about contraception. Silvia did not return to school after the birth of her first child. Instead, she got a job in Windhoek while her family took care of her baby. A year later she entered a training program for primary school teachers in a town close to Fransfontein. But she was forced to leave the training course in 1973 when she became pregnant with her second child. Luckily, however, she found employment at a health clinic soon after the birth of her second daughter.

Most of Silvia's present-day female neighbors in Fransfontein also found permanent occupations at the same time, albeit only as low-skilled domestic workers in one of the newly established government institutions. Silvia, in contrast, worked as a receptionist. When she spoke about this time of her life one could tell that she was proud of her accomplishments. Because of her academic qualifications and her language skills, especially her fluency in English, she never struggled with work. Silvia stayed in the health administration sector until her retirement in 1999. At this point she began to take care of her aging parents in Fransfontein and several of her grandchildren.

Her "almost marriage," Silvia said, developed over the course of several years. She started her narrative with the father of her first daughter. He was a first cousin, and her father strongly opposed the relationship. He argued that Silvia could not marry within the family. After Silvia gave birth, her father did everything to stop the relationship and sent Silvia to Windhoek to work. The father of Silvia's second daughter was a quite different story. He was one of the powerful big men, *kai aogu*, working in the Damaraland administration (Pauli 2017). She met him when she was attending the teachers' training course. She was madly in love, but he already had a fiancée he was about to marry. He treated her very well, giving her lots of attention and presents. He was also much older than Silvia. When he learned that Silvia was pregnant, he was happy and supported her. This was especially important as the pregnancy meant that Silvia had to leave the training course. Nevertheless, he made it very clear to her that he was not going to leave the woman who had by then become his wife. Thus, after giving birth to her second daughter, Silvia split up with him. She told him that she was still young and wanted someone who would marry her. She had high hopes that this would be Peter, as I call him here, the father of her last two children.

Peter fell in love with Silvia while she was still seeing the father of her second daughter. He proposed to Silvia a number of times. Eventually she agreed, and they moved in together. Peter was working in house construction. Silvia became pregnant for the third time. After the birth of their son, Peter's parents came to ask Silvia's father for marriage. Marriages in the region start with the elaborate *!game-#gans* or marriage asking ritual (Pauli 2019, 136–145). A date was set, and everybody prepared for the event. However, two days before the ritual was due to take place, Peter and Silvia had a big fight. Peter was drinking heavily. Silvia did not tell me the reason for the fight, but it ended with Peter severely beating Silvia and the neighbors calling the police. Silvia's father was furious, Peter's parents were disappointed, and the wedding plans were canceled. Sometime later, however, Silvia and Peter reunited and moved to a town further south. Silvia managed to get a transfer from the clinic she had worked at and so immediately continued working. While her professional life went very well, her relationship with Peter became ever more strained. He started seeing another woman. With great sadness, as she said, she kicked him out of the house. The separation lasted several years, until they met again in 1984. He promised that he had changed; promised a new take on marriage; promised so many things: Silvia remained skeptical. Still, she got pregnant again from Peter and in 1985 gave birth to her fourth child, a daughter (Mara). She told me that she had longed for another baby. She also hoped that the birth of Mara would ease and intensify her relationship with Peter. However, this hope was not fulfilled. Peter continued to be unfaithful and eventually Silvia left Peter for good. Reflecting on the men and children in her life, Silvia concluded that in the end, what remained for her were her four children. Her feelings toward men were now mostly negative: she did not trust them anymore and had enough of them.

To what extent had Silvia really opted out of marriage? There were indeed several times that she had decided against a relationship, and once she and her family even canceled marriage plans. And yet, despite clearly stating that she had enough of men, she did not completely opt out of marriage. Had any of the three fathers of her four children been a more appropriate marriage partner—not a relative, not already married, not unfaithful, and not violent—she might have married. She rather practiced judicious opportunism, carefully looking at the options that came with the moment. She was not unconstrained in her evaluations, however: kin, such as her father, repeatedly intervened in her life.

Although many of Silvia's actions must be understood within these specific circumstances, they are also framed by possibilities and narratives that go beyond the situation. Like many other economically independent and unmarried women in Fransfontein, Silvia was pleased to be independent from a stressful relationship. She enjoyed, she said, that she was the boss in the house. She also compared her situation with that of married women her age. In the 1970s and 1980s female gender roles were reconfigured in several ways. Women like Silvia were the first generation of independent, working, single mothers. At the same time, another new female gender role emerged—the housewife (Pauli 2012). Silvia viewed housewives with ambivalence. On the one hand, they were economically well-off: to be a housewife, the husband had to be wealthy enough to finance such a living so that the family did not require a second income. Housewives took pride in this status. On the other hand, being a housewife also meant a significant loss in agency and decision-making power. Married women often stressed over the troubles they had with their husbands, most of whom were unfaithful. With the fear of being infected by HIV, this could lead to fierce quarrels. Lina, a married woman the same age as Silvia, was so depressed by her husband's cheating that she tried to burn herself to death. Silvia told me how much this shocked her.

That Silvia was not married was not the result of any deliberate plan. Her singlehood emerged out of larger economic and educational possibilities that enabled her to lead the independent life she lived. At the same time, her narrative shows that there were several moments in her life when things could have developed differently. In Silvia's view, however, such contingencies framed marriage much more than motherhood. In telling me her stories, Silvia never questioned becoming a mother. In her self-making, being a mother was the base from which marriage might have emerged (Gockel-Frank 2007). It did not. In all her stories, motherhood was first. And motherhood lasted.

Silvia was close to her children, especially to her youngest daughter, Mara. When I met Mara for the first time in 2003, she had just finished school and was working for a nongovernmental organization. When her contract expired at the beginning of 2004, she moved in with her mother. During a long conversation we had in February 2004, she told me how desperate she was to leave the village and "start with her future."

Mara Built Her Future

In 2004, Mara was in a liminal stage. She knew that she wanted to leave the village but had no idea how. During our talks she told me about her previous boyfriends. She had not slept with any of the three and only laughed when I asked whether she had ever thought of marrying one of them. Mara had worked in AIDS counseling and told me that abstinence was her way of protecting herself from an infection. Imagining her ideal partner, Mara said that he should be good at communication and be a "one girl guy," not dating other girls. She was also certain that she wanted to have at least one child. Mara left the village in 2004 and moved to Windhoek. Although we communicated by email, I did not see her again until November 2015, when we met in a Windhoek restaurant for dinner.

When Mara stepped into the restaurant, I was taken aback by her beautiful appearance. During the last ten years, she had changed a lot, not only in style but also in self-confidence. In 2004, she spoke with reluctance and so softly that I often struggled to understand her. Now the words flowed out of her mouth. There was so much to talk about.

After moving to Windhoek in 2004, Mara stayed with her oldest sister. The sister was married and lived in one of the capital's middle-class neighborhoods. Through contacts of her sister's husband, Mara got into college and started training in administration. Her teachers were impressed by her skills and, once she finished college, recommended that she work for the South African High Commission in Namibia. When we met, she was still working there. Next to her full-time job she was attending evening classes. She also told me of several ideas she had for businesses. She emphasized several times how important it was to build a future, to work on her future. Career-wise, Mara said, things were working well. Love-wise, however, things were not going so well.

As she talked, I noticed some parallels between her own and her mother's life. Through our email communication I already knew that Mara had given birth to a daughter in 2013. I asked about the father. With a sigh, Mara told me that he was now out of the picture. Before meeting him, she had a few short-lived affairs. Then in 2010 she met Robert, as I will call him, through her sister. They liked each other and exchanged numbers. Things developed rather quickly, and after only a few months she moved into his apartment. It was located in the same middle-class neighborhood as her sister's home. Mara said that he was good looking, nicely built, and had a good job. After less than two years, they decided to get married. But, as with her mother's "almost marriage," Mara's wedding came to nothing. The *!game-#gans* ritual was performed in Fransfontein in April 2012. It ended with their official engagement and the setting of the marriage date: December 2012. In September 2012, Mara learned that she was pregnant. But she had a growing suspicion that Robert was cheating on her. She said that there were too many occasions when he hid her cell phone from her and behaved strangely. Using her pregnancy as pretense, she asked him to postpone the wedding. He was disappointed but agreed. At the end of 2012, Robert bought a house and they moved in. Despite all hopes that their new house would even out the difficulties they were having, the fighting continued. When she was five months pregnant, she left him and the house and moved back to her sister. From there, she was rushed to the hospital. Her baby was born prematurely and had to stay in hospital for three months, including one month in an incubator. A difficult time in her life began. Mara said that without the help of her mother and her sisters she would hardly have made it. Her "female linked" family (Preston-Whyte 1978), and not the child's father, helped her to cope with the crisis.

When Mara went back to work after three months, her mother took care of the baby. When Silvia returned to Fransfontein six months later, Mara hired a nanny. However, the nanny was often not on time. A couple of months later, when her daughter was almost a year old, Mara decided to give her to her mother to take care of in Fransfontein. Mara said this was a very difficult decision to take. She had always imagined her family life would start differently. Another parallel to her mother's life emerged when, in late 2013, Mara and Robert reunited and Mara moved back into his house. At first things went well. Mara had high hopes that he had truly changed. They talked of marriage again, and a few months later Mara's daughter was relocated to live with them. During the day, while both parents worked, Robert's mother took care of the toddler. Life as a mother-father-child family, however, was not long-lasting. After only six months, Mara again noticed that Robert was hiding something from her. The fighting started again, and Mara left him and the house for good. For a second time, Mara gave her daughter to Silvia.

When we met again more than a year later, Mara reported that she had not dated anyone in the meantime. There were men who had proposed to her. But she was enjoying being single, explaining that "it is a stress-free life." She said that at the moment her future was more important to her than men. She had rented a small apartment close to her sister: "At the moment I think I'll be better off by myself." Similar to the changing forms of intimacy and the increasing importance of romantic affection that Barbadian women have expressed in Carla Freeman's (2014) research, Mara wanted only a marriage that was emotionally fulfilling. If that was not available, she preferred to stay single. Additionally, the intergenerational solidarity, care, and support between herself, her sisters, and her mother further deemphasized the importance of a domestic heterosexual partner.

Regarding motherhood, she was happy with the one child she had. She considered getting pregnant again only if this should be important for a future husband. Otherwise, she would be happy with only one child. She did not at all regret the end of her "almost marriage" and said, "It was a good decision. Yes, it was, because otherwise we would either be divorcing, or I would be crying myself to sleep every night." Like her mother, she was not against marriage. Yet marriage was not the only thing she wanted in life. Many other things, like her daughter, her mother, her sisters, her friends, her career, were equally important.

As in her mother's story, specific circumstances led Mara to opt out of an "almost marriage." While in the process of getting married, Mara, like her mother, realized her future husband had some fundamental flaws. But, like her mother, these realizations did not hinder her from reuniting with him, after the cancellation of the wedding and the breakup. And then breaking up again. Yet Mara's judicious opportunism was also different from her mother's. In comparison to other educated and economically successful women in their twenties and thirties, Mara's skepticism toward marriage was significantly influenced by her mother's experience with marriage (see Medeiros 2018, 138–146 for a comparable generational perspective).

In 2004, I met with a group of young women in their twenties in Fransfontein to talk about love, marriage, and motherhood. All of them had finished high school, and most of them were working. Like the generation of their mothers, they expressed skepticism toward marriage. I asked them why so many young people their age were not married. Was it a question of money? Vanessa, a self-confident single mother, replied, "Everything has changed, things have gotten expensive. The parents themselves are not married. They are still with a boyfriend or a girl-friend, and they still want to get married. And then the child wants to get married, those money problems." Picking up on her last sentence, I asked whether this meant that if they had money, they would all be married. They looked at me with wide open eyes and in unison replied, "No." They elaborated that they would marry only someone they called "Mr. Right." Mr. Right was a trustworthy, faithful, wealthy, good-looking, and educated man. Mr. Right also had to accept their economic independence after marriage. All wanted to continue working. Two of them emphasized that even in a marriage a woman should not stay with a partner out of necessity. If things go wrong, she should leave. All of them were clear that their mothers, married or single, had endured far too many humiliations from men. Their mothers had also told them this repeatedly, encouraging them to not suffer such indignities. This resonated with a conversation I had had earlier in 2004 with Mona, a teacher. Mona was very unhappy in her marriage. When asked if her daughter should ever marry, she said, "By my side, I don't know. My daughter should learn for herself and be independent. During marriage, you sometimes have to stay in the house, have to be silent, silent until your heart becomes sick. I do not want that for my child." While mothers like Silvia and Mona were the first women in Fransfontein to think about a life outside of marriage, their daughters' thinking, their judicious opportunism, is also framed by the experiences of their mothers. The daughters reflect not only on their own options, including opting out of marriage, but also on the outcomes of their mothers' judicious opportunism. While larger political economic transformations have fostered the decline in Namibian marriage, it is this kind of intimate osmosis of experiences, hopes, and mistakes between mothers and daughters that has made opting out of marriage increasingly desirable.

Looking Back and Looking Forward: Situating Single Mothers in Time

To understand the different judicious opportunities of mothers and daughters, it is instructive to interpret the lives of women like Silvia and Mara against the background of their generational belonging and the wider historical transformations taking place. Faye Ginsburg shows how life stories can be used to study the intersection between lived experience and historical change. In her work on discourses and activism for and against abortion in the United States, Ginsburg uses life stories of pro-choice and pro-life women to understand their positioning: "In the narratives, all the women are struggling to come to terms with problematic life-cycle transitions, but in each group, the way they experience those as problematic is associated with very particular historical situations" (1987, 625). Experiencing a crucial historical situation together can lead a group of people to identify as one generation. Renato Rosaldo emphasizes the relational nature of this process. Identifying as a generation (or a cohort) depends on "the extent to which a number of individuals have become self-conscious about their identity as a group in the face of life chances terribly different in appearance from those of their elders and their juniors" (1980, 111). The "life chances" of women like Silvia differ substantially from those of women like Mara. The women are aware of these differences and reflect upon them.

Unlike Silvia, who did not know what was happening to her, Mara did not get pregnant while at school. When Silvia grew up there was no sexual education in school. Contraceptives became available, slowly, only during the 1970s (Pauli 2019, 193). In contrast, by growing up in the midst of the HIV/AIDS crisis, Mara had learned in detail about contraceptives and sexuality. Contraceptives were easily available. Although Mara had never questioned becoming a mother, her motherhood, unlike that of Silvia, was much more shaped by her own decision making. Silvia learned about contraceptives only after she already had two children. Mara had known her options from the start, and she had used that knowledge: she first abstained and later used contraceptives, such as condoms. Mara's pregnancy was planned insofar as she deliberately stopped using the contraceptives, knowing that this might result in pregnancy. The differences between mother and daughter thus are not only situational but have to be understood against the larger context of different life chances these women of two generations had.

Equally, although there are several parallels in Silvia's and Mara's behavior toward marriage, there are also crucial differences, based on belonging to disparate generations. When Silvia opted out of marriage, staying single was still unusual. The decline of marriage started only with her generation. This might explain why Silvia had the need to justify her singlehood and did so rather vehemently in many of our conversations. On one occasion she said that it almost felt as if she had to excuse herself for not having married. Mara, in contrast, did not excuse herself. She was proud of the life she lived and the future she was making. Staying single had become a common, and accepted, way of life.

Finally, it also is important to take into account that the two women were in different phases of their life courses. Silvia was looking back, while Mara, for the most part, was looking forward. Silvia reflected on her life, the possibilities it had offered her, and the ways she had reacted to them. The narrative of the independent and unmarried woman, which became prominent in Southern African ethnographies from the 1960s onward, was also her narrative. It framed how she perceived and justified her life path. Mara's life path, on the other hand, was still very much in the making. Her self-making was an ongoing process, shaped by judicious opportunism, her own specific life chances, and her reflections on her mother's story.

Conclusion

Within the past four decades, marriage in Namibia has changed substantially. With the strong decline in marriage rates since the 1970s, the institution has transformed from a widespread rite of passage, socially ordering society, into a rare event conspicuously celebrated only by the middle and upper classes. Nevertheless, although marriage today is out of reach for many, most Namibians continue to aspire to it. Parallel to the decline in common marriage and the rise of exclusive marriages, alternative life paths have emerged. This is especially true for women. Today, single mothers are widespread in the country. It is remarkable that motherhood has remained compulsory, while marriage has become optional. More research is needed to understand this continuity (Mkhwanazi 2014; Upton 2001).

While the first generation of single women in the 1970s and 1980s was still plagued by feelings of inferiority relating to their singlehood, their daughters live their single lives with confidence. Furthermore, women today in their twenties and thirties are more outspoken about enjoying their single lives than was the case for their mothers. Nevertheless, women of both generations did not oppose marriage. Quite the contrary, many women described moments in their lives when they almost married. That the women eventually did not marry was the outcome of specific individual and generational circumstances.

It is important to note that my findings are framed by gender and class. I am focusing on women from the emerging middle classes. My in-depth treatment of two women's life stories shows that the rise of the Namibian middle classes started much before the changes brought by independence in 1990. Many of the young women who are successful and single today are the daughters of the first generation of economically independent single mothers from the 1970s. There are, of course, also many single mothers who are impoverished (Pauli 2012, 2017). Their singlehood has to be understood on its own terms and needs further research (see also James 2017; Niehaus 2017). The judicious opportunism of men, both wealthy and impoverished, and the ways they marry or stay single also need much more attention. My assumption is that while being an economically successful single mother is now an accepted and common alternative way of life for women, this is not the case for men. The figure of the economically prosperous single father does not exist in Namibia. Economically successful men are not independent and single but married. This creates a lot of pressure for men to marry (James 2015, 53; Smith 2020). Comparable pressures on men in Senegal to prosper economically and then marry have increased male labor migration to Europe (Hannaford 2017).

Seeing beyond marriage also means questioning marriage and its relevance for the social order. Joanna Davidson describes how, without much ado, widows in Jola villages in Guinea-Bissau reconfigure gender relations by not remarrying. Contrary to the common perception of widowhood as a vulnerable and problematic state of being, Davidson highlights that "widowhood is not aberrant but attractive." She concludes, "These women suggest a haunting of marriage because they embody the prospect of a new material formation that is working outside it" (2020, 55.

What this "new material formation" outside marriage looks like depends on the ethnographic context. In Guinea-Bissau, marriage remains obligatory. Only after marriage and motherhood and with widowhood can women opt out: "Put starkly, who really needs a husband, especially after having children?" (Davidson 2020, 52). In contrast, marriage and motherhood are largely disentangled in Namibia and Botswana (Pauli 2012, 2019, 199–226; Solway, this volume; Upton 2001).

In addition to the "new material formation" scrutinized by Davidson, looking beyond marriage also makes visible a "new social formation." In her seminal paper on "what it means to be alone," Catherine Allerton (2007) convincingly argues that it is a very Euro-American perception to view unmarried people, especially women, as "alone," "lonely," and "needy" (see also Lahad 2012). She draws on her ethnographic findings of unmarried older women in Indonesia. Referring to Erving Goffman's (1971) distinction between "single" (a person by him—or herself) and "withs" (a person together with others), she concludes, "Although unmarried women may have a 'single status' with regard to marriage, in terms of wider social life they are most definitely 'withs,' whether connected with another unmarried sister, their parents, or their brother and his children" (Allerton 2007, 21). Comparably, single women in India (Lamb 2018, 64), the United States (Edin and Kefalas 2007; Stack 1970), Brazil (Medeiros 2018), and Namibia are very often embedded in complex and dense kin networks. They are not alone but actively take part in female linked webs of caring and reciprocal relations, especially to their sisters, mothers, and daughters (Pauli 2013).

The findings I present here add to this literature as they highlight the importance of generation, gender, and class. During a specific moment in time, the 1970s, economically independent Namibian women were able to reconfigure gender roles and the female life path, creating the option of becoming an accepted single mother. Their daughters have continued along this path, adding their own life chances and reflections.

Acknowledgments

My gratitude goes to Joanna Davidson and Dinah Hannaford for inviting me to their panel at the 2019 American Anthropological Association (AAA) meeting in Vancouver. I also thank Michael Schnegg, Maren Jordan, Dumitrita Lunca, Rijk van Dijk, Koreen Reece, Janet Carsten, Susan McKinnon, the anonymous reviewer, and the participants of the 2019 AAA panel on "Opting Out" for comments and advice on the chapter and on the topic of marriage in general. I am very thankful to my interlocutors in Fransfontein and Windhoek for sharing their time, experiences, and insights with me. The research has been funded by two grants from the German Research Foundation (DFG): project C10 within the Collaborative Research Centre 389 (2002–2009) and project PA 848/3-1 (2015–2019).

NOTE

1. To protect the anonymity of Silvia and Mara, I have changed their names and some identifiable information.

2

Single in Botswana

JACQUELINE SOLWAY

If asked, most women in Botswana would say that they wish to be married. Yet many are reluctant to do so. In the abstract women desire marriage; in reality they will engage in it only on particular terms and conditions, some of which they have more control over than others. Why do increasing numbers of women remain single? It is a not a new phenomenon in Botswana but, as I demonstrate, a growing one. In the past, observers often attributed the existence of single mothers to familial disruption brought on as a consequence of labor migration and the dismantling of "tribal" customs such as initiation (Schapera 1940/1971, 43–47). In more recent times HIV/AIDS prevalence was added to the familial disruption mix (see Reece 2019). I do not view the rise in single women as pathological and question whether marriage is the necessary "natural" and ideal adult condition for women against which other conditions are to be described or evaluated (Solway 1989; Davidson 2020). Nonetheless the decline in marriage constitutes a significant demographic shift that requires examination and explanation, which I offer in this chapter.

Exploring women's reluctance to marry requires examining the broader context of Botswana's evolving political economy as well as more specific issues such as shifting forms of conjugality and residence, shifting attitudes regarding the social and moral legitimacy of these forms, and the nature of contemporary weddings. Most contemporary wedding organizers strive to be "modern" and showy while at the same being "traditional" and thus culturally "authentic." These seemingly contradictory mandates entail great expense and the imposition of patriarchal disciplinary rules and practices upon the participants, especially the brides, which impact marriage's desirability (see also Mupotsa 2015).

Any change in marital patterns must be considered first in light of transformations in Botswana's political economy. At independence in 1966 Botswana was virtually completely rural and livelihoods were almost exclusively based on agropastoralism and oscillating male labor migration to the South African mines;

patrilocal residence was the norm. Within a few short decades, Botswana's formal sector expanded dramatically (funded mostly by massive windfall diamond wealth), labor migration declined, and urban neo-local residence became a new norm although multigenerational patterns still predominate and people retain multiple residences.[1] As Botswana became increasingly wealthy it also became more unequal, but class, while important, cuts in contradictory ways in relation to marriage possibilities. As noncommercial agriculture rapidly declined in economic significance and alternate livelihood options not based in agriculture opened for women, many felt less pressure to marry for economic security (see Pauli, this volume).

Remaining single has long been an established option in Botswana for women. Indeed, Botswana has been an outlier with respect to rates of marriage not only globally but even within Southern Africa, where marriage rates are generally low (Solway 2016; James 2017; Hunter 2016; Pauli 2019). Almost a century ago, Isaac Schapera, in his 1933 article on "Premarital Pregnancy" in Botswana, spoke of the moral alarm raised by "un-wed" mothers. Subsequent anthropologists also addressed the issue (Comaroff 1980; Comaroff and Comaroff 1981; Gulbrandsen 1986). Kuper (1982) suggests that many current single mothers might have been junior wives in polygynous unions in previous decades when polygyny was a norm. Yet Botswana's marriage rates continue to decline dramatically, an observation from fieldwork confirmed by the census.[2] Now, by the evidence of this volume, the rest of world appears to be catching up to Botswana.

Weddings and Their Discontents

In recent decades the phenomenal rise in wedding costs has been a key factor contributing to lower marriage rates. Julia Pauli (2019) argues in *The Decline of Marriage in Namibia* that extravagant weddings have become the means by which the elite demonstrate their distinction and wealth. The elite's increasingly opulent weddings have set an expensive norm that very few can attain. Couples, actually more often the parents of the bride, reject cheaper wedding options, seeing these as calling into question their own status and worth as well as the value of their daughters, which is, in large part, a reflection of their own value. The elite's power to define the wedding agenda such as to virtually exclude the vast majority of people is profound. The situation is similar in Botswana, where lavish "white weddings" have become the norm and where the ability to perform wealth and status better enables aspirants to actually acquire such status (Livingston 2009). These weddings have a potlatch quality, with new weddings attempting to outdo previous ones, leading to an escalation in expectations (Solway 2016; van Dijk 2017). Several couples told me that they wanted a simple wedding but their parents, especially the bride's, continued to demand more wedding extravagance, so much so that some young people, particularly men, have described getting married as a war between the sexes and the generations. In contrast to Pauli's (2019) research area, credit is more readily available in Botswana, which puts greater pressure upon young working people to accede to their family's requests. Despite help from relatives, grooms and often brides take out exorbitant loans, frequently up to five times as much as the couple's annual salary and from more and less scrupulous sources, to pay for their weddings (van Dijk 2012, 145). Wedding debt takes years to pay off, often at steep interest rates. Most people cannot afford white weddings even with loans and stay single or participate in other forms of conjugality.

Interestingly, there appears to be an emerging countertrend (for which I have limited data) that points to alternatives available primarily to the elite who choose to express their distinction by defying the "crass" display of white weddings. Some couples and their parents who can socially "afford" it are opting out of white weddings and instead marry at the magistrate's office (and often at church as well), followed by a "nice" luncheon attended by close friends and family. I am told that such couples wish to avoid the crippling debt that accompanies white weddings but still have a formal wedding/marriage recognized by the state, the church, and their circle of invitees. Such weddings usually include the transference of *bogadi* (bridewealth—often eight cattle or their agreed-upon cash equivalent), but bogadi costs are standard and not subject to inflation as compared to those for a white wedding. White and magistrate weddings are not mutually exclusive, but couples who reject white weddings may be making a statement not only about avoiding ostentatious consumption and debt but also about avoiding aspects of patriarchal discipline instantiated during the "traditional" component of white weddings as discussed below.

While the importance of social recognition of life cycle events, especially marriage, in Botswana is hard to overstate, some recognition is sacrificed in magistrate weddings. Yet enough is preserved and ripples outward to satisfy those involved. In addition to a stated concern about debt, many magistrate-wedded couples are in a socioeconomic, educational, and status position where they can eschew the conspicuous consumption and excess of white weddings, thereby casting a negative light over the ostentatious display and exhibiting a "less is more" (Mies van der Rohe) attitude with its imbrication of arrogance and modesty (Veblen 1924; Meneley 2018; Bourdieu 1984).

Magistrate weddings that reject the fuss and expense of white weddings can now validate elite standing for both the couple and their parents, although it might be a hard sell for the latter. I often heard them described as "with a ring and paper."[3] However, whether the "ring and paper" weddings will trickle down the status hierarchy remains to be seen. They may be more common among second- or third-generation elite families where the status of the parents and the couple do not require white wedding validation. However, even if magistrate weddings become more accepted among middle-class couples and the rate of marriage increases, this will still be within limits. Many couples at the bottom end of middle-class status and the majority below that remain unable to afford a magistrate wedding, bogadi, or a ring.[4]

I have emphasized the cost of contemporary weddings as an impediment to marriage, but in some instances the prestige emanating from holding a showy wedding might be a greater prize than the marriage. In what might be a limited trend but nonetheless notable to anthropologists and to many of my local interlocuters is a rise in white weddings among very young couples, especially young women, thereby bucking the pattern of women delaying marriage, or at least white weddings, until later in life. Kubanji (2014, 228) reports that the average age at marriage for women was 24.8 in 1971 and 32.0 in 2011. The status and pride attached to ostentatious weddings has led some eager young couples and their families to allow weddings to go forward without extensive negotiations, wide kin involvement, or the sociality inherent in the time lags that are usually considered necessary to launch a successful marriage. Reece in Carsten et al. (2019) notes this visible trend among young couples who manage to rush through normally accepted "prerequisites," such as examining past kinship history and "transactions" in order to fast-track weddings. Especially prevalent among "AIDS orphans," the practice enables them to circumvent deep kinship negotiations and norms that would be difficult due to the relatively ambiguous identities and statuses of their parents (5).

Many of my interlocutors speak with some alarm of the rise in younger people engaging in flashy white weddings and of a concomitant rise in divorce, in which settlement often entails difficult property negotiations. Most distressing to them is how frequently the divorces led to very painful custody disputes that, despite court rulings, rarely resolve well. Fast track weddings are often discussed as cautionary tales, implying that the couples, and especially the young women, wanted the wedding more than they wanted the marriage. Spouses are simply too young and neither sufficiently socialized nor sufficiently committed to the "long-haul" necessary for a functioning marriage.

Some officials, NGOs, and clergy have championed simple customary court-based wedding alternatives, often as group events for mostly older couples who have cohabited for many years (see also Setume 2017, 18, Reece in Carsten et al. 2019). The large group weddings, called *Re a Nyalana* (literally "we get married"), have taken place mostly in the larger villages of eastern Botswana. While not recognized as "real" or "authentic" Tswana marriages, they serve a critical purpose, namely, to provide civil and legal protection to spouses (and children) with respect to issues of property and inheritance. While important for both spouses, the marriages are most important for women. There have been many instances in Botswana, some resulting in very high-profile court cases, and most in ordinary everyday practice, in which a cohabiting "wife" is "widowed" and the "husband's" patrilateral family arrive and seize all of the couple's estate regardless of the fact that the couple may have built up the property together over decades and even regardless of the fact that the "wife" may have made the primary material contribution to the estate. I am told of cases in which the man's kin assert that they "don't know" the cohabiting "wife." Of course, they know her in the English sense of the term but argue that they don't "acknowledge" her as kin in the absence of a socially recognized marriage. Technically, this accords with Tswana customary law as it was recorded in colonial times (Schapera 1938/1984, 231), but with urbanization, displacement of agropastoralism as the primary livelihood practice, and female employment this law now has little purchase. Formerly, most widows continued to reside with their husband's lineal kin, who would, ideally by this time, include her children, especially sons.[5] Re a Nyalana is a "modern" reaction to patriarchal practice and structures, many antiquated, but that reveal the difficulties "unmarried" women encounter in moving through the life cycle. Re a Nyalana offers a means by which senior women can gain legal protection for their homes and property. However, the group weddings and resulting marriages have not provided an acceptable alternative to more conventional forms of marriage, especially for younger women.

Mothers and Other Single Women

The vast majority of Tswana are officially single, but this is an appellation that encompasses multiple sorts of relationships and residential circumstances. As depicted by Hunter (2007, 2010) for South Africa and by me for Botswana (2016), many poorer women do not marry for reasons of choice, force of circumstance, or some combination of the two. Given the unemployment crisis in Southern Africa, few men have the means to provision a household let alone give bogadi (G'Sell, this volume). Marriage is also risky for women, especially poor women, who cannot rely upon one man alone to provide for them and their children and who, by design or default, participate in what Guyer (1994) has aptly termed "polyandrous motherhood." The more children a single woman has, the less likely she is to marry (see also Griffiths 1997). It is less that single mothers or their children are stigmatized (almost all women have children while single)[6] and more that the children's welfare can be called into question if a single mother marries. Despite promises to care for the children as their "own," not all husbands and/or their kin do so, often making care decisions based upon limited resources and jealous (lefufa) kin. Theoretically, if a single mother marries and bogadi is transferred, all of her children, unless specifically agreed upon, become legitimate children of her husband, but sometimes they remain in an inferior position in relation to children conceived with the husband (Schapera 1933, 84). I know of one marriage that began when the wife was already pregnant by another man. After the child was born, the husband said, "If the child is not your own, its nose is too wide, its urine smells too strong, and its cry is too loud." The child was sent to live with the wife's parents as soon as it was weaned. A child might be more secure if he or she lives with maternal kin, but this is uncertain.

Many women leave their nonmarital children with their natal kin after marrying; it is an attractive option but also presents risks. Grandmothers, often in their forties themselves, might also have young children and find caring for grandchildren difficult or, as is increasingly the case, grandmothers have jobs outside the home and cannot easily take in children. Young mothers often enjoy a period of relative ease while still living in their natal homes, particularly in rural areas (G'Sell this volume). They and a young child are often indulged by immediate family and allowed to call upon the labor of their junior kin, especially sisters-in-law, for child care and other domestic duties. I recall in my early fieldwork in an agropastoral village, gossip that wives of a set of brothers just become babysitters for Agnes, their unmarried sister-in-law in her late teens. However, Agnes knew that her privileged situation could not continue. Eventually her brothers' wives would have children and her natal family's labor, attention, and resources would be directed toward the new families of their patriline. By staying, Agnes would place her parents and siblings in a series of conflicts of interest out of which discord would emerge. Increasingly, she and her child would be "out of place." In Agnes's case, she married and her child was fully absorbed in her new household. Agnes had a small window in which to act, and she did well by her own account, but that window and outcome are not always available and not always desirable. After a first or second child comes a time when many women face what Johnson-Hanks identifies as a vital conjuncture, "when socially structured zones of possibility . . . emerge around specific periods of potential transformation in a life or lives" (2006, 23). Vital conjunctures are time limited, full of potential but also uncertainty; the degree to which women can choose a path toward marriage or single motherhood and the degree to which that path is overdetermined by encompassing structures and circumstances vary according to numerous factors discussed throughout this chapter.

While single mothers and children are much more the norm than the exception and are rarely subject to harsh stigmatization (cf. G'Sell, this volume), many women, especially those from the middle class, the educated, and/or the elite, attempt to remain childless until marriage or the attainment of economic self-sufficiency (see also Setume 2017). For many higher status women, such restraint is a symbol of strength and self-valor. However, to never have a child is a source of great personal sadness and humiliation. Without a child a woman is considered incomplete. Bearing a child is a central component of achieving womanhood; children bring great joy, they extend lives and descent lines forward, and infertility can render a woman suspect, as a sign that she might either be practicing or be a victim of witchcraft. A childless woman is also suspicious because she may become envious and dangerous; envy can cause harm regardless of its bearer's intent.[7] Ideally children provide labor and eventually care for their aging parents. Thus, single women who choose to "wait" for children eventually face a decision between their desire to remain childless until conditions are "right" and their virtual social mandate to have a child. These women tend to have fewer children overall, and many would rather remain single than marry a man who they believe might be disrespectful, irresponsible, or abusive (Pauli, this volume; G'Sell, this volume). Some prefer to have no relationship with their child's father. In addition, women of such status have very few potential marriage partners. As I have been told repeatedly, men do not wish to marry "women who own houses" or have as much or more education than themselves; generally, they wish to marry women whose status does not exceed their own and who will be submissive to them and their parents. Women at both ends of the class continuum face difficulties making a marriage.

Residence, Cohabitation, and Conjugality

There are many forms of residence and conjugality that compete with marriage in Botswana. Following Setume (2017), alternate forms of living and/or establishing a household need to be examined in their own right and not as a deviant form or as a prelude to the supposed norm of marriage, a view she critiques as "methodological nuptialism" (2). Cohabitation, long and short term, is extremely common in Botswana; indeed, cohabitation without formal nuptials is becoming the new norm and the new normal despite the articulated aspirations of many women to marry (see also Posel and Rudwick 2014a; Pauli, this volume). Cohabitation arrangements vary enormously; for some couples, long-term cohabitation resembles an incomplete marriage in which parental and family negotiations have begun but there has been no "wedding," bogadi is yet to be transferred, and social recognition is uncertain.[8] Such indeterminacy is common in Botswana, where ambiguity is valued for its social productivity (Comaroff 1980; Solway 2016). Comaroff (1980, 170) speaks of a proclivity for ambiguity in marital relations. Until recently transferring bogadi was delayed sometimes for a whole generation, and sons gave bogadi for their mothers. Marriage incompletion keeps relations open and encourages ongoing sociality, harmony, gifts, and exchange between the affinal families (Mauss 1950/2002). In addition, as long as bogadi is not yet transferred, the wife and children remained technically part of her natal lineage who often play a role in ensuring her well-being (Solway 2016, 311).

More commonly, cohabitation occurs in the absence of any marital arrangements or little thought of marriage. Parental assent to cohabitation also varies considerably. Parents often allow a man to live with their daughter without marital intentions but under certain agreed-upon terms, usually with respect to the financial contribution of the man and his treatment of their daughter and her children. However, a young woman's parents may prohibit their daughter from living with or even maintaining ongoing relations with a man they distrust, even if he is the father of their daughter's child. If forced to choose, it is more likely that younger daughters remain loyal to their parents than to their partners. Parents are often more reliable sources of support of all kinds. But many couples simply live together for as long as they wish without seeking explicit parental assent.

A number of women cohabit serially, neither wishing nor able to establish a stable heterosexual household. Some, as discussed earlier, do so for reasons of poverty and the risks of relying upon one partner. Many women wish for a companionate marriage, but these are difficult to establish and sustain. In my observation, relatively few couples of all classes socialize together regularly; women are more likely to remain home or socialize with female friends and family while men are often out. Men exert more control over household resources and join friends for drink and food, and many "congeal" their resources into cattle, rendering the resources not only indivisible but resistant to pleas of household need (Ferguson 1990). While women own cattle (Solway 2017), they are primarily men's property and a source of masculine pride and power. Many men go to the cattlepost to work but also to get away from domestic work and to pursue other leisure activities. Of course, I know of numerous exceptions, but the pattern prevails. Even if the husband is not the primary breadwinner and the wife largely controls her own property, she can be subject to male control. An older woman whose assets include a modest house, fields, and a small number of livestock was recently widowed. She told me that she would never marry again and still had nightmares of her husband asking her to make tea for him at any time of day or evening In this case the husband, neither the woman's first nor father to her children, had moved into her home, yet he still felt the ability to command her obedience. Botswana remains a patriarchal society; according to official reports two out of three women have experienced gender-based violence (SADC 2015, 65), and men often have multiple girlfriends or concubines (*bonyatsi*) whom they support. Wives are meant to be submissive to their husbands and his family; more and more women chafe at this prospect.

Women often weigh the advantages and disadvantages of cohabitation relative to marriage. Botswana newspapers regularly run articles about women and children who are left dispossessed of property (house, furniture, land, etc.) that they built or purchased with their partners but which is seized by his patrilateral kin upon his death (see discussion of Re a Nyalana above). Civil marriage offers a woman and her children property protection via recognized legal inheritance laws. Since at least 1994, leading legal scholars and practitioners in Botswana (Othlogile 1994) have argued for legal recognition and protection of cohabitants and their children. While courts have occasionally supported such women's right to household property, outcomes are uncertain, and lawyers are expensive (cf. Werbner and Werbner 2020). Mark Hunter (2016) makes a similar case for legal and social recognition of cohabitants in South Africa who have completed an early stage of marriage transfer.

Opting Out, Opting In, But . . .

Many women either refuse marriage or wish to influence its terms; for some the choice is constrained, absent, or overdetermined, as noted earlier for poorer women and for women who have many children. Women of socioeconomic means are often reluctant to marry if they are not confident that they will enjoy a companionate marriage. Parents often agree. I know of a professional young woman whose parents understood and explicitly advised her to wait until her late twenties to have children and establish a home as a single mother. Some very poor women refuse marriage out of fear. Some poor women in western Botswana (Ghanzi district) who took advantage of government gender empowerment programs to acquire cattle are determined to build their herds, at times sacrificing their own nutritional needs to ensure that the cattle are fed. They often refuse marriage, preferring to retain their independence and property (A. Petitt, personal communication, 2016). Similarly, some single middle-class women state that they would marry only "outside the community of property" in order to ensure their control over their property, especially in event of divorce. This is ironic, as several decades ago leading Tswana feminist lawyers advocated for women to marry "in community of property" in order to protect themselves in the event of divorce or abandonment. In the 1980s it was hard to imagine that, except for a very few elite women, women might earn or bring substantial material resources into the marriage (apart, of course, from the monumental domestic and agricultural labor they provide).

Many women delay marriage or its completion in order to maintain closer ties to their natal kin. Patrilocal residence occurs, but is much less common than it was forty years ago when Botswana was almost entirely rural. Still, marriage usually entails a shift in affiliation and authority for the wife. During the wedding she is instructed to obey and listen to her husband's family and to serve them. If urban based, the couple are expected to align with and visit the husband's family on weekends and during vacations more often than with the wife's. Many women do not desire to have such a rupture with their natal kin who provide them with love, security, and support. I know women who have asked their husbands to delay transferring bogadi to their parents so as to not sever the relationship or to be "owned" by in-laws and suffer the expectations of service and subservience that come with it (G'Sell, this volume; Hannaford, this volume; see also Hunter 2016). Prior to the latter decades of the twentieth century, most marriages entailed a lengthy process of rituals and exchanges with bridewealth usually transferred a decade or more after the early rituals. Marriages solidified more gradually and both the wife's and the husband's family remained more involved. Not only do many women wish to retain stronger ties to their natal kin, but parents of marriage-age children complained to me that limiting ties to the wife's natal kin increased marital instability and too often led to divorce (which an interlocuter from my first days of fieldwork recently explained to me was "twenty times worse" than when we first met).

Family lawyers claim that a leading cause of divorce centers around a wife feeling "crowded out" by the extended family, her in-laws, especially her mother-in-law. This is true in a physical sense as more and more kin come to stay with the new family, particularly if they are urban based. It is also true in an emotional sense that is often more difficult for the wife to abide. A man is said to remain too attached to his mother, to pay more attention to her concerns and interests than to those of his wife, and to be inordinately influenced by his mother. The lawyers' statements resonate with my own decades-long observations of the powerful bonds between mothers and sons and the great deference shown to mothers on the part of sons. Patrilocal residence facilitates this kind of affect and loyalty; it blends in with the landscape and is part of general habitus, but it can be jarring and feel oppressive to wives in other circumstances.

Neither men nor women wish to escape their kin; they are not seeking to be the autonomous liberal subjects of modernity's imagination (Solway 2016; Lamb 2018; Pauli, this volume), but they do wish to exert more control over the nature of their kinship ties. Research in South Africa illustrates creative ways in which women are increasingly setting their own terms for marriage or avoiding it altogether in new ways. Eric Bähre (2020) offers an account of Sylvia in South Africa, who, through a complicated set of circumstances, came to raise a child of her deceased close kin as her own son. The boy did not know to the contrary. Eventually when she married, "Sylvia . . . like so many other African women living in South Africa today . . . objected to customary law preferring only a judicial marriage [and she objected to] *lobola* (bridewealth)," which would give her husband and in-laws, in particular, "more rights over Sylvia as well as her son" (270). There is an ironic twist to this story that reveals the risks entailed by women who buck the rules. As a teenager the child wished to be initiated, but where and among which kin? Sylvia had divorced, but that was irrelevant since her husband had not transferred bridewealth and the "son" was not affiliated to his lineage. Given the boy's complicated parentage, he was not "properly" affiliated to any kin line. Sylvia could have arranged for the boy to be initiated amongst a group of her kin but, as she stated, "You cannot fool the ancestors" (271), indicating that no ideal solution to her and her son's dilemma existed. Eventually he was initiated among her matriline, but the consequences of her "freedom" rendered the outcome of his initiation uncertain in Sylvia's eyes and those of others in the lineage, some past and some "not yet born" (273). Sylvia's son's life did not "go well"; he did not achieve adulthood as he and his family had hoped, and he took his own life while still relatively young but after having fathered a child. The extent to which Sylvia and others attribute his decline to her kinship choices and the ancestors' displeasure with them remains an open question. Of course, as many have observed, achieving adulthood especially for males in a world where their labor is in little demand is a fraught, contingent, and poorly defined process, although vernacular attributions of the elusiveness of adulthood have their own logic (Durham and Solway 2017).

Rice (2020) offers a compelling case from South Africa (Eastern Cape, Xhosa) in which female aversion to marriage amplifies men's declining role in social reproduction. In the rural area where Rice conducted her fieldwork, some jobs have become available that young women can obtain more easily than men. The jobs require skills that women are more likely to have since they tend to remain in secondary school longer than their male counterparts. While these young women are mothers, they refuse to marry despite the desire of some of their parents for them to do so and for bridewealth to be transferred. The young women argue that they are better able to support their families as breadwinners than as wives. Some behave outside the home in ways that disrupt gender norms such as going to a bar with friends but do not compromise their ability to support their families materially and otherwise. They trouble gender roles in this way but also, and ironically, reinforce patriarchy at the same time as they challenge it. They recognize that their employment keeps them away from the domestic work at home that accompanies their roles as mothers and daughters. However, they prefer to resolve this dilemma by encouraging their brothers and sons to marry so that they will have sisters-in-law and daughters-in-law to fulfill domestic responsibilities. Thereby, they simultaneously support patriarchal household structures while selectively undermining gender meanings. Women evoke the discourse of human rights as enshrined in the post-apartheid South African Constitution to support their choice to remain single, while men often argue that as traditional rural people their rights are being "trampled upon" by women in cahoots with the independent state government.

Livelihood, Production, and Reproduction

Joanna Davidson (2020), in her analysis of widows, argues that one must attend to transformations in the politics of resource control in order to apprehend any long-term changes in kinship and gender relations. Local processes of resource use, control, and value and their role in evolving livelihood opportunities are connected to Botswana's rapid and profound changes in national resource and welfare policy. In the latter decades of the twentieth century, Botswana achieved rates of economic growth (GDP) second to none and went from being one of the poorest countries in the world at independence (1966) to becoming an upper-middle-income country in 2005 (Leith 2005; Gulbrandsen 2012). Samatar's portrayal of Botswana as the "African Miracle" (1999) illustrates how an effective state was able to absorb new wealth and expand infrastructure, education, and services of all kinds while limiting corruption. Just as the new wealth began flooding the country, opportunities for men to work in the South African mines virtually disappeared and, with extensive state subsidy, arable agriculture became mechanized. However, agriculture's prestige and economic importance for households and for the nation declined significantly.

Prior to this period, women gained access to agricultural land and the harvests that they controlled as wives; single women could gain access to land as sisters or daughters or through a form of sharecropping or "putting in hands" (*majako*), but access to these latter options was unreliable. Some women had their own fields, but this was rare. At independence men had almost exclusive access to land and salaries,[9] although this began to erode in the final few decades of the century. Men continue to control cattle and cattle remain an important component of masculine power, although less so than in the past century, and more women exert control over cattle now.

Urbanization and formal sector opportunities expanded dramatically in the late twentieth century. While women had been dependent upon men for access to their mine wages, once women had their own employment, they gained greater control over their earnings. At the same time, urbanization resulted in a decline of patrilocality, which enabled women to obviate the constant scrutiny and regulation of their affinal kin. Men and their patrilateral kin were thereby less able to socialize, control, and discipline wives through daily practice and subtle invocation. Opportunities for senior kin to socialize the spouses through rituals have also declined with the rise of "fast bogadi" marriages in which rituals and exchanges that may have stretched over decades in the past century are now usually completed within a few days. While not simply cause and effect, changes in the larger political economy, regimes of resource control, and residential patterns together have lessened many women's economic dependence upon men and concomitantly increased their ambivalence about marriage. This may account for the strong emphasis placed upon invoking, often harshly, discipline and the law during the actual weddings (see also Reece in Carsten et al. 2019).

Marriage and Discipline

Weddings and marriage inscribe generational and gendered patriarchal discipline in both men and women, and not just the spouses. Patriarchy is reproduced through numerous practices that continually revalidate and sometimes reinvent the value of marriage, but these practices—and patriarchy itself—are increasingly contested. The example of women attempting to maintain close links with their natal kin makes the point. Part of the discipline of marriage is to break or diminish the wife's connection to her natal kin. *Go Laya*, giving advice, is a central component of weddings. Spouses may receive such advice on more than one occasion, but most importantly at the wedding itself and especially, but not exclusively, from their lineal kin. Here the bride, surrounded by her married, mostly senior, female maternal kin, is advised on how to behave as a wife. Almost all the advice reinforces patriarchal structures: brides are told to care for the home, but most of all they are told how to behave and to serve their husband and his kin. The woman must be subservient, obey commands, not ask questions, and accept a husband's transgressions. She must not "talk too much" or complain even if the circumstances might lead to her own harm. Ellece (2011, 46) quotes a mother's sister at a wedding advising her niece "to be a fool like me" and not leave the marital home if mistreatment occurs. A woman must be silent during go laya, just as she is meant to be passive during the marriage. Grooms receive go laya as well from their paternal married male kin, during which they are instructed to be proper husbands, to provide for and protect their wives and home. They are encouraged to foster harmonious marital relations but are held to less account than their wives. For instance, they are told to consult their wives but not necessarily to abide by their wishes (2011, 51).

Single people usually experience social humiliation and stigmatization during the negotiations, throughout planning, and especially at the wedding itself. The danger begins during the negotiation stage when sensitive issues arise, such who has or has not previously exchanged bogadi and therefore would be able to accept it at the wedding.[10] Tswana customary law excludes single people from involvement in many martial processes such as negotiation, giving advice (go laya), and participating in various wedding activities, especially the latter two. For instance, an unmarried middle-aged man who is an extremely highly educated successful professional told me that he is theoretically excluded from most marital events. He explained how although he is not meant to enter the kraal when the bogadi cattle are received, despite the "noise" of his relatives, he does so anyway. His status and wealth enable him to violate the rules. But he is constantly reminded of the rules and how he has not yet achieved full "social" adulthood. He told this to me with a bit of a grin, but few people can endure such an assault on their integrity and adulthood with the same nonchalance. Other single adults "break" the rules as well; some can do so more easily than others, but they face gossip and varying levels of disapproval. Throughout the whole process of marriage, single people are identified and marginalized; they are disciplined by being reminded of their deviance in this context and marginalized or excluded as a consequence. They are shamed. For some this validates the value of marriage, perhaps in a similar way that revived "tribal initiations" do, mostly for males, but there is also a rise in female initiations. These require personal sacrifice, endurance, and submission to patriarchal rules but engender a feeling of accomplishment and pride for oneself and one's culture once complete.[11] But for others the process relegates aspects of "traditional marriage" to an anachronistic past.

One single mother whose daughter married in an elaborate wedding claimed that her in-laws were happy when she paid the bills but that they insulted her by critiquing her participation in some of the rituals and excluded her from others. Out of step with the fact that the spouses were middle-class professionals who were to assume urban neolocal residence, the groom's family insisted upon a precise set of rituals for the bride and her family, most of which were reinventions, or simply inventions, of an antiquated rural past. When the bride and her family were inevitably unable to perform them to the imposed standard, whispers about the marriage's doom began to spread. By the end of the wedding, a young highly educated professional close female relative of the bride just threw up her hands and stated, "I'm never going to get married." Instead of reinforcing the value of weddings and being married, the advice, practices, and disparagements had the opposite effect—further alienating young people, especially women. In sum, the patriarchal discipline delivered at weddings can backfire, undermining instead of valorizing marriage and further promoting "opting out."

Acknowledgments

This chapter is based upon four decades of research in Botswana, beginning with early intensive fieldwork in a Kalahari village, repeated visits, shorter fieldwork periods in other rural localities, and ongoing fieldwork in Botswana's capital. I wish to thank the government of Botswana for granting research permits to Trent University and maintaining an open research environment and Social Sciences and Humanities Research Council (SSHRC) of Canada for several grants over the years. I am indebted to the people of Botswana for their kindness, patience, and hospitality that was generously provided to me. In particular, I wish to thank Jeffery Tsheboagae and family, Doreen Moeletsi and family, Dimpoetse Khudu and family, Lydia Nyati Saleshando (Ramahobo), Kelone Khudu-Peterson and family, Gagarin Segwagwa and his parents, as well as many others, for their critical intellectual and personal support while I pursued this research. I wish to thank Joanna Davidson and Dinah Hannaford for organizing the double session "Opting Out" at the 2019 meeting of the American Anthropological Association and all of the participants for their intellectual stimulation. I have enjoyed and learned from critical engagement with Koreen Reece, Deborah Durham, Kathleen Rice, Mark Hunter, Julie Livingston, Julia Pauli, Josef Ehmer, Janice Boddy, and especially Michael Lambek.

NOTES

1. Based upon the most recent census in 2011, Botswana was 64 percent urban, and the percentage is surely higher than that now (Gwebu 2014, 169).

2. According to Botswana's most recent census in 2011, 17.9 percent of women claimed to be married, down from 42.9 percent in 1971. And 53.4 percent of women claimed to have never been married in 2011, up from 37 percent who claimed the same in 1971 (Kubanji 2014, 224–237). Numbers and trends for men are similar. Census data invite questions of methodology, not all of which I can answer. According to the census, "A person should be regarded as married if he/she is married, or when he/she has been through any form of marriage ceremony, whether tribal, civil, religious or other and is still married" (Mokomane 2006, 87). It is possible that Batswana are increasingly less willing to acknowledge the early stages of "traditional" marriage as "marriage" and recognize only civil/magistrate marriages. Civil marriage has been available for close to a century (Schapera 1940/1971) but not widely practiced until the late twentieth century (Solway 2016).

3. The ring, often a diamond or diamond alternative, is sometimes substitutable for bogadi.

4. While bogadi is virtually sacred in that it is subject to neither inflation nor litigation and its cash equivalency remains equal or lower than the actual monetary cost of a bovine, extra fees and damage payments in cattle or their equivalent are added alongside but remain distinct from bogadi. Grooms are charged a beast for "jumping the fence" (impregnating the bride prior to the wedding), for making too many arrangements via cell phone instead of in person, for not collecting enough firewood for the bride's parents, and so on, and I know of one groom who brought an extra animal for eating at the wedding.

5. The circumstances of widows and property now and then are much more complicated but beyond the scope of this chapter.

6. Motswapong et al. (2018) discuss "showering a first-time mother" with love, goods, support, and community at urban baby showers. Of attendees, 70 percent are unmarried, and all new mothers are celebrated regardless of marital status.

7. See Lambek and Solway (2001) on *dikgaba*, a plant and a corresponding condition that can cause harm to others as a result of sadness, jealously, or envy on the part of a person, usually a woman, who cannot control the consequences of the condition.

8. Mokomane (2005) considers relationships in which *patlo*, early-stage marriage negotiations, have occurred as marriages.

9. Many women, married and single, accessed men's wages indirectly by brewing and selling *khadi*, a beer-like drink.

10. "Slow" or process marriage in which bogadi was transferred often decades after the initial marriage ritual has given over to "fast bogadi," in which virtually all of the marriage rituals occur over a few days period (Solway 2016). Many men give "preemptive" bogadi to forestall their daughter's bogadi from being transferred to their wife's kin. However, not all men have the material means to do so. Marriage negotiations bring such embarrassments and sorrows out into the open, into recognition via the news (*dikgang*) that they produce (Reece 2019). Sometimes marriage negotiations fail or are avoided altogether for fear of the humiliation and disgrace they may bring, which adds another possible factor that might contribute to declining marriage rates.

11. I am indebted to Koreen Reece for helping me think this through.

3

Freedom to Choose?

Singlehood, Gender, and Sexuality in India

SARAH LAMB

In India, social transformations seem to be making opting out of marriage for women increasingly possible. A 2019 *India Today* cover story, "Brave New Woman," celebrates "a demographic fact that is fast becoming an economic and political force to reckon with—the single woman" (Sinha 2019). This woman is "single by choice" and represents "the rise of the unattached, independent woman, who has rejected the socially sanctioned default setting of a married life" (Sinha 2019). Other upbeat news stories feature portraits of the new single women as "happy with their status and not wanting the burden of marriage on them" (Kuriakose 2014) and of single women celebrities conceiving and adopting children on their own (Singh 2018). An Amazon reviewer from India comments on the anthology *Single by Choice: Happily Unmarried Women!* (Sharma 2019), "Young girls [reading this book] would learn marriage is something they can choose or opt out of, not a fate they have to be resigned to."

At the same time, the imperative to marry in India continues as a tremendous hegemonic force, and nonmarriage remains extremely rare. A 2019 "Families in a Changing World" United Nations report finds that less than one percent of all women aged forty-five to forty-nine in India have never married, one of the lowest nonmarriage rates in the world (UN Women 2019, 54). For women, marriage is the only familiar path toward achieving economic and social security, respect, and a socially legitimate way of being sexual. Primarily only the most privileged, city-educated, and cosmopolitan elite are the ones who can now embrace single lifestyles by choice; even then, many battle to make their singlehood accepted in the wider society.

In my own fieldwork with fifty-four never-married women across a range of class, caste, and rural-urban backgrounds in the Indian state of West Bengal, I found that a celebratory notion of autonomous individuals making free choices to opt out of marriage and live singly does not well capture the constraint, struggle, and ambivalence most single women highlight in their own narratives. Complex personal, sociocultural, and political-economic contexts lie behind women's lives and choices, and evading marriage is often an unintended consequence of other pressing life decisions. Further, even when purposefully choosing to live singly, most women find it difficult to escape constant reminders and doxic ideologies that marriage is right and normal for women and required for secure social and economic belonging. Tine Gammeltoft writes of how "the concept of choice is, in many respects, empirically misleading; it tempts us to overemphasize people's freedom to shape their world as they want to" (2014, 15).

So, even if we as anthropologists may wish to think outside marriage and decenter marriage from our analyses of gender, kinship, and personhood, I have found that we cannot engage in such a project without also probing the immense force the norm of marriage exerts upon so many interlocutors' lives and communities. Nonetheless, many single women do contest social norms in small and larger ways, expanding conceptualizations of normalcy and inciting changing social landscapes.

In this chapter focused on West Bengal, I explore both the gendered marriage imperative and the stories of single women who have evaded marriage for both intended and unintended reasons. Their stories compellingly reveal the ways single women, by crafting lives outside marriage, are powerfully subject to—while also provocatively working to redefine—conventional notions of gendered personhood. Their stories also illuminate the intersections of social class and gender in a changing Indian society.

Methodology and Meanings of "Single"

In 2014, I began to focus fieldwork in West Bengal, India, on the lives of never-married women, to date making eight fieldwork trips lasting two to four weeks to Kolkata and nearby towns and villages for the project, while enjoying ongoing WhatsApp video and text conversations in English and Bengali with several of my closest interlocutors. I also draw on the narratives of single women gathered over years of ethnographic fieldwork conducted in the region since 1989. I combine formal, open-ended interviews with ethnographic research involving hanging out with women in daily-life contexts, in their homes and while going marketing, dining out, gathering with friends, attending single women's support groups, taking weekend getaways, talking and texting by phone, and (with the English-speaking elite) conversing by email.

I was often accompanied by one of three research assistants during the fieldwork, choosing other Bengali women as assistants who were either single themselves or, in one case, living quite independently from her husband.[1] The presence of other women researchers helped facilitate lively and intimate conversations and ensure that I did not miss the nuances of Bengali discussions. Most conversations took place in Bengali, although peppered with English terms as is common. I use single quotes to indicate English terms in an otherwise Bengali conversation.

On the Meanings of My Choice of the Terminology "Single"

In India, "single" has been emerging as an emic, local category, referring to adult women and men who are not married. The category can be used to signify young cosmopolitan adults in their twenties and thirties who are dating and still likely to marry; formerly married widowed and divorced individuals; and those who have never married, including gay or lesbian persons in long-term relationships, since same-sex marriage is not yet legal in India.

I recruited as interlocutors fifty-four never-married women across social classes and rural-urban contexts, whose ages span from thirty-five to ninety-two.[2] I chose thirty-five as the lower age limit, generally the age at which women are regarded as no longer marriable (an age cutoff that implicitly connects marriage to a woman's reproductive capacities). I came to find that the *condition of never marrying* puts women into a unique and anomalous social category, distinct from formerly married widowed, separated, or divorced women (Lamb 2020).

Although many other Bengalis I spoke with about my project, especially men, would express skepticism—"*Are* there really single women in our society? Even in villages?"—I could always find at least one or two never-married women in any urban neighborhood or village region. My explorations also revealed that forgoing marriage for women is not a new phenomenon, despite its rising popularity, as I was able to locate ample never-married women in their seventies, eighties, and nineties who shared compelling life stories. Most single women I encountered were very interested in the project and happy to participate, as many feel under-represented and misunderstood in their wider societies and are eager to share their stories as part of their endeavors to "find a way to count in the social body" (Dickey 2013, 219).

The Question of Why: Reasons for Not Marrying in a Changing Society

One aim of this volume is to engage in an ethnographic deep dive into the situations that permit the growing prevalence of evading marriage around the world, even in places where marriage has long been obligatory. In India, the most important contemporary situation making the opting out of marriage possible for some women is growing recognition of the value of educating women and fostering their desires to work.[3] Education and work for women are often regarded as two pillars of a gendered revolution taking place around the world leading to delays in or avoidance of marriage (Inhorn and Smith-Hefner 2020).

Recognizing the value of education for girls and women as the foundation of a strong, progressive society and economy, West Bengal's chief minister Mamata Banerjee instituted in 2013 a cash incentive scheme to keep girls in school while delaying marriage until at least age eighteen. (Nearly half of all girls in India are married by that age.)[4] Public posters advertising the girl-empowerment education

FIGURE 3.1 An advertisement for West Bengal's girl-empowerment education program.
Source: Kanyashree Prakalpa.

program, called Kanyashree Prakalpa, are displayed across West Bengal in both
English and Bengali, depicting smiling schoolgirls in uniform, often riding bicycles,
declaring, "I am a Kanyashree Girl. I am Progress," "I am Courage," "I am
Determination," "I will read, write, and advance."[5]

Partly because of this scheme and the public dialogue surrounding it, Bengalis
in both rural and urban areas are widely discussing how girls and women now have
life-path and economic-security options beyond marriage. "These days, girls are
saying, 'I'm going to study. Then I'm going to work. I'm not going to get married
now,'" one conversation unfolded among a mixed-gender group of village neighbors, their tones mostly implying approval. "Our daughters are becoming much
more aware. They all want to become independent." In public media, the new
Indian single woman is described as "armed with an education and a career and
the empowering financial independence it brings" (Sinha 2019).

Yet other reasons for not marrying have little to do with contemporary
situations of social change or gendered transformation, such as parents and other
natal kin depending on an unmarried daughter's income, or impoverished parents
unable to afford wedding expenses. Table 3.1 portrays in plain strokes the reasons
for not marrying conveyed by my fifty-four primary interlocutors through their life
story narratives and our fieldwork conversations. Note that most participants
conveyed several overlapping reasons for not marrying, so the figures add up to
more than fifty-four.

We can see from this table that nearly one-third (sixteen) of my participants
articulated that they had purposefully chosen not to marry. Many in this group
expressed confidence in their decisions to evade marriage, even if single life is not
always easy. Of those who deliberately chose to evade marriage, their most common
reasons for making this choice included what I call "conveying a feminist

TABLE 3.1
Reasons for Not Marrying

	Participants (out of 54)
Purposefully chose not to	16 (~30%)
Conveying a feminist sensibility: perceiving marriage at odds with gender equality	15
Parents/kin failed to arrange marriage (due to financial problems, death, incompetence, selfishness, and/or intoxication)	13
Too engrossed in education and/or work	13
Natal kin needed income (responsible for supporting siblings and/or parents)	10
Body/appearance problems (regarded as disabled, ill, infertile, too dark-skinned, and/or unattractive)	9
Too educated, and/or achieved an individual class status much above natal kin, meaning no suitable match could be found	6
Could not (yet) find the right man	5
Uncomfortable with arranged marriage process but no real access to finding own partner	5
Too attached to natal kin; feels that own family or father are better than would be in-laws or husband	4
Identifies as lesbian	4
Expresses some gender dysphoria, such as now or in childhood wearing masculine clothing or "feeling kind of like a boy"	4
Disgusted by or uncomfortable with sex and/or men	2
"No one liked me"	1
Tarnished public sexual reputation (became pregnant out of wedlock)	1
Pursuing a spiritual life instead	1

sensibility" or feeling reluctant to be subsumed within a sexist marital family, potentially facing triviality, oppression, and/or abuse (seven people); natal kin needing one's income and feeling very attached to one's own natal kin (six); being too engrossed in education (five); identifying as lesbian (four); and being too busy with work (three).

We can see that many more women—70 percent in this study—did not see themselves as having purposefully chosen to opt out of marriage. Even those who pursued education with passion usually did not in their early years realize that gaining an MA or PhD degree would mean they would never marry. Instead, for many, "age happened" gradually as they pursued their studies or they became "too qualified" to find a suitable match. Aarini recalled, "I never thought that getting a PhD would mean I would not marry. But time passed, and then I was too old."

"Too much" education and success can lead both to women becoming too old to marry and to a dearth of eligible grooms. Medha pronounced derisively, "In Indian society, the groom must be superior to the bride in all ways, in *all* ways—except for looks!" Popular author Bhaichand Patel similarly articulates, "To put it crudely, men generally, and Indian men especially, don't like to marry high achieving women. They become undesirable marriage partners" (2006, xii). A joke in China pertaining to so-called leftover women who have not married by their late twenties implies that too much education even transforms a woman's gender into something else: "There are three genders in China: men, women, and women with PhDs" (Fincher 2014, 43).

For women from poor and working-class families, another common reason for not marrying was that their natal kin were so dependent on their income and care labor that they did not feel they could depart in marriage. Marriage in a virilocal Bengali context means that a woman's income and domestic labor belong to her husband's family rather than her natal kin. Although some married women continue to support parents and siblings through visits and gifts, the prevailing sense is that once married, a woman may well not have control over her own movements and financial decisions, forcing her to loosen supportive ties with natal kin.

The force of ideologies about the value of the beautiful, sexual, fertile, fit female body within heterosexual marriage underlies the experiences of nine women in my study who did not marry due to perceived body problems—being regarded as disabled, infertile, ill, or outside prevailing standards of feminine attractiveness, such as being too dark-skinned or "Black" (*kalo*). Even an illness from the past, such as having survived cancer (even with no reproductive impacts) or having survived polio and being left with a limp, can make it difficult or impossible for a woman to marry, especially if the family cannot provide a substantial compensatory dowry.

Among the four who expressed some gender dysphoria—a conflict between their assigned gender and the gender with which they identify—two identify now as lesbian, and one told of being disgusted by the idea of sexual relations with men as a reason not to marry. One told of feeling "kind of like a boy" when growing up, often preferring boys' games and at times wishing they had been born a boy. Another interlocutor now in her eighties told of dressing up in boys' clothing and screaming relentlessly each time her parents arranged to have a prospective groom and his family visit.

The four women in my study who identify now as lesbian tell of growing up being unaware of gay and lesbian identities as a category but knew they loved women and managed, surmounting immense family pressure, to avoid marrying.

Importantly, I found that even among those who chose deliberately to opt out of marriage, many convey ambivalence about this decision—as life for most single women is not easy. Single women face tenuous kinship ties, housing insecurity, sexual harassment, (often) sexual and social isolation, and not being regarded as a normal person. Pratima, a retired schoolteacher who had chosen not to marry, reported, "I would not advise my students now to be single—I tell them to think about it very carefully." This leads to the next topic.

The Gendered Marriage Imperative

It is hard to get away from marriage in India. One aim of this volume is to move beyond implicitly situating marriage as a normative referent in the anthropology of gender and kinship. But what if the emic perspectives of so many of my single interlocutors and their community members underscore that marriage is unavoidably the normative referent in women's lives? Prevailing ethical imaginaries of a normal life and valued subjectivity are that women will be firmly located within families and marriage.

Medha, a single professor of Bengali in a provincial college, sent me an incisive email on this point. She had been raised in an impoverished village family, yet succeeded in pursuing education up to the PhD level. She was now in her fifties and keenly interested in my project. She wrote by email, "I would like to draw your attention to some customs/conducts of Indian/Bengali society that I am facing in my everyday life and sometimes make me irritated. You know in India every Indian girl is addressed as Ma (mother) by others. They may be their family members or other persons from outside the family or even by strangers! The girl should be a mother anyhow as early as possible. Indian culture has no acceptance that they could deny the motherhood!" Further, the Bengali practice of calling people by kin terms in everyday interactions reinforces a sense of compulsory motherhood and marriage, as Medha articulated: "Another point should be noted that when I am traveling by public bus or train or meet people in the vegetable market or other places, . . . everybody addresses me as *kakima* [wife of father's younger brother] or *jethima* [wife of father's elder brother] or *boudi* [wife of elder brother]. People do not allow the womenfolk to be unmarried even in their subconscious mind!" Sexuality is key to such societal and personal perceptions of singlehood and the doxic force of marriage. Prevailing ideology is that a woman's sexuality must be firmly contained within marriage and reproduction and that a woman outside marriage is sexually vulnerable and dangerous (see also Walters, this volume and Medeiros, this volume).

Amid such ideologies, many landlords will not rent to single women. Some Kolkata apartment complexes even maintain written rules forbidding single women tenants. The Government of West Bengal Working Girls' Hostel, where several of my interlocutors reside, maintains strict rules—a nine o'clock curfew and no male visitors indoors, not even a father or brother. The government's choice to name this a hostel for working "girls" reflects implicit conceptualizations that never-married women have not achieved mature adulthood, even though many hostel residents are in their thirties through seventies. The fear in such housing complexes is that single women might bring in lovers or secretly be prostitutes or tempt the upstanding married men in the environs or be subject to sexual assault. Then the reputation of everyone else in the building and community also suffers in a form of social contagion.

In village regions, the only viable residence for a never-married woman is with natal kin. Such women tell of the policing their kin and neighbors wage, to prevent the threat of any potential sexual liaisons. In one small village, I met Nabami and Srabani, two Scheduled Caste sisters in their thirties who had not married due to their family's poverty (their father had died, and there was no money for a dowry) and to continue to support their widowed mother. They brought in income working as day laborers in the rice fields and as nursing home aides in a nearby town. While her younger sister quietly listened, Nabami described their cloistered life as unmarried women: "If we go out and mix with anyone, people will criticize us. They will slander us, saying, 'She is vulgar!' So, we don't mix with anyone at all. At least I have my sister here; together we can talk a little." Nabami went on to tell of being excluded even from mixed-gender family events: "We can't go to anyone's house where there will be boys or men, either married or unmarried. Even if it's a family event, like a festival or a wedding! We face this kind of problem. We can't really mix with anyone at all."

Such practices and ideologies have profound implications for many single women's sexual lives. In North America, single might signify not currently sexually active, but not never sexually active. Some U.S. research even suggests that single (as in unmarried) people are having sex more often than married people are (DePaulo 2017). A few of the most cosmopolitan elite women in my study did tell of enjoying romantic partnerships and sexual pleasure beyond marriage. Media buzz also touts the free and agentive sexual lives of today's cosmopolitan single Indian women (Sinha 2019). However, the vast majority of women in my study, especially from the nonelite classes, found themselves contending with and internalizing the strong societal expectation that a woman who does not marry should not be sexually active at all, ever, not even with herself.[6]

Rinku, a recently retired schoolteacher in her sixties with an elite family background, had been narrating her life story in English to both Medha and me, when Medha suddenly interrupted to ask intently in Bengali, "Not having any sexual relations your whole life, how difficult was it to control your 'urges'?" Medha, my "best informant" or closest interlocutor, often accompanied me on research visits, as she was personally interested in the project and keen to meet other single women with whom to connect and share experiences.

"Hugely difficult!" Rinku replied.

"Me, too!" Medha rejoined.

Rinku reverted to English to continue: "The older I grew, I became more conscious. I gradually began to feel a loneliness. Then I gradually realized this to be a sexual loneliness. To recognize this as a physical urge comes a little later. First, there is an inchoate desire; you don't know your desire. . . . This is something that tormented me when I was younger—tormented me like hell. Sex, society, social attitudes about sex, and taboos about sex—all used to torment me. Now my knowledge is more whole."

Medha exclaimed later, "People in this society are obsessed with controlling women's 'sexuality'! This is why there is such pressure to get them married, and why we cannot accept if a woman is single! 'Society' exerts a huge pressure on single women to control all their sexual urges—to not even 'masturbate'! This is a huge problem for single women! . . . People do it; they do do it sometimes; but then they feel like they did something filthy."

"One thing in this society that you have been seeing," Medha continued, "is that women are not supposed to pleasure themselves! Not for sex, or anything! You are supposed to focus on your family! Sexual pleasure is for having children—and especially for a son!"

Sanjaya, age forty-five, who had not married due to being left with a limp after surviving polio as a toddler, told of how she would still be very happy to find a male partner, if such an occurrence could be possible. But she added, "If I were to live with a man, or bring a man home, the whole neighborhood would immediately talk! 'What a girl!' They would start beating me; their perceptions would absolutely change. They would start saying very bad things about me, behind my back, and to my face as well. 'Our children will be ruined!'"

Further, regarding the marriage imperative, the only normal, sure way for a woman to belong to a family after adulthood is through marriage. Sons and brothers have lifelong rights in their natal homes, but in this virilocal society daughters are to be displaced from their childhood homes when given away in marriage. Although half of the women in my study (twenty-seven of fifty-four) continued to live with natal kin, their parents worried about how their daughters would manage, kinless, in old age. Two professional women in this group had earned enough income to build their own flats, legally in their own names, above their parents' homes, giving them long-term security. Yet other working-class and poor women slept on mats in the corner of halls or storage rooms in their brothers' homes—increasingly marginalized after their parents' deaths—clinging to maintain their rights to even these small spaces. Aarini, from a well-to-do Kolkata family and living with her parents in her ancestral home, felt highly insecure about her future vis-à-vis her brother. She commented, "Bengali parents will say, 'I love my daughter so much, but *still* she wants her share in the assets?'" Sanjaya commented similarly, "Regardless of the laws, Bengalis believe homes rightfully belong to sons and wives. If parents die and there are brothers, the unmarried sister is a soft target. For some time now, the law has stipulated that daughters and sons are to get an equal share of their parents' property. But in reality, brothers throw away their sister or get her to sign away her portion."[7]

Making lives with fellow sisters may seem an option, as other chapters in this volume explore. However, in West Bengal, strong sisterly support and coresidence can usually work only in the rare occurrence when both sisters remain unmarried. Sukhi-di, who at age seventy-eight had resided in the government working girls' hostel for thirty-one years, worried about where she would go when she could no longer climb the three flights of stairs to her room or if the hostel expelled her for no longer being a "working girl." She articulated Bengali gendered kinship norms pertaining to sisters: "If they are both unmarried, sisters can live together; but that has not happened [in my case]." The eldest sibling of twelve, Sukhi had helped arrange and fund all her little sisters' marriages, while working as a telephone operator and UNICEF field researcher. In Bengali kinship systems, once a sister or daughter leaves her natal kin in marriage, she becomes *por*—"other" or "someone else," no longer "one's own" (*svajan*). So if Sukhi were to try to move in with one of her married sisters now, she explained, "I would put *them* into trouble. If I go to someone else's house like that, it would be extremely inconvenient! Strained." Without marrying, an adult woman often faces a precarious kinship future.

Amid all this, never-married single women face the social stigma of not being "normal." Medha remarked, "I have to fight with hostility in every step of my life due to my not being regarded as an ordinary person."

Storied Lives

I turn now to four portraits to illuminate diverse experiences of singlehood. No one story should be regarded as "typical," as single women lead highly varied lives situated by social class, rural-urban contexts, family kinship situations, sexuality, life experiences, and personal aspirations. Yet stories of individuals have the capacity to illuminate, with much more nuance than a table or summary analysis, the intersecting aspirations, obstacles, and opportunities at play in women's lives, as they negotiate singlehood and work to extend notions of what women, belonging, value, and normalcy can be.

I begin with Subhagi, a day laborer in her fifties from the countryside, who demonstrates that never-married singlehood is not limited to the urban or middle classes. Subhagi's exuberant glowing manner convinces one that she is telling the truth that she chose not to marry, so that she could remain living with her own family to help care for them through her labor and love. "This is my fulfillment— that we are all together and having enough to eat," Subhagi declared.

Subhagi was born into an impoverished family of the Lohar caste, one of West Bengal's Scheduled Caste groups of historically disadvantaged people. She came in the middle of four sisters and one younger brother, and while the children were all still very young, both parents fell ill, her father with a paralyzed hand and her mother with cancer. They struggled to have enough to eat. Subhagi worked hard to support the family—through caring for the village schoolmaster's children, washing dishes and clothing in other people's homes, catching and selling fish, and working as a day laborer in the rice fields. "*I* was the one who worked so that they could eat," Subhagi declared with pride.

Subhagi herself took the steps to arrange her sisters' marriages, with her uncle's help. "Everyone came to look!" she recalled. "And my sisters were very attractive and fair-looking. I would say, 'Whoever you like, you can choose and take away.'"

I asked, "And did some also like you? It's not like no one liked you?"

Subhagi exclaimed, "Yes! They did! But if I were to go, then my sisters and brother would have to go from house to house begging. *I* was the one feeding them by working!"

"I would tell [the men]," Subhagi recalled, "'Please forgive me, brother. Please forgive me,'" pressing her palms together in a prayer gesture. "'For these children, there's no one else to look after them.' . . . I would say, 'Even if you take me without dowry, I will not go. I will not go.'

"So, men *did* want to marry me," Subhagi affirmed, "but if I went, who would look after my siblings and parents?"

Over her years while young and unmarried, Subhagi took care to not dress up at all, "so that people [i.e., men] would not do anything to me, 'touch' me or anything."

"Someone might have fallen for her!" women neighbors listening in exclaimed. "People might have looked at her, and something might have happened!"

"Until today, the whole village knows!" Subhagi laughed with pride. "Still today, the entire village knows what I did for my siblings."

"With all this, I am happy, I am very happy. *This* is where I was born!" Subhagi exclaimed, conveying the same privilege men have to remain belonging to just one family and place. "Since I was young we were all together here, so I am so attached to this place. I have never left this place since I was young—from here I haven't gone *anywhere* else at all! And here there are grandchildren now," she said, hugging her brother's son's daughter to her chest as she spoke.

By now, Subhagi's parents have died and her sisters have been married off to other villages. She lives in her natal home with her brother and his wife, their married son, and their grandchildren. Subhagi still works hard so they all can eat, describing serving her family as a moral-spiritual practice. She avowed, "Serving [*seva kora*] the people in this family, the happiness I receive is incomparable. Compared to serving a husband, and compared even to serving God, then serving one's family is the best!"

Subhagi's story illustrates several key themes. First is that her natal kin needed her income and labor, a common theme in many Bengali never-married women's stories from working-class and poor households. Second is how attached Subhagi feels to her natal kin as a positive life aspiration and source of value and intimacy. Through her efforts, Subhagi successfully sustained lifelong ties to her natal home and place—like a brother and son can. Third, Subhagi conveys a glowing pride in her own work and labor. We do not see here a profound shift in gender norms away from a primary focus on family toward self-actualization; Subhagi's work is less for self-cultivation than for serving family. Nonetheless, very significant for Subhagi is that she is serving her "own" lifelong natal family rather than a husband's. This in itself represents a major transformation of conventional gendered kinship norms.

I now turn to Medha, a professor of Bengali living alone in a provincial city in her mid-fifties. She was born into a poor family of a midlevel caste and raised in a remote village. Her family often went hungry. Her mother sold vegetables on the footpath. Yet Medha was the first girl in the village ever to complete secondary school. They didn't have money for books, but Medha would read the shopping bags made from old newspapers and would walk after school to a village library four or five kilometers away, returning in the evening carrying books through open fields as the sun set and her mother worried. Medha is now a tenured college professor.

When she was young, Medha resisted marriage. She recalled, "Other girls wanted to get married, dreamed of having husbands, having guests over, wearing jewelry. I never thought this way. . . . Other people in the village would say to my older brother in front of me, 'Why are you letting her study? What will she become? Why aren't you getting her married? What is she going to do—get a *job*?' After hearing all this, I would think, 'Yes, I *will* get a job.'" She loved to read about faraway places and dreamed of putting on wings to fly away.

Later, after completing her BA, MA, and PhD and securing a prestigious job as a college professor, Medha thought she might like to marry. But she came to realize that her social class limbo made it nearly impossible to find a suitable match. As Medha put it, "I'm a professor now with a good salary—but I don't belong to that kind of family that another professor could marry me. . . . I also can't marry a village boy from an uneducated family."[8]

Now living alone in a rented flat in her university city, Medha finds the condition of solo living highly unfamiliar, even unnerving. She sometimes hires another woman, an abandoned mother of two, to spend the night on the floor next to her bed, so that she won't have to sleep all alone.

Indrani, from an elite Kolkata family, returned to India when her grandmother became ill, after receiving an engineering PhD and working for several years in New York City. Having had enough of U.S. corporate life and wishing to be with her grandmother during her dying days, Indrani created a lovely flat with a rooftop garden above her parents, while securing a good local job. She never gave too much thought to marriage while pursuing her education and career. But as she approached her forties, she began to long intensively for a child.

Indrani recalled, "My mother used to say that love can happen even at ninety-seven, but there is a time for having a child. I also very much longed for a child."

Adoption is legal for single parents in India, but Indrani faced an uphill battle against stigma, passing through multiple adoption agencies over a three-year period, while accompanied by her parents.

"Why aren't you married? Why didn't you get married?" the adoption agencies always asked. "I was just studying all the time," Indrani reported replying. "You know, presenting myself as a real nerd."

"'Well,' now glaring at my mother, 'a daughter may be able to forget such things as marriage, but a mother never should!'"

Some of the adoption agency staff also found Indrani too pushy, or not demure enough, or needing counseling. So Indrani with her parents went to several counseling sessions and returned to report that they had completed the counseling.

Finally, just weeks before she legally aged out at forty-five, Indrani was approved fit to adopt—due to Indrani's good professional position and the fact that she lives with her parents. So, she is not really entirely "single"—singlehood makes it near impossible to be approved, amid the strong sense that no one can raise a child alone and that a child needs a family. But would there be an infant available before Indrani turned forty-five? The last weeks were very stressful. Finally, just a day before her birthday, Indrani was given a child! The infant was six weeks old. They named her Nandini, "daughter who brings joy." Nandini has grown into a wonderful little girl, beloved to both mother and grandparents.

Six years later, Indrani wonders how and what she will tell her daughter about her background. People ask continually, "Are you married?" "No," Indrani replies simply. Then they wait for an explanation, as to how there is a child. Indrani says little and leaves them guessing. Another problem is that Indian identification systems—for school IDs, high school exams, driver's licenses, passports—all ordinarily require providing a father's name, in this patriarchal setting.

Indrani gives hints that she might still like to marry, if it can happen. She commented: "In the United States, nobody would think that a woman past thirty-five years would be unmarried forever. But here the pressure to marry stops after that age because people think you are old."

Ajay, from a middle-class Kolkata family, identifies as a single woman, lesbian, and transgender person with a chosen male name and preference for masculine-style clothing. Since Bengali's third-person pronoun *se* is already gender neutral, I never felt the need to ask Ajay about their preferred pronouns, but I am choosing the English "they" here as most in keeping with Ajay's nonbinary gender expression.

As a child in high school, Ajay began to fall in love with a beautiful girl classmate, Anindita. The two became intimate friends and began to make love before they had ever encountered the concept of lesbian, thinking they were the only ones. Later in college, Ajay recalls seducing other women in the girls' dormitories, while always frightened that they might be caught and expelled or, worse, arrested and imprisoned. Years later, Ajay's group of lesbian friends celebrated when the British-era law criminalizing homosexual sex was finally overturned in 2018.

In their twenties, Ajay began to express themselves in increasingly masculine terms, taking on a male name and dressing largely in masculine-style clothing.

These forms of gender expression helped Ajay evade marrying, convincing Ajay's family that they were not really the marriageable type. Ajay's longtime girlfriend Anindita also convinced her parents to avoid arranging her marriage, by pointing out how her sister's arranged marriage had ended in divorce and arguing that she could support herself economically.

So, Ajay and Anindita established a printing business together, and both now in their forties they continue to live in their natal homes while caring for their widowed elderly mothers. While making deliveries, Ajay drives a motorcycle dressed in shirt and pants, their partner Anindita riding in back, her long black hair and brightly colored scarves flowing behind her.

It is still not easy to live openly as a lesbian or queer couple in Ajay's home city of Kolkata. Yet Ajay and Anindita have found a way to cultivate a lifelong relationship, economic independence, and an active circle of supportive single women and lesbian friends. Watching Ajay and Anindita together, I sense possibilities for women's independence and queer love expanding.

Conclusion: On Singlehood, Social Class, and Subjectivity

The single women's stories and voices shared here invite us to actively reflect on the ways people forge meaningful lives out of intersecting situations of possibility and constraint. Their narratives help us begin to imagine what it can mean for anthropologists, and for our interlocutors, to decenter marriage as an unquestioned norm.

"India is in the middle of an independence movement. For women," Deepa Narayan asserts (2019, 4). One feature of this women's independence movement is the expanding possibility for women to say no to marriage. However, my research with Bengali single women reveals how complicated is the condition of opting out of marriage.

In closing, I highlight the ways social class and gender so powerfully intersect to shape women's marital choices and possibilities. I then turn to probe public and academic discourse on choice and singlehood, wishing to complicate naïve and overly celebratory models of unfettered free subjects able to choose their life paths.

Even with all the hype about expanding opportunities for women to opt out of marriage, such as in the 2019 *India Today* cover story "Brave New Woman," I found that it is mostly only women from highly privileged, educated, and cosmopolitan classes who are able to embrace singlehood as a distinctive lifestyle emerging from a claim to freedom of choice. Recent media stories and anthologies celebrating the rise of single women in India focus almost exclusively on the cosmopolitan, highly educated classes.[9] Further, these stories often seem aimed more at promoting new ways of thinking about women and marriage than at describing actual widespread societal transformations taking place beyond the most elite.

Because the elite constitute only a small minority of people in India, I instead sought out for this project never-married women across social class and rural-urban contexts. I found that, true to the public narratives, women among the most cosmopolitan, educated classes did experience a relative degree of freedom from prevailing societal norms of gender, sexuality, and marriage. Especially when elite single women were successful at establishing professional careers, which provide both economic security and societal respect, they were often able to craft secure, pleasurable, and socially respected lives beyond marriage. Further, because some members of the elite participate in a cosmopolitan public culture emphasizing modern ideals of sexual freedom, and due to their privileged access to private spaces such as independent apartments and cars, a few among this elite group in my study were successful in creating satisfying romantic and sexual relationships outside of marriage.

At the same time, women across social classes in West Bengal contend with many shared gendered norms. One is the ongoing near-ubiquitous expectation that women (and men) will marry. I met no woman of any social class who had not faced forceful social and familial pressure to marry. Other pervasive gendered norms concern ideals of feminine respectability, such as that nonmarried women should not be sexually active or spend time having fun in public spaces (Phadke 2020). And as we have seen, single women across social classes can find it difficult to secure housing and kinship belonging. To forge a life path outside of marriage is not, at this point, straightforward or simple for women of any social class in India.

For women not born into the most elite, educated classes, the avenue of education and/or work can open up possibilities for nonmarrying, as evident in the stories of Medha and Subhagi. Yet, I would not want readers to come away with the impression that Medha and Subhagi provide typical or common examples of what is happening among the laboring classes in India today. I had to search hard to find never-married women from nonelite families in urban, semiurban, and rural contexts. In Subhagi's whole large village of around five thousand residents, only Subhagi and one other woman, born with congenital dwarfism, had forged the path of never marrying. In Medha's natal village, which she took me to visit, we were able to locate two women who had never married. One had become pregnant out of wedlock when she was nearing thirty and still unmarried because of her family depending on her income as a live-in domestic servant in Kolkata. This woman gave birth to her son and raised him amid much difficulty as a single mother in village society. It was her public, nonvirgin sexual status that made her unmarriable. The only other never-married woman from Medha's village, a woman in her mid-forties, lived with her widowed mother. Her father had died when she was only fifteen, leaving the family near penniless and without money for a dowry. Medha could be said to be the third unmarried woman of this village. One could deem that she had achieved a remarkable success story, as the first girl from her village ever to graduate from high school, let alone then go on to receive a BA, MA, PhD, and prestigious job as a university professor. But Medha's ensuing mismatched class status—born into a poor, rural family but now with the education and professional position of an urban elite—made her highly unusual and virtually unmarriable.

In her examination of changing cultures of gender in India, Deepa Narayan explains her choice to focus on highly educated, urban, elite women "because these are the groups that can bring about change" (2019, xvi). Whether more women across social classes, rural-urban contexts, and generations will choose the life path of nonmarriage in coming years, time will tell.

I wish to close with a few words about the idea of choice flourishing in public, academic, and feminist work on the dramatic rise of singlehood around the world today. In *Happy Singlehood: The Rising Acceptance and Celebration of Solo Living*, Elyakim Kislev advocates that societies develop a "clear and more benign image of singlehood," to "allow individuals to freely choose whatever lifestyle fits them best," in accordance with their "true feelings," as opposed to "attitudes enforced by social norms" (2019, 5). Eric Klinenberg, in his best-selling *Going Solo: The Extraordinary Rise and Surprising Appeal of Living Alone*, asks, "Why has [living singly] become so common in the world's most affluent societies?" His reply: "Because . . . living alone helps us pursue sacred modern values—individual freedom, personal control, and self-realization" (2012, 17). "Singledom is a choice," Catherine Gray asserts simply in her preface to *The Unexpected Joy of Being Single* (2018, 9). *India Today*'s featured story "Brave New Woman" declares, "The urban Indian single woman is answerable to no one but herself. . . . Her life choices are her own. . . . More than economic independence, it is the freedom to be who you are that is the attraction of singlehood" (Sinha 2019).

Such language of choice seems often to rest on a neoliberal model of self-determining individuals, painting a celebratory vision of people's ability to make themselves and their worlds according to their own desires. Yet, I find this model of autonomous individual subjectivity both misleading in its simplicity and ethnographically dissonant. As Lata Mani argues in her critique of the ideal of personal freedom underlying much neoliberal contemporary discourse in India, "We live in an interdependent world with finite resources, in obdurate sociocultural contexts that we are compelled to negotiate at every turn, and within a matrix of possibilities shaped by these constraints as well as our own personal inclinations, strengths, and weaknesses" (2014, 27).

Further, most of the Bengali single women I have grown to know—more than striving to cultivate an independent subjectivity "answerable to no one but herself"—are working hard to foster modes of interrelationality and social belonging, including forms of kinship, companionship, friendship, security, and respect and ways to care and be cared for. Finally, the paradigm of choice is not ethnographically accurate for the many single women in India who do not see themselves as having purposefully chosen to opt out of marriage.

Nonetheless, whether they see themselves as having deliberately "chosen" to forgo marriage or not, the many single Bengali women I have grown to know—through living unconventional lives outside of marriage—are fostering important forms of social change. Positioned outside the norm on roads less traveled in both daily life and ethnographies of gender, never-married single women are able to recognize and speak penetratingly about their society's sociocultural norms. In so doing, in large and small daily ways, they are working to redefine the normal, expanding social visions of what living well for women can be.

NOTES

1. These invaluable research assistants, friends, and collaborators are Hena Basu, MA, Anindita Chatterjee, PhD, and Madhabi Maity, PhD.

2. The group included thirty-five women living in Kolkata, ten from smaller towns, and nine from rural villages. Regarding social class, the group included nine elite, twenty-one middle-class, fourteen working-class, and ten poor participants. Nine participants were from Scheduled Caste communities, designated by the government of West Bengal as historically facing socioeconomic discrimination.

3. Recent figures indicate a drop in the proportion of women in India's paid labor force, however, from close to 61 percent in 2004–2005 to below 54 percent in 2009–2010 (Mazumdar and Neetha 2011, 118). Bhandare (2018) reports, though, that "as Indian women leave jobs, single women keep working."

4. According to UNICEF, 47 percent of girls in India are married by eighteen years of age, and 18 percent are married by age fifteen (Times News Network 2018). This is despite India's Prohibition of Child Marriage Act of 2006 prohibiting the marriage of girls under age eighteen and boys under age twenty-one.

5. See Singh and Dutta (2017) and www.wbkanyashree.gov.in.

6. See also Narayan (2019), Phadke (2020, 283), Phadke, Khan, and Ranade (2011), Trivedi (2014), and Twamley and Sidharth (2019).

7. See Agarwal (1994) and Basu (1999) on women's property rights in Indian law and practice.

8. See Lamb (2018, 59–61) on the problem of "gendered mismatches of class." If through education and employment a woman achieves a class status much higher than that of her family background, she becomes practically unmarriable.

9. In addition to the examples provided in this chapter's opening, see Kundu (2018).

4

Single Women's Invisibility in South Korea's First Decades

LAURA C. NELSON

At the end of the twentieth century a smoldering incredulity burned across South Korea as a growing minority of young women openly began to question the desirability of marriage and motherhood. Marriage and parenting are deeply normative in both historic and contemporary Korea. It was nearly unthinkable that marriage and raising children would not be the foundation of a young woman's life. The *inevitability* of marriage was built into Korean social structures and cultural practices, as well as myths and stories. Marriage universality was reinforced through repetitive representation in fiction and nonfictional media, in the wedding-dress-lined streetscape in front of the major women's university and the many wedding halls whose sole business was to host weddings, in the commercialized matchmaking industry, and in the constant hectoring of unmarried young people by parents, friends, teachers, and coworkers. The repetitive reinforcement was bolstered by the erasure of any sign of marriage-divergent life trajectories. Nevertheless, in the years following the first tentative expressions of intentional marriage resistance, patterns of marriage and parenting have undergone a dramatic shift. Following changes in the national Family Law in 1991 that allowed mothers to argue for custody of their children in the event of a divorce (Yang 2008), divorce rates surged and remain high (Park and Raymo 2013). Moreover, the average age of first marriage has also climbed, leaving the majority of young adult South Koreans unmarried until their thirties (Jones 2018; Statistics Korea 2021). These changes have been portrayed as unprecedented sacrifices to economic exigencies and as an unhealthy adoption of foreign lifestyles. Yet while it is a significant cultural transformation that marriage and child rearing are now viewed as matters of individual choice in South Korea, it is untrue that in the past every adult Korean got married.

In this chapter I suggest that marriage, while highly normative traditionally for Koreans, was not as universal as it has been perceived and portrayed and that this assertion of marriage universality produced positions of extreme social marginality for those individuals, especially women, who remained unmarried but who contributed in hidden ways to the economic and cultural trajectories of contemporary South Korea. Particularly in the first decades of the second half of the twentieth century, the contention that marriage was universal is contradicted by the fact of the demographic impossibility of matching marriage-age women to the smaller population of marriageable men. The life stories of these unseen, unmarried women both shed light on the structures of the social economy during the period of South Korea's intense industrialization and also offer insights into the underappreciated rewards of marriage resistance and of less intentional marriage omissions, in a culture of compulsory heteronormative marriage.

Korean Traditions of Heteronormative Marriage and Reproduction

The particularly intense importance of marriage in Korean culture is rooted in the imposition of Confucian hierarchical values and structures during the Chosôn era (1392–1910). Martina Deuchler has traced how marriage became woven into the establishment of patrilineal, patriarchal neo-Confucian Korean society. According to Deuchler, "Marriage was the precondition for adulthood and to remain unmarried was socially inconceivable" (1995, 243). This applied in equal measure to men and to women who both were expected to marry and procreate, but the marriage of daughters was a particular focus of formal rules.

> It was of continuous concern to the Confucian legislators that economic reasons might prevent a family from marrying off its daughters at marriageable ages. Near the beginning of the dynasty, a law was passed that held a girl's closest paternal and maternal relatives responsible for getting her married at an appropriate time. Negligence was to be severely punished. The *Kyŏngguk taejŏn* [state code of laws] contained assurance of government help for needy girls [to subsidize their marriage prospects] and also carried a warning to family heads to keep within the prescribed time limits. For a woman, the wedding signified a rite of passage from a childhood during which she received little attention to an adulthood during which she could become a full member of society. (243)

Deuchler documents the gradual historical erosion of pre-Chosôn-era daughters' inheritance rights and women's rights to independent property that undergirded this system, making women financially, as well as culturally, reliant on men. Women were interpellated into a gendered hierarchical structure of dependence upon their husbands and in-laws: "A woman thus could not lead an independent existence. Her point of orientation for livelihood and domicile was at all times a male member of her family or household" (265). Although the household shared both production and consumption, there was no recognized role for unmarried adult women in their natal home, and in the premodern era the options for self-sufficiency outside the family were limited for men and even more tightly constrained for women, comprising the nearly unspeakable social roles of Buddhist nuns, shamans, entertainers, servants, and women who traded sex for financial support.

As Korea opened to outsiders in the late nineteenth century and early twentieth, foreign observers documented their perceptions of the extreme importance of marriage and its presumed inevitable corollary, parenthood, in Korea. One example is in the 1902 ruminations of the American missionary Homer Hulbert, who wrote for and edited *Korea Review: A Monthly Magazine*: "The chief occupation of the Korean woman, whether of the high or low class, is motherhood. . . . This springs from the instinct for self preservation. The Confucian code renders male offspring a *sine qua non* of a successful life and a woman who brings her husband no children is doubly discredited. There is no more valid cause for divorce in Korea than barrenness. There are no 'old maids' in this country. It becomes a matter of public scandal if a girl passes her eighteenth or twentieth year without settling in a home" (Hulbert 1902, 1). Hulbert went on to note that parents of disabled women might have a harder time finding a husband but that "many a young man takes his bride home only to find that she is a deaf mute or cross-eyed or humpbacked, or partially paralyzed. This is a triumph for the old woman, the professional go-between, who 'works off' these unmarketable goods without the groom or his family knowing anything about the deformity until too late. But the balance is even as between the brides and the grooms, for a nice girl as often finds herself tied to a drunkard or a case of non compos mentis. The Korean woman's main business then is wifehood and motherhood" (1). Note that while Hulbert considers men in the context of marriage, the focus is on getting women married at any cost: women are the subject of the project of marriage—both for Hulbert and for Koreans.

But was marriage universal? In the same publication, Hulbert noted (with a pitying comment regarding the "awful price" of their independence) the existence of unmarried women: "The Koreans say that among the very lowest classes are to be found the most unfortunate and the most fortunate women but this would not be our estimate for the Koreans mean by this that the *mudang* or sorceresses and the courtezans and the dancing girls, being unmarried, are the most independent women in the land and are cared for and dressed the best of anyone in Korea" (Hulbert 1902, 100–101). And Deuchler as well suggests some fraction of the female population must have somehow managed on their own. Weddings would be officially ordered postponed when girls were being selected as tribute to China early in the Chosôn period and throughout the Chosôn era when girls were being sought for the royal palace *kan t'aek* (Deuchler 1995, 243). Presumably some matches were lost simply due to the deferral of marriages during these pauses.

Further evidence of the incompleteness of universal marriage is found in concerns around care of ancestors and protection of the lineage. After death, unmarried persons and persons without descendants haunt lineage members as needy ghosts. In her study of supernatural conflict in a South Korean village (carried out in the late 1970s and early 1980s), Laurel Kendall distinguished ghosts from proper ancestors, whose successful procreation means they receive ritual tribute from male descendants: "Ghosts died badly: as bachelors or maidens, without descendants, violently, or far from home. These unhappy souls are filled with resentment and envy, usually directed at living siblings or at a youthful niece or nephew. Bachelor ghosts bring sickness to a surviving brother or cousin and sometimes hamper his career prospects. . . . Married women are harassed by a sister or a husband's sister who died unmarried. These virgin ghosts cause much marital strife and set a husband's affections wandering. A woman in labor is vulnerable to the envy of a sister or an aunt who died in childbirth" (Kendall 1984, 217). Anxieties around this haunting, and the development of shamanistic rituals to propitiate the ghosts, are evidence of the historical fact that not every young person was successfully married off while they underline the importance of marriage into the afterlife.

Yet even official documents asserted the universality of marriage well into the second half of the twentieth century. This is reflected particularly in studies about South Korean fertility, the management of which became the focus of international and Republic of Korea governmental family planning efforts beginning in the late 1950s. A report prepared for a 1975 conference in Kyoto on fertility transition stated that historically, "The custom of early marriage prevailed, and marriage was universal. . . . Marriage patterns did not go through any substantive change throughout the entire [Japanese] colonial period especially in terms of age at marriage and its universality" (Lee 1980, 7–8). After the end of colonial rule and the Korean War armistice, however, extensive family planning programs were implemented throughout the new nation, with significant assistance and involvement of the United States (DiMoia 2013). In a U.S. National Academy research report from 1982 on the determinants of Korean fertility, the authors stated that "prospects for future fertility trends are uncertain. All of the variables examined in this report indicate favorable conditions for further fertility decline, except for three factors: (1) the *universality of marriage*, (2) the reduction of the incidence and duration of breast feeding, and (3) the continued strength of son preference" (Cho, Arnold, and Kwon 1982, 11, emphasis added). But while marriage appeared to remain "universal," another paper published in 1974 (Lapierre-Adamcyk and Burch 1974) examined the role of the rising mean age at first marriage from the early twentieth century through the late 1960s on total fertility. This study, drawing on government census and survey data, does not even consider women who remain unmarried. The authors argued that social change factors such as rural to urban migration patterns and different opportunities for women to work both before and after marriage, alongside changing structures of multigenerational households, which offered alternatives to maternal child caring for wives, were stronger influences on fertility than family planning programs per se and unfortunately facilitated fertility. The report includes a graph of women in five year birth cohorts (starting with those born before 1896) depicting the percentage of each cohort remaining single as they aged from fourteen years old to forty. The fraction of unmarried women captured in this report is admittedly small, but the existence of these never-married women over forty received no notice in the text. This focus on reining in population growth and managing women's fertility reproduced as an artifact the continued assumption of marriage universality in the later twentieth century; it is notable that these studies reflected a complete lack of attention to the possibility of children born out of wedlock (an unmentionable problem well into the late twentieth century in South Korea). This bioadministrative approach reinforced, through the authority of demography with its tacit lack of interest in women who remained unmarried, the presumption of universal marriage.

This same study looking at fertility and age cohorts noted a critical demographic problem, however, pushing the average age at first marriage upward: "The steady rise in average age at marriage and the constant difference in average age between men and women have remained, despite sharp changes in the sex ratio of persons of marriageable age" (Lapierre-Adamcyk and Burch 1974, 256). Historically, Korean male/female birth ratios followed the normal pattern of a slightly greater number of boy babies born, with a trend toward near equalization in late adolescence and early adulthood. This (and an even distribution across geographic and social spaces) would seem to be a prerequisite for universal marriage in a society with rules of monogamous marriage. A demographic gender imbalance locally or regionally, particularly among unmarried adults, would generate challenges to matchmaking. This is exactly the circumstance found in South Korea in the 1950s and 1960s: not only did men and women migrate from their rural homes to the cities in gender-differentiated patterns, but there was also an absolute disparity in the population of single men and women of marriage-normative age. The authors of this report focus on the resolution over time of significant gender disparities, but their focus is on the drivers of fertility; they comment that despite the reduction of disparities, age at marriage had climbed: "Kim (1965) noted that in 1955 there were 62 single males aged 20–34 for every 100 single females aged 15–29, compared with 102 single males per 100 single females in the respective age groups in 1935. He suggested this imbalance in the sex ratio as a partial reason for the rising age at marriage. But in the 1960 and 1966 censuses, the ratio increased to approximately 82 males per 100 females, while age at marriage continued to rise. It thus appears that basic changes in marriage patterns occurred independently of changes in the sex ratio of persons of marriageable ages" (256). This anodyne observation that the problem of wildly imbalanced sex ratios in 1955 (in the wake of colonial-era forced labor migration, deaths of Korean soldiers in the long period of the Japanese imperial wars in the 1930s and 1940s, and further deaths of soldiers and civilians in the Korean War in the early 1950s), alleviated only somewhat by the mid-1960s, led to a longer average time for women to find a husband fails to grapple with the fact that time alone could not solve the deficit of marriage-age men for the women who outnumbered them for at least a decade of marriage opportunity years. Putting these data a different way, in the mid-1950s, demographically, for every three women of marriageable age, one would be left without a man to marry, and while the situation improved in the 1960s, the ratio was still six marriage-age women for every five marriage-age men.

For demographers interested in reducing fertility, the extra unmarried women are not problematic as it is assumed (correctly or not) they will not give birth. But for the rest of South Korean society, what are we to make of the fact that a significant fraction of a generation of women would have faced formidable obstacles to marriage and that in fact many would never be able to fulfill the universal requirement of marriage? Where did those women go, and what was their impact on South Korean history? How are their contributions remembered?

The Real Unmarried Women of South Korea

Before the 1990s in South Korea, lifelong unmarried women—not single women who had not yet married, but women who would never become married—were essentially invisible. Single women were almost never depicted in fiction or films of the time, except as women on the path to marriage. I can find no trace of news media discussion of the problem of the midcentury demographic sex-ratio imbalance and the extra hurdles of finding a husband. In the course of my own research, I asked a wide range of friends, and strangers, if they knew any older women (women born between 1935 and 1960) who had remained unmarried. Invariably, the answer was no. When pressed, people often offered a few categories they thought might be promising for me to investigate: Nuns? College professors? Widows? Lesbians? Perhaps prostitutes? But another phenomenon emerged in the responses: many of those same people would come to me later, remembering an unmarried older aunt or cousin. This inability to call to mind a close relative who had not married was striking, and the pattern of amnesia did not change after I learned to prompt people to think of their extended family.

Not all these unmarried relations were hidden away. Several had played key roles in the well-being of the family. The women I spoke with were all born in the 1940s, 1950s, or 1960s. Chi-myung, for example (all names are pseudonyms), was the unmarried aunt of four young adults, the children of her two brothers. Her life path had been shaped by her parents' sense of the importance of their sons: despite her love of studying and her high marks in school, Chi-myung was sent to a technical (rather than an academic) high school so that she would find employment at an early age and support her two brothers' pursuit of higher education in the 1970s. At the age of eighteen she got a job as a secretary at one of the large corporations and worked there for more than twenty years. Indeed, her income not only contributed to her brothers' educations, but she supported her widowed mother after her ne'er-do-well father passed away, and the fact that she continued to live at home relieved her sisters-in-law (once her brothers married) from the responsibility of caring for her mother. I asked her if she had wanted to get married herself, and she explained in a pensive voice, "It's hard to say. I liked one or two of

the men in the company, but I knew they wouldn't marry a high school graduate."
The white-collar men hired by this company held sufficient prestige that they would
normatively prefer to marry a woman with a college degree. "I didn't like the men
my parents wanted to match me with. I was happy as I was. I had a few romantic
fantasies, but no, I never really wanted to be *really* married." Chi-myung's emphasis
on the contrast between her romantic fantasies and her sense of what it meant to
be "really" married reflected her experience of her parents' marriage. Her father
was unfaithful to her mother, profligate in his use of money, and he spent as little
time at home as possible. Chi-myung expressed surprise and delight that her
brothers did not emulate their father's behaviors, and over the years her brothers'
families have become her social centerpiece; she is clearly a beloved aunt in the
extended family. Chi-myung's life has had its own hardships. She was pushed to
retire from the corporation before she turned forty, and since then she has operated
a series of small businesses with varying success. She's concerned about her future,
but she has built a close relationship with her nieces and nephews and is confident
she'll have family around her as she herself grows older.

Other women related similar stories of wandering into unmarried middle age
while taking care of their parents. I met Hyun-sun after a friend confessed that
his aunt was unmarried, days after he told me he knew no unmarried older women.
Hyun-sun met me at a department store café. She told me that after college she
had continued to live with her parents and was apparently on target for a normative
married life. At home she enjoyed reading and housework and carefully studied
her mother's cooking to prepare herself to be an accomplished wife. She went on
several arranged dates but hadn't found the perfect match when, unexpectedly,
her father was diagnosed with stomach cancer. This was just at the point she was
aging out of the most marriageable period of her twenties. She threw herself into
caring for her mother, who herself was devoted to her own husband's care. At that
point, Hyun-sun's family simply stopped suggesting she get married. After her
parents had both died, and rather than selling the apartment where Hyun-sun had
been living since high school, her younger brother allowed her to stay on there,
and he continues to provide her with money for essentials. Hyun-sun also has a
financial cushion from some investments in stocks and real estate she made in
the 1980s, so she has been able to maintain a comfortable lifestyle. She frequently
meets old school friends, whose children are now all grown up, and travels widely.
She told me that sometimes she feels lonely but that she still loves nothing more
than an afternoon reading a good book.

Chi-won was called into service when she grew tired of phone calls from her
mother complaining about her older brother's wife. Although Chi-won's brother
wasn't living with his parents (as was still at the time expected for many eldest
sons), Chi-won's sister-in-law was demonstrably unhappy with the burden of labor
demanded of her as a daughter-in-law. Chi-won explained, "Actually, my mother
wasn't an easy person, and she grew up in a conservative family so she asked a lot
of her daughter-in-law. I think if she had been gentler it would have worked out.

But I had a lot of energy and I didn't want to hear the complaining, so I took over a lot of the work my sister-in-law should have been doing. In the end, I was exhausted by working full-time and then doing the work of a daughter-in-law." Chi-won's parents lived about two hours south of Seoul by bus, and Chi-won was commuting from her apartment on Sundays and one night during the week to cook and run errands for her parents. "I had no time for meeting men, or even for seeing my friends. I was caught in the middle. For a while I was frustrated, but then when I saw that my friends who had gotten married were exhausted by caring for their husbands and their children as well as their own parents-in-law, I realized that my situation was alright." At that point in our conversation, Chi-won paused. "I have never told anyone before," she said. "It's good. It's good not to be married."

These three women had all lived relatively quiet lives, slipping into spinsterhood as an unplanned outcome of taking on parental care work. This occurred at a time when the pattern of caring for aging parents in South Korea was shifting from a responsibility of the wife of the eldest son to other relatives, in the context of the massive shift of the young population (including sons) from farms to the cities. Joint households of eldest sons, their wives and children, and the parents became less common, and daughters-in-law became less dependable as caretakers. The availability of extra daughters was an obvious cushion against this structural tension, facilitating a cultural change that otherwise would have been a source of even greater social tension. None of these women actively resisted marriage; their never-married trajectories resulted from various permutations of extensions of the ways women were expected to care for their birth families in this period of social change.

But there were other reasons, aside from filling the roles of care workers, that women remained unmarried. Seung-ki, for example, grew up poor, in a family with five children, in a village five hours south of Seoul. Her parents suggested she find work to help support the family, so she moved to the capital as a seventeen-year-old and took a job in a factory, living in the factory dormitories for several years. She was active in the labor movement, but she worked long hours for little pay, and after a few years she felt worn out. She quit her factory job and took up work in a friend's tea shop. "Usually I enjoyed talking to the men, but they often bullied me with inappropriate language. Sometimes they would assume they could pay me to have sex with them. They were all married men, and it disgusted me. So I decided it wasn't worth it to get married to that kind of man." Her entire adulthood she has worked in cafes and restaurants in various roles, but Seung-ki has never worked her way out of financial precarity. When I spoke to her, she was imagining retirement to a rural village where no one would know her, but the cost of living would be cheaper; she has occasionally wondered if she would have been better off settling for an unhappy marriage with more material comforts. "I don't know," she said. "It's not easy for women."

Illness factored into several of the stories, often drawing women to care for parents, grandparents, or siblings, but sometimes their own illness impeded marriage. Suk-hi fell into a depression in her early twenties and has been depressive on and off her entire adult life. Her parents were unable to find a match for her. Similarly, Chi-young was left with a limp after a case of polio as a young child; her parents tried half-heartedly to marry her off, but without success. With a surplus of women, it took only a minor disability to make marriage unlikely. Eunjung Kim (2017) has deftly examined how disability and illness, alongside and entangled with entrenched patrilineal patriarchy and heteronormativity in South Korea, produced the tendencies to implement what she terms "curative violence" exercised against women who did not fit normative standards of health, fertility, and attitudes, leading to violence, ostracization, or hiding nonconforming family members from view. Into the 1980s, "health" was often the primary characteristic South Koreans said they were looking for in a spouse; little had changed since Hulbert's observations on ableism in the marriage market at the turn of the century.

Only a few of the women I interviewed knew, as children, they did not want to get married. Hee-sun was one. She was the oldest daughter in a large family living on the outskirts of a provincial capital. She was tasked from an early age with the work of being the extra mother and wife, caring for her siblings, cooking, and doing the laundry, in addition to her schoolwork, which suffered. She avoided marriage because she did not want to have children of her own. She moved to Seoul as a teenager and was able to save enough money working in tea houses to open her own small cafe, which she has run since the early 1980s. Yoon-hee was another. From a young age she simply did not like the idea of a man touching her body, and she framed her life choices around a strategy to support herself. She worked as a seamstress in the sewing area of Seoul for a few years and then bought a portable sewing machine, which she set out in an outdoor market to do tailoring and cloth-ing repairs on demand. She liked the independence, and her happy disposition gained her a loyal clientele. Over time she was able to buy a stall in an indoor mar-ketplace, where she continued to offer repairs as well as clothing of her own design.

The routes that brought all these women to permanent unmarried status include intentional and unintentional choices, aversion to marriage or child rearing, or simply a lack of commitment to the project of marriage seeking, as well as new arrangements for ensuring economic viability in a socioeconomic context structured to compensate women as though they were secondary workers. Several faced challenges throughout their lives to support themselves in the context of a patriarchal labor market in which women systematically were paid lower wages. Others managed more easily, buoyed by family support and, often, a more secure family class position.

As single women, many were able to play important roles in the social reproduction of their extended family, including shouldering parental care work ordinarily required of daughters-in-law, and providing extra financial and emotional support to siblings, nieces, and nephews. It is important to note that none received significant pressure from their families to get married. In a society where nonnormative behaviors were stigmatized, an unmarried daughter might attract unwelcome comments from neighbors. The fact that these women were not pushed into unwanted matches makes sense if we situate these women in an environment of constrained marital opportunities. But there still remained the problem of family reputation management, which leads us to consider the erasure of these women from memory.

Eclipsing the Unmarried

During the 1950s and 1960s, at least 18 percent of the population of young women were excess supply in the South Korean marriage market (as reflected in the statistic of 82 marriage-age men to 100 marriage-age women in 1966, at the tail end of the period of demographic imbalance described above). This is smaller than the proportion of women who have recently shocked public attitudes by remaining single into their early thirties, but it is nevertheless a significant fraction of the total population of young women. This scale of unmarried women, in a society that saw marriage as universal, should have attracted notice at the time. The unmarriageable women might have been seen as pitiable or a threat to existing marriages or, simply, as helpful to their extended families or even as a sign of cosmopolitan female independence. But there is hardly a trace of commentary or representation of this phenomenon from the period, and so, at the turn of the millennium, South Koreans reacted as though not being married was inconceivable and unprecedented. This lack of history was produced through a combination of invisibility at the time and erasure from memory.

Premodern Korean social structure and philosophy made marriage essential for women before the twentieth century. The patrilineal traditions of the Chosôn era were imposed over centuries. Historically, although the rules were not static (as a Japanese colony, in 1909 Korean lineage authority was replaced by the imposition of the Japanese-style household registration system for colonial administration), Korean women had few socially legitimated opportunities to live outside of a family household unit led by a father, father-in-law, husband, or adult son. Women were allowed few inheritance or property rights and had little public authority. Sungyun Lim's detailed analysis (2019) of family law disputes in colonial Korea demonstrates both the importance of marriage in defining women's social standing and the ways Korean women contested those limits in the context of colonial cosmopolitan social and cultural changes. Nevertheless, through the colonial period and beyond, the defining act of a Korean woman's life remained her marriage and transfer to her husband's home, and the event that inscribed her into the lineage was the birth of her first son. Teknonymy was (and still is) widespread: women were called by their roles inside the family, most commonly referred to as Someone's Mother, that someone being their eldest son. These norms made marriage not just expected but *definitional* of being a Korean woman. A woman without a husband and a child was in a real sense almost unnamable.

Marriage was also definitional to the biopolitical administration of Korea. During the Japanese colonial period, family head laws were altered but strengthened and customary practices around inheritance, divorce, and property were central in legal disputes that resulted in some gains for women's rights but solidified the administrative importance of family registry (Lim 2019). Management of movement, marriage, and fertility were central concerns of the Japanese colonial administration (which viewed Korea as a source of labor), as they were to the American government of the southern Korean zone after liberation and the Republic of Korea after the formation of national independence in 1948 (DiMoia 2013). Given the extremely low rates of childbirth outside of marriage, any attention to fertility management encouraged a focus on marriage, and in the period before widespread use of contraception. specifically on age of marriage, as a key demographic indicator. Years of fertility while married was the strongest indicator of the likely number of children a woman would bear. The residual data, unmarried women, particularly women unmarried after the age of fertility, were of little interest to this birth-focused orientation.

The concentration on biopolitical fertility management in South Korea generated a focus on married women as the defining category in the production of the future labor force. Other aspects of the South Korean labor structure during the period of rapid industrialization in the second half of the twentieth century intensified the emphasis on heteronormative marriage: gender differences in pay and in employment opportunities were legal and widespread, men were often paid "family wages," and South Korean workers regularly clocked among the world's longest work weeks. The labor of social reproduction—pregnancy and childbirth, food preparation, shopping, care work of all kinds—presumed the continual availability of a family member, particularly if children, elders, or persons with disabilities lived in the household. Even after the economy had expanded employment opportunities for women, it was hard for single women to support themselves on the wages they were likely to earn; men needed wives to feed them, do their laundry, raise their children, invest their earnings, and inhabit the homes from which men were absent much of the time. The historical legacy of the concept of "universal marriage" underwrote the evolution of a social structure that exerted strong pressures on women to see heteronormative marriage as their only option.

Yet in the 1950s and 1960s, for many South Korean women it was not a realistic option at all. While the experiences of those who remained unmarried demonstrate that, despite challenges, it was possible to survive and even to thrive in a lifelong unmarried state, these exemplary lives did not eliminate the stigma for that cohort of women. Although the care and labor of unmarried relations was a buffer for families during a difficult period of social and economic transition, those same families discouraged one another from talking about single aunts or sisters for fear the failure to marry one daughter would tarnish the marketability of other single women in the family. Family members considered the existence of an unmarried relative as shameful to that individual and to the family as a whole. Several of the women themselves told me about elaborate lies they used to hide their single status from strangers and acquaintances both to protect their family name and to prevent prying questions or assumptions about their health or their chastity. The women I spoke with were aware that commercial sexuality may have absorbed a significant fraction of the extra women in their cohort, and so they were careful to present themselves in ways that would not leave them open to suspicions. Yet, on the whole, as mature women, they were coming to terms with their closeted lives. Several of them had never told anyone that staying single had been a satisfying choice, but all of them compared their lives to those of married women they knew, and none of them was envious of them. The stresses and constraints on South Korean wives and mothers were clear to them.

The anxieties expressed in recent years around a trend toward higher numbers of women and men in South Korea voluntarily choosing to remain unmarried focus on the economic pressures that have led to what is seen as a generation characterized by three "losses": courtship, marriage, and children. Yet for some, these are not losses at all. Jesook Song's study of the day-to-day challenges single South Korean women face in even such simple tasks as securing housing illustrates the value some women now place on independence. "Unmarried women [active in the women's movement] attempted to address the marginalization by creating and circulating a new category of single women: *pihon yôsông*, meaning literally 'unmarried,' but with the added connotation of being 'unassociated with marriage'" (2015, 21). As the numbers of single and divorced women have grown in South Korea, and their stories are featured in dramas and news media, increasing numbers of women believe that marriage is no longer necessary for their happiness (Lee 2019).

The older women, who have spent their lives unmarried in an era when their society not only did not believe that their unmarried circumstance was desirable, but did not even acknowledge their existence, have distinct stories to tell about their unseen lives, and about the society around them they helped to form. Their invisibility resonates with the widows discussed by Joanna Davidson in this volume, and as in the Jola villages, the lack of recognition covers up the misfit between the ideology of heteronormative marriage universality and the reality of nonnormative-compliant social structures in a dynamic context of cultural change. The women in South Korea share many similar circumstantial factors with the women Sarah Lamb (also in this volume) has encountered; like the women in West Bengal, the women I spoke with in South Korea offered various stories of nonmarriage, ranging from failures to achieve matrimony to active resistance to the institution of marriage. Whether their lifelong single status was intentional or the outcome of circumstances, both the fact of their independence from marriage and the fact of their erasure from view contributed to the character of contemporary South Korean culture, and their obscured lives simultaneously contest and reinforce the ideological power of heteronormative marriage.

Just as it was not convenient to recognize them when their single status threatened the promising image of South Korean future prosperity, their perspective on the changing pressures on women to marry has not been sought out, and they are unlikely to offer it. As one of the women said to me, "I know I shouldn't be so grateful for my bad luck, but I am. I think it would make my married friends sad to know what they missed. So I let them pity me, because I pity them." As South Koreans struggle to make sense of the rise in women who actively opt out of marriage, replacing pity with recognition and appreciation would facilitate understanding of how nonmarriage has always fit into Korean society.

PART TWO

Outside of Marriage

5

Pathivratha Precarity

Sex Work on the Other Side of Marriage in South India

KIMBERLY WALTERS

Many communities in South Asia understand women to be interdependently subordinate to male kin—initially to fathers and brothers and ultimately to husbands. In the abstract, these men are ideally expected to wrap their women in a cocoon of material support and protection while daughters and wives strive for worth through devoted service, motherhood, and deft domestic management. One of the various terms for chaste wives who succeed at remaining cocooned in this way is *pathivratha*, literally meaning one who is devoted to her husband. As I outline in what follows, pathivratha women emulate Sita from the Hindu epic the Ramayana, by remaining inside a metaphorical *Lakshmana rekha*, the circle their male kin draw around them at home for bodily and reputational security. All too often, however, this idealized system of female encompassment miscarries, just as it did for the goddess Sita, whose story I recount below. Fathers and husbands die or, in India's liberalized economy, find themselves unable to support wives and daughters who remain at home in the orbit of global cities where rising costs rapidly outstrip wages. Men may desert their families physically or economically, and wives and even daughters may find themselves forced outside their cocoons in search of a subsistence.

In this context, women and girls encounter a market for feminine labor in the high-tech economies of places like Hyderabad that can offer better earnings through paid sex than through other forms of work traditionally done by women. Even middle-class work typically gendered female that requires formal education (such as teaching) does not pay as well as sex work (Walters 2016a). But beyond the hydraulics of economic necessity, South Indian women may also find themselves propelled into sex work when they lose or cross the Lakshmana rekha in other ways—especially in the pursuit of romantic love. For women in South India, opting or being pushed out of marriage often results in opting in to sex work. This chapter situates sex work as both an effect of and—perhaps counterintuitively—a partial antidote to the precarity of marriage.

The Lakshmana Rekha and the
Mythos of Female Encompassment

The goddess Sita, pathivratha to Lord Rama, devoted herself so completely to her husband that she insisted on accompanying him into exile in the forest for fourteen years. While there, Rama, Sita, and Rama's brother, Lakshmana, encountered a mysterious golden deer. In an attempt to protect Sita while he and Rama pursued the deer, Lakshmana drew a magical boundary, the Lakshmana rekha (rekha literally meaning line), in a circle around Sita and their shared hut. He told Sita that if she would remain at home inside the circle, she would surely remain safe. Sita promised to obey her brother-in-law's instructions, but when she began to fear for Rama's life, she chose to overstep the magical boundary and run (she thought) to Rama's aid. But Sita's choice to disobey Lakshmana's command to remain encircled immediately subjected her to being kidnapped by Ravana, a foreign king bent on wooing Sita. When Rama and Lakshmana discovered that Ravana had tricked and abducted Sita, they pursued them and eventually defeated Ravana in an epic battle, reclaiming Sita. And yet, after having gone to such lengths to rescue her, Rama insisted that he no longer wanted Sita, whom he suspected had lost her wifely chastity during the abduction. Sita offered to walk through fire to prove her purity, and she emerged from the flames unscathed (in some versions of the tale the flames turn to flowers). With this evidence, Rama agreed to accept Sita back as his queen. But after returning to his kingdom in apparent triumph, the gossipy doubts of Rama's servants began to perturb him, and he again banished Sita in fear of losing the respect of his subjects.

Years later, Rama once more reversed his stance and pleaded with Sita to return to his palace to raise their twin sons and reign as his queen. This time Sita responded, "I have been doubted once, twice, and I do not care to be doubted again" (Arni and Chitrakar 2011, 145). The earth itself, Sita's mother the goddess Bhudevi, cleaved open and Sita returned to her belly, never to return to the earth's surface.

Myths play key roles in organizing intimate relations and their affective circuitry (Nuckolls 1993; Berlant 2008). The epic of Rama and Sita has gained both ritual and social saliency across the majority of South and Southeast Asia. Its characters and stories have become not only objects of religious piety but the everyday fare of children's cartoons and nightly television serials and a powerful engine for Hindu nationalist politics (Pollock 1993; Baber 1996; Rajagopal 2001).[1] While other myths also structure Adivasi (Indigenous), Dalit (oppressed caste), Christian, and Muslim communities,[2] Rama and Sita continue to model idealized (if increasingly contested) relations between husbands and wives across much of India. Guests at Hindu weddings sometimes affectionately tell a resplendent bride that she reminds them of the goddess Sita or one of Sita's related avatars, the goddess Lakshmi. In Telugu they say, "Sitadevi laga unnaavu, thalli" (You are like the goddess Sita, my dear). This idiomatic utterance acts both as an endearing tribute to the bride's radiance and as reminder of the role she is about to undertake, oriented toward the example of Sita's loyal purity. Sita's model of wifely devotion that was doubted once she crossed the explicit boundary of her home continues to structure conflict arising in the lives of many women whom I interviewed from 2009 to 2018 in Andhra Pradesh and Telangana in South India.

The South Asian idealization of female domesticity, dependence, and devotion to husbands precariously perches women who cannot or who do not wish to fulfill the expectations of the normative Telugu female life course outside the protections that such encompassment is understood to provide.[3] The ideal of the encompassed pathivratha wife structures the anticipation of imminent danger (figured by the greedy Ravana) as located outside the circumscription of home and familial direction.

In what follows, I illustrate how women who lose their protective encompassment after being widowed, separated, or financially abandoned, or those who wantonly cross the limits set for them by their families in order to pursue romantic love, find themselves so unmoored both financially and reputationally as to be vulnerable to entrance into sex work, the logical inverse of the protectively encompassed pathivratha woman.[4] The women whose lives I draw from in this chapter came from largely rural, working-class backgrounds and often (but not always) hailed from oppressed castes. Among the 136 workers whom I interviewed and spent time with from 2009 to 2018, the majority of them conveyed to me that their options at the time of making their initial foray into sex work seemed to them such that no other choice felt sensible.[5] Marriage, then, too often fails at its promise of permanent sustenance. For many women, the instability of marriage itself becomes the liminal antechamber to the deeper halls of sex work. Women unexpectedly find themselves needing to become self-reliant in order to sustain themselves, their children and parents, and often their husbands. The experience of transforming precarity into self-reliance, in turn, can prompt additional changes in gendered expectations as women begin to push other boundaries.

Exiting Monogamy: Wives without Husbands as Sexual Targets

While a husband's death or abandonment may spark additional financial troubles that often predispose women to turn to sex work, losing a husband's physical presence also creates something of a power vacuum around a woman as her Lakshmana rekha is altogether erased. While living in Hyderabad, I heard from other widowed women whom I encountered outside of my fieldwork among sex workers that friends of deceased men often propositioned them. The sex workers I interviewed mentioned similar events in their own lives: no sooner had their husbands died than their husbands' friends began to stop by to "look in" on them. Such eager visitors sometimes offered to take care of them permanently as their *chinna illu* (small house) or what is referred to in Telugu English as a "second setup." Some women, especially if they had already turned to sex work, accepted such offers not just for financial reasons but because they felt that they were safe only when they lived "under a man" (*bhartha kinda*). The expectation that women are precariously dependent on men for their safety as well as their sustenance and are therefore in danger when alone permeated many women's sense of themselves.[6] More practically, as Sarah Lamb also notes in this volume, women who live alone face extreme difficulty in finding homes to rent. Partnering with a man in some capacity can help assuage these problems.

Widowhood as a particular door to sex work or the presumption of sex work has been noted by many South Asian scholars (e.g., Das 1979, 97–98; Harlan 1995, 218; Lamb 2000, 221; Minturn 1993, 235–236). In North India, the Hindi word *randi* (literally widow) has lost its original meaning and has become synonymous with "prostitute," indexing the easy slippage between these categories. In Telugu, the word for widow, *munda*, has a similarly salacious tinge. It is seldom used other than as an insult. The slur *munda kodukaa* (son of a widow) is something equivalent to "son of a bitch" in English. Widows are rarely explicitly named as such. Instead the phrase *valla ayana leru* (her husband is no more) is used to communicate a widow's status while avoiding the uncomfortable term itself (see parallels in Davidson, this volume). Writing of rural Bengalis, Sarah Lamb suggests that "a widow, especially if young, was disturbing not only in her possibly uncontained sexuality but in her liminality—someone who has forsaken her husband by remaining on earth, but who yet cannot ever be truly free from him to move on to form new or independent relationships and identities" (2000, 237). It is this quality of indeterminacy and instability that marks widows and divorced and separated women alike—which I have elsewhere termed "wives without husbands"—as ready sexual targets for nearby men (Walters et al. 2012). Expelled from the boundaries mapped through marriage, wives without husbands appear to the men around them to be readily available, like free electrons in need of a nucleus to orbit. As a result, Telugu women who have lost a male partner may find themselves transformed into objects of sexual predation (see also Braun 2014 for a similar discussion regarding women in the Congo).

Lakshmi was one such example.[7] She was thirty-five when she spoke to me about her entrance into sex work. She came from a Madiga (Dalit or oppressed caste) family in a town in Telangana and had received no formal education. Her parents married her at fifteen, and she gave birth to a daughter at seventeen and later to two sons. Despite being one of the few sex workers I knew who was in the enviable position of owning her own home and possessing a government ration card (which provided her access to monthly food supplies), a voter ID, and a bank account before her husband died, she nevertheless turned to sex work once she found herself widowed. She explained how her predicament began despite her seemingly secure life: "My husband kept bad company with whom he used to drink and gamble. He borrowed ten thousand rupees from his friends, but then he could not repay it." These associates used to pressure Lakshmi and her family for money. One day, they got angry and in the heat of an altercation they hanged Lakshmi's husband by the neck. Lakshmi's mother-in-law and father-in-law fingered Lakshmi as the ultimate cause of their son's death, saying that she had brought bad luck to the family upon setting foot inside their house. Without their support, Lakshmi was left with no money to feed her children, and her husband's friends began forcing her to have sex with them.

Word quickly spread of Lakshmi's dire situation, and an *aunty* from another district caught wind. The English loan word "aunty" is used generally in India to respectfully refer to any older unrelated woman. However, among many South Indian sex workers the term has also come to mean a woman who brokers sex with customers while splitting their fee with the sex worker. This aunty came out to Lakshmi's village and offered that she could begin sex work at a house in Hyderabad. Lakshmi told me that she accepted because she needed the money, and almost as an afterthought she added, "I also thought, 'Anyway, my husband's friends will not leave me in peace. Why not do it for myself? If I go to another town, no one in my village would know about my business.'" Having made the decision, Lakshmi accompanied the aunty to Hyderabad and stayed in her house for a week while selling sex. She found the money good, but with her children in the village under the care of her mother, she could not remain alone at the aunty's house. So, she hired her own room in Hyderabad for fifteen hundred rupees a month, moved her children in from the village, and started life in the city as a full-time sex worker.

In Lakshmi's rendering of the story, she mentioned that her husband's associates had been forcing her to have sex with them in passing as if this outcome was not surprising under the circumstances. Also noteworthy was that Lakshmi drew a sort of moral equivalency between being raped by her husbands' friends and engaging in sex work. Being forced to have sex and being paid for sex were both modes of stepping (or being pushed) outside the ring of obligatory faithfulness to her dead husband. In Lakshmi's reckoning, it seemed that *exit* from monogamy mattered while the *mode* of exit was less important.

Another interlocutor, Preethi, echoed this calculus of female worth measured through monogamous circumscription when she explained to me her fear that her family would never take her back again after she ran away from home and was then brutally trafficked into commercial sex:

KW: Why don't people understand? When it is not your fault, why do people blame you?

P: Whether it is our fault or not, generally—If a wife and husband are walking together, and if *pokirivallu* [miscreants] rape the wife against the will of the husband, would the husband accept his wife again?

KW: That is what I am asking.

P: He would not.

KW: But, it is not the fault of his wife, you know? She has done nothing wrong. Really, it is the fault of the pokirivallu.

P: But society does not think like that. Very rarely can we find people who think thoughtfully. People would not think that the woman is not to blame.

Preethi's account of contemporary wifely precarity clearly parallels the tragedy of Sita. According to Preethi's example, a woman's worth as a wife is located in her perpetual monogamy, and it is neither her intention nor her action that bears weight in the balance of opinion, but rather the vagaries of public (dis)belief in her bodily monogamy. Once there is cause to doubt her monogamy, the rekha has been crossed, and banishment looms on the horizon. For my informants, after crossing the rekha, taking up sex work became the passing stuff of "anyway," as women looked back on what seemed, in retrospect, inevitable. As a result, they expected to be rejected by their families and unable to obtain other employment that paid a living wage. As I show elsewhere (Walters 2016a), many women who resort to sex work use it as a means of contending with their forced exit from monogamy to resourcefully make a living for themselves and their dependents.

The Perils of Love: Romantic Agency as Precursor to Sex Work

While many women I interviewed communicated a sense of the economic inevitability of sex work when husbands (dead or alive) failed them, there was another sense of the inevitability of sex work among girls who crossed the Lakshmana rekha by choosing to deploy their sexuality for love rather than on behalf of their families. Damaging her family's standing in the community (*paravu povadam*) by dating or eloping often meant that a girl could not return to them for the foreseeable future. By eloping, then, she might be forced to cut ties with her natal family (possibly permanently). Without the support of natal kin, the young woman forgoes access to dowry, wedding expenses, and ongoing gifts that most affinal families expect to gain from a daughter-in-law, and there is little chance of their welcoming her into their home and family without these expected forms of wealth transfer. Choosing against the grain, she opts for the risky prospect of a future tethered solely to the object of her romantic love sans family support.

The idea of young romantic love is prominent in the vast majority of Telugu films, and it functions as a site of intense friction and social change in South India as elsewhere (Cole 2008, 2010; Cole and Thomas 2009; Hirsch and Wardlow 2006; Hota 2020; Padilla et al. 2007). But among Telugu speakers, romantic love can also become a portal to sex work. By choosing to cross the Lakshmana rekha, a girl who wrests control of her own sexuality by dating or eloping is considered morally audacious enough that a further step into the business of sex may seem probable to her community, or ultimately to her. This may be true even if she did not at first consider the possible linkage to sex work when she initially set off to marry her lover.

Priyanka's story illustrates this point. She was fifteen, hailed from a poor rural Dalit family, and was yet unmarried when she eloped with her lover. She was a tall, thin girl with glowingly smooth skin the color of dark chocolate. Despite her exquisite features, Priyanka's deep skin tone preempted her from being considered beautiful by her family and friends. Additionally, Priyanka had never received any formal education. Her parents were illiterate construction laborers, but on their few attempts to send her to school, she had insisted that she would rather take the cattle for grazing. Priyanka's rural childhood upended when she fell in love.

The man who wooed her was short but fair and thus, Priyanka had thought, very good looking. "We should never marry for looks," she said to me in retrospect, "but only for good qualities." At first, their clandestine intercaste romance was storybookish: Priyanka's boyfriend brought her gifts and told her that he loved her. He promised her that he would take care of her for life. Later he convinced her to secretly accompany him to a Sri Rama temple in their town where he tied a *mangala sutra* (marriage necklace) around her neck with no family or friends there to witness their religious wedding ceremony. Priyanka returned home to her parents' house and the two continued to meet without his or her family knowing. She would occasionally steal things her new husband asked for from her parents' house when they rendezvoused.

After two or three months of their clandestine marriage, Priyanka's husband told her, "Let us go someplace and get work. Your parents will not let us live if we remain here." They boarded a train for Hyderabad and disembarked at Secunderabad station, one of the hotspots for sex work in the city. There in the train station itself, Priyanka's new husband began talking to another man whom he introduced as a friend of his. After the men finished their conversation, Priyanka's husband told her that she was to wait with the man for a moment while he went to drink some tea. "When I said that I too want to drink tea" (meaning that she wanted to go with him), "he hit me and said, 'What do you need a drink for?!' [*Emi thaguthavu?*] and then he left." Priyanka tried to wait for her husband to return, but the man she'd been left with told her that her husband had just sold her to him and that she must come with him now. When Priyanka refused, he caught hold of the long black braid at the back of her neck and hit her again. She struggled with him, broke loose, and made an escape. Among the hundreds of sex workers I have met and interviewed since 2009, stories like Priyanka's are by no means unheard of. However, experiences like Priyanka's of being tricked by a lover, husband, or family member and sold into sex work were a minority. A few girls who ran away from home for reasons other than romance have also recounted to me having been picked up in train stations and physically forced into prostitution.

Later, as the escaped Priyanka sat alone crying in this strange new city, a group of sex workers associated with a nearby sex workers' community-based organization (CBO) found her. She told them that she had no one, and she called them "aunties" and asked them to take her along with them. They ferried her to the CBO office. Priyanka told me, "The Big Madam [meaning the CBO president] is a good person." She continued, "When she saw me, she said, 'Come with me. It will be like this: I will take care of you and you will not face any problem.' Until now there is no problem. She is taking good care of me." What this arrangement meant was that the sex worker CBO, which ostensibly worked in part to end sex trafficking, effectively introduced Priyanka to sex work after she narrowly escaped from being sold into what many observers would term "modern slavery." The CBO sex workers told Priyanka that she could better subsist on the earnings in this profession than any other. The CBO president assigned her to a woman whom Priyanka began calling *atthamma* (father's sister and mother-in-law). Clients phoned her atthamma, and she invited them over to purchase sex from Priyanka or herself. Sometimes Priyanka and her atthamma went out to work at bus stops together. Priyanka had been working for the CBO atthamma for two years when I met and interviewed her. Whenever the police caught them, Priyanka told me, representatives would come from the CBO office to negotiate their release by telling the police that they "belong to them" and that they "work for the doctors," in reference to their status as an HIV-prevention project with government backing. These connections shielded them from police interference.

When Priyanka found herself dodging a trafficker and stranded in the Secunderabad train station, crying and alone, why had the CBO not transported her back to her parents in her hometown? Why had that not been the moment when her life transformed again—when she returned to something resembling the more valorized Telugu female life course that sex workers often referred to as belonging to "house women" (*intlo unna aadavallu*)? Here, clearly, was a victim of trafficking even by stringent definitions, and yet, crucially, Priyanka had been found in that preliminary moment before ever being forced to perform sex.

The CBO sex workers had also stumbled upon Priyanka before she learned of sex work's quick and lucrative earnings and well before she had formed what I elsewhere refer to as the *aalawaatu* (habit) of sex work (Walters 2016b). Why not return Priyanka back to what sex workers often refer to as a "family girl" (*family ammayi*, in a mix of Telugu and English), especially given that the CBO claimed to prevent anyone below eighteen from entering the profession? Priyanka seemed to present them a valuable opportunity to score a trafficking rescue.

To me this initially appeared a liminal moment. Yet neither the CBO women nor Priyanka had equivocated. Upon encountering a crying Priyanka in the station, the CBO held no powwow of deliberation to consider a plan for safely delivering Priyanka back to her former life. Instead, Priyanka's future seemed overdetermined, and they immediately introduced her to commercial sex. In retelling her story to me, Priyanka did not pause at this juncture in the narrative to explain how and why this crucial decision had been made—why it was that the CBO president and she had chosen the path of sex work over an attempt at return. She did not mention even considering a journey back to her family or a moment of looking back over her shoulder before choosing sex work as the better option. The option to return did not seem to have occurred to her. It was not, effectively, an option.

The lack of equivocation reveals a dimension of female precarity and the propulsion toward sex work: a shared set of expectations about the thin line that circumscribes a "virtuous," marriageable Telugu girl and delineates her from a "spoiled" girl who has lost her virginal exchange value. In her mind, Priyanka's fate as a sex worker had been sealed when she cast her lot with the man whom she married and who eventually sold her. It was the very fact that she had made a choice *for herself* rather than allowing her parents to choose her future for her by arranging a marriage on her behalf that was the crucial moment at which Priyanka crossed over from the magical protection of her status within "family life" to the inevitability of sex work. Since she had eloped without their permission, her parents would no longer welcome her back. Priyanka told me: "They said, 'You better not come back to us.' My mother is not a good person. She says that she will kill me. None of my people are good natured. They are saying that they will kill me if I go back. My father, mother and others are not good people. That is why I am staying here [in sex work]." It was the very choice to violate what her community regarded as the right of her parents to direct the use of her sexuality that Priyanka considered her point of no return, marking her as permanently other than respectable. It occurred well before the choice to sell sex. Thus, being sold by her husband to a stranger was not the ultimate reason that Priyanka never looked back to try to recoup her former life. In her mind, it was her earlier choice to spurn her parents' prerogative to deploy her sexuality through a marriage of their choosing that mattered to the further journey into sex work with the CBO women after her husband's treachery.

What my informants understood to be the moral overlap between women who take control of their own sexuality by falling in love, eloping, or running away and sex work is crystalized in Kondamma's story. When Kondamma (a girl from a poor Dalit family in a small town) was in fifth grade, her father, a quarry worker, suffered a heart attack. Her mother tried to support him in his recovery and the rest of the family by working for a gas company. Kondamma soon decided to drop out of school to add her extra earnings to her mother's by working alongside her at the gas company. There Kondamma fell in love with a coworker, and although she was still a teenager and unmarried, she started having sex with her boyfriend (a highly unusual experience among my informants, who had largely remained virgins until marriage):

> We used to meet now and then secretly in parks and in deserted places like old vacant buildings. But he never gifted or paid me anything as a lover. At the same time, my family situation remained the same, and I shared my problems with my close friends. One of my friends in the gas company introduced me to an aunty who convinced me to enter into sex work for extra money. I thought that I could support my parents besides getting good food. I also thought that I could wear good clothes to impress my lover. That was the first time I earned a thousand rupees in one day and that was how I started to entertain clients now and then. My lover got suspicious of my behavior and questioned me about it in front of many people. People started talking about me. When my mother learned about me, she hit me like anything but then kept quiet because of our poor financial condition. I entered sex work completely because I was anyway stamped as a *lanja* [whore].

Kondamma's story is instructive because of the extenuating "problems" she shared with her friends, which are perhaps not immediately apparent to readers. She and her mother were both working to support their family and seemed to be getting by in their small town. Yet what mattered more to her trajectory than her economic situation was that her friends discovered that she had begun having sex with her boyfriend. The news of this transgression ("crossing over") was enough to hasten a propositioning aunty to Kondamma's side. And once Kondamma had but dabbled in sex work, the resulting rumors that her boyfriend spread about her were enough to propel her into full-time sex work, and she soon quit her low-paid job in the gas company. Like so many other sex workers I interviewed, Kondamma deployed the term "anyway" in retelling her story. "Anyway" she'd been having sex with her boyfriend; the algebraic inevitability resulted in her consequent entrance to sex work. Kondamma's story illustrates the expected outcome of female waywardness in a widespread Telugu moral imagination.

Sex Work as Self-Reliance and Self-Determination

As I discuss at length elsewhere (Walters 2016a), many women who resort to sex work use it as a means of actively contending with the consequences of opting out or being forced out of monogamy. Such women use it resourcefully to make a living for themselves and their dependents. Sex workers regularly told me that it was not just better earnings but self-determination that appealed to them in sex work. In South India, most sex workers decided for themselves if and when they would work based on many personal factors. If they received clients via an aunty, they usually had the prerogative to decline work when it did not suit their schedule. I was surprised to learn how much sex work in Hyderabad occurs in daylight hours rather than at night. The flexibility of sex work left women able to work around family members' school and work schedules. Some could even hide their work by leaving home to "shop." engaging in a brief paid encounter, and returning home without having been gone long enough to rouse curiosity. Like gig economy workers, they might choose to work only when they needed extra cash in addition to other forms of work. Except in rare circumstances, there was almost always opportunity to earn; work was theirs to refuse. Sex work offered many women a (stigmatized) security in contrast to the precarity of pathivratha encompassment.

Most women's explanations of how they had entered sex work seemed straightforward enough to them: they encountered financial problems (sometimes severe, sometimes not), usually due to a husband's or father's death, inability or unwillingness to support them, and a friend or acquaintance recommended sex work as the best means of getting by or even ahead. These kinds of stories accounted for about three-fourths of the more than 130 sex workers whom I have interviewed. Stories of financial calculus and women who claimed to have entered sex work because other work "does not pay" are so common that they became unremarkable to the sex workers themselves. Witness the remarkable consistency in the following examples of how these women turned to sex work for the self-reliance it offered.

Saiamma was a thirty-year-old woman with a tenth-grade education from a Reddy (privileged caste) family. Saiamma's parents married her at the age of sixteen to a man who worked for Hyderabad city as a road and drainage cleaner. Her husband and his family lied to her family about his position with the city before they fixed her match with him, claiming he had a loftier job working in an office. They also lied that he was a bachelor. In truth, he was already married, and Saiamma became his second wife when she married him—a situation that became technically illegal for Hindus in India only in 1956 but remains somewhat in practice. He also proved to be a drunkard, and he often hit Saiamma while demanding she bring money from her parents, something that her parents could seldom afford. After two years of marriage, Saiamma gave birth to a girl just as her husband lost his government job due to his involvement with organized crime. When we spoke, Saiamma's husband was in Cherlapalli jail. Saiamma at first began work as a laborer at a blade factory called the Topaz Company. At the factory, men regularly pestered her for sexual favors. The salary that the company paid her was not enough to sustain her household. She felt that she could not continue to support herself and her small daughter on the wages that she earned, and so she started trading sex for money in addition to her wage labor at the factory. She explained, "I started it myself. No one suggested that I enter sex work. I just watched women in sex work at the Topaz Company and learned about it from them."

Durga was twenty-two when I interviewed her in 2013. She had a ninth-grade education and came from a Dalit family in rural Telangana. Her parents had married her a few years before at the age of nineteen to an auto-rickshaw driver, and she gave birth to a daughter a year later. She was happy with her husband, but in 2012 he died in a road accident. At that time, Durga was pregnant with her second child. After her husband's death, she stayed with her mother and brother, where she gave birth to a son. Her brother and sister-in-law began to feel irritated with the extra burden she posed to their household, and Durga's parents-in-law offered her no refuge. She was left with no money and insufficient food to be able to nurse her newborn son. She was offered a job as a sales girl in a textile shop with a salary of two thousand rupees plus a 10 percent commission on the sales, but she turned the job down because she could not sustain herself and her two children on such meager wages.

At that point, Durga met an aunty who was visiting relatives in Durga's town when she became friendly with Durga. As their friendship developed, Durga confided her troubles to the aunty and asked her to locate a job for her in Hyderabad, the nearest big city. The aunty in turn suggested that Durga enter into sex work in her home-based brothel in Hyderabad. At first, the idea scared Durga. But because of her uncomfortably tight situation at home with a brother who was angrily begrudging her support, she decided to try it just once. "So that I could feed my children well," she explained. Leaving her children in the village with her mother,

Durga came to Hyderabad along with the aunty and tried sex work for three days. She was immediately and pleasantly surprised to discover how much money she had made even after sharing her income with the aunty. And so Durga rented a one-bedroom apartment in the Kukatpalli area of Hyderabad for fifteen hundred rupees a month and moved in her children. Durga also brought her mother out of her brother's home—where Telugu ideals suggest she ought to ideally remain. Durga has secretly supported herself, her mother, and her two children ever since with no man in the house through her earnings from sex work.

In Meena's case, sex work offered her a means to thrive after she chose to leave her alcoholic and abusive husband. Along with her three children, she secretly boarded a bus in their hometown in West Godavari, Andhra Pradesh, and departed for Hyderabad. Once there, she realized that working one full-time job would not suffice to support the three of them. The year was 2000, and Meena was then a thirty-year-old illiterate woman from one of the many Telugu agricultural castes. At first, she sought out construction work (*taapi pani*). The foreman offered to pay her sixty rupees, at the time worth about seventy-five U.S. cents, for a full day of physical labor. This was then entirely typical pay for unskilled female labor in the booming city, but it was not enough for Meena and her children to subsist. After a few days of taapi pani, one of Meena's fellow workers said to her, "How long can we work like this? Let's go to Secunderabad. Let's see if anyone falls." With this elliptical invitation, she took Meena to the bus depot near the city's main train station where men pick up women for paid sex, and she showed her how to find a customer and bargain for a rate.

That day, instead of spending hours carrying bricks on their heads, Meena and her new friend together provided the same customer with sex. He paid each of them two hundred rupees for their services, and Meena went home with almost as much money as she would have made in four full days of taapi pani. The next day, skipping the detour to the construction site, she headed directly back to the same spot in the bus depot with her coworker. There, Meena got picked up by a man who asked her if she wanted to go for a movie. They bargained out a rate of two hundred rupees for the date and went off together to a dark theater. Afterward, Meena's customer bought her two kilos of ripe mangoes to take home with her and then asked whether she had eaten her main meal of rice yet that day (*annam tinnaavaa*). When she said no, he took her to Alpha Hotel near the train station and ordered a chicken biryani for the two of them to share. In addition to her two-hundred-rupee fee, Meena went home with India's favorite fruit for her children and with her belly full of Hyderabad's most prized cuisine. Meena, who had left her unsupportive husband in the village to seek sustenance in the city, never returned to construction work.

Many Telugu sex workers use their earnings to amass wealth, buy gold, rent nice apartments, acquire land in their natal villages, send their children to private schools, provide dowries for their sisters and daughters, offer gifts and large loans to their family members, and buy the affections of their once frosty extended relatives. Sex work enabled some of my interlocutors to transcend circumstances of abandonment, utter rejection, and abject poverty. While the consequences of participation in sex work were highly complex and often challenging, those who navigated the social and physical risks well were able to leverage their careers into lives of relative comfort and even social standing.

Conclusion: Out of Bounds

In my interlocutors' retellings of their lives, once a woman had crossed her Lakshmana rekha, whether by eloping, engaging in romance, or being abandoned or widowed, there was no need to look over her shoulder as there could be no ready return. That line had been crossed, pathivratha respectability was now behind her, and a new need for economic self-reliance lay in front of her. Labor, wages, and the cost of living are a large but only partial window into Telugu women's exit from the normative expectations of marriage. While it is extremely difficult for a working-class Telugu woman to support her family in Hyderabad on the wages available to her through legally recognized forms of labor, any simple calculation of more cash for less work in commercial sex misses the simultaneous and intertangled workings of gender, marital status, and romantic love that many sex workers index when recounting their histories. Economics alone obscures Telugu notions of what it means to be a woman without support (see also Kapadia 1994). Stories of crossing out of bounds that are understood as predisposing a woman to sex work in turn complicate any merely materialist explanation of sex work as a straightforward strategy to cope with poverty. The mythical figure of the goddess Sita, the loyal but tragically suspect wife of Lord Ram in the Ramayana, maintained its saliency for my interlocutors in modeling Telugu female monogamy and the precarity of female reputation. Indeed, reputational precarity figured as prominently in stories of beginning sex work as financial precarity.

The precarity of marriage would seem to suggest that its inverse, sex work, may be quite common among Telugu women, and many of my interlocutors indicated as much. I often asked sex workers with whom I spoke to imagine the neighborhoods where they lived and the women whom they knew there and to estimate the number of women there who sold sexual services at least occasionally. Estimates ranged a great deal, with answers from "very few" to 75 percent, but on average, sex workers suggested to me that more than 25 percent of the women who lived in their urban working-class neighborhoods sold sexual services at least occasionally.

For those women who succeeded at the business and managed to financially secure themselves and their families in the process, the loss of pathivratha reputation and the crossing the Lakshmana rekha meant traversing other forms of encompassment as well. Some left behind gendered expectations about moving about at night, drinking alcohol like a man, speaking like a man, dictating decisions like a man, amassing wealth, and supporting one's parents like a man. For others, success in sex work allowed them to traverse classed expectations as they hobnobbed with politicians, turned down the romantic advances of men in their own class, made their own romantic choices, or snubbed the patronizing interference of middle-class work colleagues. In this sense, sex work acted as both a seemingly inevitable outcome of pathivratha precarity and an unexpected means to redefining cne's own purview and possibilities.

Once a woman crossed outside the protection of domestic honor and marital security, she found herself in largely uncharted territory. While for some this left them vulnerable to being trafficked for sex work, for others it became the very grounds on which to resist many of the normative expectations of gender, class, and caste that otherwise constrained their everyday lives. They harbored, housed, and fed family members. They provided loans to their relatives. They paid rent, private school fees, dowries, and wedding costs. For some, earning, saving, and paying out like men also prompted them to transgress into the timings, spaces, and linguistic registers inhabited by men. For a few, it meant dictating decisions to their male partners like a husband might to a wife or demanding a show of respect from *peddavallu* (people of higher socioeconomic status). The increasing precarity of pathivratha marriage put other ideals at risk by extension. As women pushed or were pushed past the Lakshmana rekha, what had once seemed a deep abyss between genders proved far easier to traverse than the myth of Sita predisposed them to imagine.

Acknowledgments

I have taken sections of this chapter from my 2016 article in *Signs* titled "The Stickiness of Sex Work: Pleasure, Habit, and Intersubstantiality in South India."

NOTES

1. For example, physically locating and memorializing the events of the Ramayana on contemporary Indian soil is one of the driving preoccupations of Hindu fundamentalists, who now dcminate India's parliament.

2. See, for example, Illaiah (1994), Nuckolls (1993), and Ramberg (2014), among others, for accounts of myths that organize relations in South Indian *avarna* (oppressed) communities.

3. See Mies (2012) for an account of how remaining cocooned may produce other forms of economic disadvantage.

4. This claim may invite accusations of figuring Telugu women as the invented foil of privileged white feminist women, as elucidated by Mohanty (1988, 2003), among others. But to analyze a shared coherence is not to deny the idiosyncrasies of individual experience, and to analyze the dynamics of female precarity among Telugu speakers is by no means to deny it among women in Europe and North America.

5. About two-thirds of these women hailed from caste backgrounds other than Adivasi or Dalit. These caste proportions among the women I encountered in my research were roughly congruent with the caste proportions of women in sex work among the large survey of cisgender female sex workers in this region reported in Dandona, Dandona, and Kumar (2006).

6. The sentiment that losing a husband makes a woman free-for-all apparently troubles more than just the poorer, Telugu women who were my informants. Several sociological studies have found that one of the primary consequences of divorce (a legal resolution to separation that is more typical of wealthy Indian women than poor Indian women, who may recouple but seldom seek a writ of divorce) is that divorced women see a stark increase in the amount of sexual harassment they face in both their workplaces and their social lives (e.g., Amato 1994; Mehta 1975; Pothen 1986).

7. All names have been changed.

6

Respectability and Black Brazilian Women's Decisions to "Opt Out" of Remarriage

MELANIE A. MEDEIROS

When I first met Karolina, she was twenty-four years old and recently divorced from the father of her four-year-old son. While sitting on the curb outside the home she shared with her sister, niece, and nephew in Brogodó, Brazil, Karolina described the thoughts and feelings she was having about her divorce. For Karolina, her decision to dissolve her marriage reflected her need to end the marital suffering she experienced due to her husband's infidelity, not her desire to be single. While Karolina did not regret her divorce, she did express her sense of loneliness and longing for an intimate partner: "I don't like to be alone. I don't feel well alone. I like to have someone to give me affection, to give me attention. I like to sleep together, wish someone good night. I like to sit at the table and eat lunch with someone at my side. This [being single] for me is very difficult." Karolina expressed a longing for the physical and emotional intimacy and companionship that she believed a partner could provide. When Karolina began dating again as a divorced woman, she was subject to local gossip. She described, "When I went out with him [her date] in the street no one believed it. Everyone looked at us with their hands on their mouths, 'Karolina is dating!' And I was like, 'Uh, huh I'm dating. Hello people, I'm alive!' Because there are people that think we've separated and we've died." Similar to other Brazilian women, for Karolina marriage offered the potential for intimacy and was also a source of respectability—the state or quality of being of good social standing and respectable. Karolina's respectability, as a divorced woman, especially one who was dating, was put into question.

Three years after her divorce Karolina remarried; however, her second marriage also ended due to her husband's infidelity. Karolina explained, "The biggest pain I had in my life was with what I went through with my second husband. Because it was a four-year relationship. I gave him my life. I stopped doing various things that I liked to do. I reserved myself to be with him. And in the end he cheated on me with some random woman." Reflecting on the marital suffering she experienced despite the sacrifices she made in her relationship, Karolina told me that she had no interest in remarrying and suffering through another marriage. While Karolina still hoped for an intimate relationship, the scale of disappointment she felt over the dissolution of her second marriage led her to reject the institution of marriage.[1]

Several years after the end of her second marriage Karolina began dating one of her brother's friends. Fifteen years her junior, Karolina's boyfriend had never been married and had no children. As they continued to date, I noticed Karolina begin to refer to this man not as a boyfriend but as a *namorido* (boyfriend-husband). When I asked Karolina to explain what she meant by a namorido, she responded, "A namorido is a mix of a husband with a boyfriend. He sleeps every night in your house." The word *namorido* is a combination of the words *namorado* (boyfriend) and *marido* (husband). It signifies a relationship in which a man spends the vast majority of his time in a woman's home, eating and sleeping there, but not officially living there (cf. Freeman, this volume). This distinction is important because one form of marriage making in Brazil is cohabitation. Karolina's story reflects divorced women's desire for a new relationship model that challenges the married/unmarried dichotomy.

Karolina's rejection of remarriage and the emergence of the relationship category namorido is remarkable given the material and symbolic value of heteronormative marriage for Black women in Brogodó. Marriage was a vehicle for motherhood, which was a critical component of women's identities, and marriage promised unemployed women financial support outside of the natal home. For younger women who subscribed to the notion of romantic love, marriage carried the potential for physical and emotional intimacy, companionship, and commitment. Marriage also afforded respectability for women and their households. In Brazil, respectability is an elusive ideal historically granted to white Brazilian women and tied to their access to formal marriage (a phenomenon Freeman also discusses in chapter 7). In Brogódó, Black women's decision making surrounding marriage and remarriage was influenced by their quest for social respect and acceptance. In rejecting remarriage, Karolina and other women I met were resisting the notion that divorced women should remarry to obtain respectability. In doing so they also challenged the conventional relationship between respectability and remarriage and instead advocated for notions of womanhood grounded in independence and self-respect. In the face of a difficult decision to remarry or not, women like Karolina forged new kinds of relationships that served as a compromise between remarrying and remaining single. Defining an intimate partner as a namorido granted women the intimacy they desired, but because the namorido relationship was not a marriage, they were able to avoid the constraints, disappointments, and risk for suffering that marriages could pose, as well as the specter of divorce if the relationship ended.

Over the course of ten years of ethnographic fieldwork (2009–2018) among working-class, African-descendent, cisgender women in the rural town of Brogodó, I discovered that many divorced women were "opting out" of remarriage, preferring to remain single or enter into nonmarital relationships with men, despite the potential social costs. In a society where divorce had become more common and accepted but marriage had historically been valued as a source of respectability, women's decision making surrounding remarrying and their efforts at carving out alternatives to marriage were complex. Their decisions were influenced by long-held racial and kinship ideologies, political-economic changes impacting women's gender roles and their identities, and global transformations in marriage norms and values. Their decisions were also shaped by their previous experiences of marital conflict, suffering, and divorce, which for some dissuaded them from remarrying to acquire the respectability of being women. Thus, divorced women's past experiences with marriage distinguished them from women who had never been married and were opting to remain single.

Brogodó is located in the rural interior of the Northeast Brazil state of Bahia. In the past thirty years Brogodó's economy has shifted from being reliant on the remnants of the late nineteenth- and early twentieth-century diamond mining industry to becoming an ecotourism destination as one of the gateway towns to a national park. This chapter presents findings from interviews, focus groups, and participant observations with working-class Brazilians of primarily African descent whose families have lived in this region for generations. Members of this community have historically been racialized and marginalized due to their class, phenotypic traits, habitus, and geographic location in rural Northeast Brazil, where the social and economic legacy of slavery and inequality persists (Medeiros and Henriksen 2019). As a result, my informants were racially marked as "Black" in Brazil. While a full exploration of the complexity of racial categories and identities in Brazil is beyond the scope of this chapter, it is important to note that race in Brazil encompasses more than phenotypic traits and does not reflect the Black/white dichotomy prevalent in North America. Instead race is imagined along a color spectrum, so whiteness/Blackness are not discrete but gradient categories—with people even in the same family falling along different points in a variable range (Hordge-Freeman 2015). Yet even though race is a fluid construct in Brazil, racial ideologies and white privilege persist. That privilege leads some Brazilians to strive for characteristics of whiteness, such as heteronormative marriage and the social status it affords.

At the time of my fieldwork, the ecotourism economy had increased social inequality in Brogodó and formal employment rates were markedly low, especially among men. However, women had used the employment opportunities available to them as hotel cleaning staff, kitchen staff, and launderers to earn an income. Whereas prior to the growth of the ecotourism industry women in Brogodó were financially reliant on men, first their fathers and then their husbands, employment in ecotourism granted women relative financial autonomy. Notably though, women's employment was precarious; they were hired into positions that were low-paying and fluctuated with the tourism seasons. And yet, in giving women a formal source of income, even precarious employment in the ecotourism industry contributed to women's ability to transform their gender roles and assert their independence (Medeiros 2018). Subsequently, the ecotourism industry had profound effects on the lives of people in Brogodó and their intimate relationships. These changes reduced women's dependence on men for financial support and made it possible for divorced women to remain unmarried.

Coinciding with socioeconomic changes that influenced women's gender roles and their identities was the spread of the global ideal of romantic love to the rural interior of Brazil and subsequent cultural transformations in the values and beliefs surrounding and expectations for marriage. In Brogodó, women described "marriage in the past" as reciprocal relationships, sanctioned by the conjugal couple's families and grounded in a husband's financial support and a wife's domestic and reproductive labor. In these marriages couples aspired to *boa con-vivência* (good coexistence), which consisted of both material reciprocity and the demonstration of respect for one's wife through the absence of physical abuse (Medeiros 2018). In these marriages, husbands performed a functional role rather than an affective one (Gregg 2003). Younger women in Brogodó contrasted these marriages with a notion of marriage that was based in the ideal of romantic love, with characteristics such as passion, emotional intimacy, companionship, and fidelity, what anthropologists often refer to as companionate marriage (Hirsch and Wardlow 2006). Younger women's descriptions of their marriage expectations reflect a generational shift from desiring marriages based primarily in reciprocity to ones combining reciprocity with attraction and emotional connection (cf. Rebhun 2007).

Younger women in Brogodó distinguished themselves from women "in the past," including their mothers and grandmothers, who they argued settled for marriages based in boa convivência. Instead these women desired romantic love and marriages that corresponded with romantic ideals, especially fidelity. Whereas in marriages based in boa convivência the absence of physical abuse was a sufficient demonstration of respect in a conjugal relationship, for younger women in Brogodó sexual fidelity was also a critical demonstrator of respect in a marriage. Interpersonal respect is highly valued among working-class Black Brazilian women, largely due to their marginalized status in Brazilian society, and being respected by their husbands, family members, and the local community, if not broader Brazilian society, is critical to their sense of personhood. Women in Brogodó described abuse and infidelity as significant forms of disrespect and sources of embodied suffering. For women who felt disrespected by their husbands and whose marriages were a source of distress, divorce was an opportunity to end their marital suffering and assert their self-respect (Medeiros 2018). Therefore, in making decisions about whether or not to remarry, women negotiated between the risks associated with marriage and their desire for intimacy, companionship, and respectability.

Race, Class, and Gender and the Respectability of Marriage

Black women in Brogodó's access to marriage and feelings about marriage were influenced by a complex historical legacy. Understanding this legacy is key to understanding their decision making surrounding remarriage. In Brazil, marriage has historically been an institution with racial implications. Since the colonial era formal (legal or religiously sanctioned) marriage has been out of reach to many Brazilians of African descent, initially due to policies that prevented enslaved people from marrying (Myscofski 2013) and later due to the cost or inaccessibility of a marriage ceremony and celebration for working-class Brazilians, of which Black Brazilians are in the majority. As a result, consensual unions, also known as common-law marriages, were and continue to be more prevalent among working-class Black Brazilians than middle- or upper-class white Brazilians (Gregg 2003). Renowned Brazilian anthropologist Thales de Azevedo (1986) argued that for working-class—read Black—Brazilians, formal marriages were fantasies and aspirations correlated with higher status and class. McCallum (1999) asserted that among some Brazilian scholars in the late twentieth century, kinship studies stigmatized working-class Black Brazilians and their conjugal relationships. McCallum compared Brazilian anthropologist Woortmann's (1987) "ideal model of kinship," which he associated with upper-class respectability and whiteness, with his "practical model of kinship," which he associated with working-class consensual unions, sexual promiscuity, and Blackness. Woortmann's and Azevedo's work in the twentieth century reflects Brazilians' social correlation of formal marriage with social status, respectability, and whiteness, as well as the dismissal of alternative kinship models.

Historically, this correlation both influenced Black women's aspirations for marriage and its associated respectability and made formal marriage out of reach to them. In her 1947 ethnography of African-descendent Brazilian women in Salvador, Bahia, *City of Women*, Landes describes Black women's notions about marriage: "Most of the women dream of a lover who can offer financial support at least to the extent of relieving her of continuous economic worry; but they do not think of legal marriage. . . . Marriage means another world, something like being a white person. It brings prestige but not necessarily joy in living" (1947, 148). For the women Landes encountered, formal marriage was inextricably tied to whiteness and the social status whiteness provides. Brazilian ideologies surrounding marriageability and respectability are rooted in colonial constructions of race and gender that exalted white women as the legitimate wives of plantation owners and heads of the plantation household, including a domestic labor force composed primarily of Black women. Thus, the subordination of Black women was a key part of the construction of white womanhood, and Black women were framed as productive rather than feminine beings (Caldwell 2007). In the 1930s, Brazilian sociologist Gilberto Freyre documented the popular adage "White women are for marrying, *mulatas* (mixed/brown women) for fornicating, black women for work" (1933/2000, 85). This aphorism highlights the ways in which racial markers dictated whether Brazilian women were associated with respectability and marriage (white women), "sensuality" and sexual intimacy outside the confines of marriage (*morena*; mixed/brown women), or household labor (Black women; Caldwell 2007, 50). In Brazil's racialized patriarchy, women's relationships to white men determined their social identities and roles (Caldwell 2007).

These historical constructions of race, class, gender, and respectability persist in Brazil, influencing Black women's aspirations for marriage and simultaneously challenging their access to marriage. Communities bestow respect on women with husbands, while unmarried women may be deemed as unworthy of respect and social acceptance, especially if a single woman is sexually active (Gregg 2003; Sarti 2011). This notion has its foundation in historical notions of marriage in which it is the husband's responsibility to ensure the respectability of his wife and household, largely through controlling her sexuality (Caulfield 2000). The desire for respectability motivates some women to marry, despite the conflict they may confront in their marriages (Mayblin 2010). Marriage may confer respectability to all women, but again white women's presumed respectability grants them greater access to the institution of marriage. The correlation between marriage and middle-/upper-class white women is perpetuated by notions of white respectability and beauty (Caldwell 2007; Safa 2005; Williams 2013), and tropes about Black hypersexuality (Burdick 1998; Goldstein 2003; Williams 2013). Whereas white women model respectability and their sexuality is considered to be honorable because it is presumed to exist within the confines of a respectable marriage, Black women are sexualized and perceived as sexually available outside of marriage, and thus less respectable (Caldwell 2007; Goldstein 2003; Williams 2013).

As a result, Black women are "the last ones chosen [for marriage] and the ones first abandoned" in the "awful calculus of the heterosexual romantic economy" (Burdick 1998, 52)—even among Black Brazilians (Hordge-Freeman 2015). Hordge-Freeman explains that some Black men perceive working-class Black Brazilian women as unmarriageable, and they demonstrate preferences, both conscious and unconscious, for marrying white women. Hordge-Freeman found that due to the complex racial hierarchies in Brazil, even marriages purported to be based in romantic love were also influenced by a desire for upward social and class mobilization. In a society where marriage confers respectability, discrimination against Black women threatens their ability to acquire respectability through the particular means of marriage. Discourses surrounding Black women's marriage-ability impact not only Black women's ability to access formal marriage but their access to consensual unions as well. Although wedding ceremonies and celebrations still hold a symbolic value among middle- and upper-class Brazilians, in Northeast Brazil consensual unions have become more widespread than they were in the twentieth century. As a result, the words "marriage/married" (*casamentao/casado*), "husband" (*marido*), and "wife/woman" (*esposa/mulher*) are used by Northeast Brazilians whether or not couples are formally married. In Brogodó, women referred to cohabitation as a synonym for marriage and used the terms "live together" (*morar juntos*) and "marriage" interchangeably. Women used the terms "marriage," "husband," and "wife" to describe their conjugal relationships with men in part to earn the respectability that formal marriage afforded (cf. Gregg 2003). As I will discuss later in this chapter, in deciding to remain unmarried, women in Brogodó rejected not only formal marriage but consensual unions as well.

The spread of the ideal of romantic love further complicates the racial calculus of marriage. In Brazil, marriage (whether formal or informal) grounded in qualities associated with romantic love, such as fidelity, has become an aspiration associated with being *moderno* (modern) and subsequently with whiteness and the privilege whiteness affords. Historical precedent and contemporary social relations afford white people in Brazil certain (perceived) benefits, including love and fidelity (Hordge-Freeman 2015; Telles 2006). Although marriage is a source of respectability, infidelity tarnishes marriages grounded in the ideal romantic love and complicates the notion that marriage inherently grants respectability. For women in Brogodó, where respect was highly valued, physical abuse and infidelity were egregious signs of disrespect, and in divorcing abusive or unfaithful husbands, women asserted their self-respect (Medeiros 2018). The spread of the ideal of romantic love and corresponding marriage expectations, combined with the growing incidence and acceptance of divorce in this community, challenged the conventional notion that divorced women's respectability was inherently tied to remarriage, especially when marriage was a source of disrespect. In the remainder of this chapter, I explore how in opting out of remarriage, Black women in Brogodó created a social framework in which divorced women who demonstrated self-respect by staying single and avoiding marital suffering could be socially accepted, or in other words respectable.

Reasons to Remarry

In Brogodó, Black women's decisions to remarry were driven by a desire for intimacy and companionship as well as social expectations that divorced women should remarry for respectability. For divorced women in particular, rather than widowed women per se, remarriage was an opportunity to reclaim the respectability that was sullied by the dissolution of a previous marriage. The women I spoke to had a clear sense of the negative social perceptions community members had about divorced women who remained single.[2] Older women especially described the stigma divorced women experienced. During a focus group discussion with women fifty years and older, participants described the need for a divorced woman to "comport herself the right way," in a way that "doesn't call attention to herself." They discussed how it was socially acceptable for a married woman "to walk alongside" a divorced woman only if the divorced woman dressed and acted in a socially acceptable manner. As an example of acceptable behavior, one woman explained, "If she [the divorced woman] goes to visit her friend and her friend's husband is there, it's no problem. But if she visits the house and the friend is not home, she needs to leave." The assumption here is that a divorced woman is sexually available and a threat to other women's marriages, and therefore unchaperoned interactions with men are potentially intimate encounters that women must avoid (cf. Douglass 1992; Freeman, this volume). Another woman explained, "She's single, but she has to comport herself in an exemplary manner. You don't see her house full of men. You don't see her going to a party. . . . She comports herself in such a way that a person can be seen with her and no one will say anything about that person." These women highlight the stigma divorced women experienced if they did not present themselves as virtuous. Their discussion also reveals the potential stigma married women could face if they were seen in public with a divorced woman who did not satisfy these social norms.

These perceptions were also reflected in the one-on-one conversations I had with older women. Giovanna and I spoke while sitting in the shade of the narrow, concrete veranda at the entrance to the home she shared with her unmarried son and grandson. A sixty-nine-year-old widow, Giovanna's perspectives on divorce were representative of older women in Brogodó: "I think men think differently of a divorced woman. She no longer has the name she did." Giovanna highlighted the local belief that marriage is a key part of a woman's identity and that it is a husband who gives his wife "a name" and respectability. In Northeast Brazil, normative ideologies surrounding gender and sexuality determine women's value in relationship to men. Divorced women lose the status they achieved through marriage, and that status is one reason why women seek to remarry (cf. Gregg 2003).

However, my conversations with younger women revealed shifts in perceptions of divorced women. Younger women were aware of the stigma and loss of respectability divorced women experienced, but they also pushed back against it. Thirty-one-year-old Deborá and I first met when she was twenty-seven and I was visiting Brogodó for the first time. I witnessed Deborá's life in the years following her first divorce, her excitement over and confidence in her second marriage, and her dismay when that marriage ended as well. Deborá detailed the story of her relationships to me while we sat on a twin mattress on the floor of her two-room home. Deborá's first marriage began when she was fifteen years old and she discovered that she was pregnant. She and her husband had two children together before she divorced him for being unfaithful. Deborá explained, "I divorced my husband because he was always cheating on me. What woman in this day and age tolerates being cheated on? He always gave me [financial] support and continues to help me if I need it, even so I could not stay married to him." For Deborá, and many other women in Brogodó, it was no longer sufficient for a husband to demonstrate his respect through financial support and refraining from physical abuse; fidelity was demonstrative of respect and an essential component of a good marriage (Medeiros 2018). Deborá's tone of voice also indicated that she judged women who remained in marriages with husbands who were having extramarital affairs.

Deborá reflected on the social perceptions of women who were being cheated on: "[If] everyone knows he is cheating on you and you stay with him. I think it's like this. . . . We pass and people make comments. . . . Brogodó is small, and everyone talks." Her perceptions demonstrate that whereas "in the past" women remained in marriages with disrespectful husbands in order to ensure their respectability, younger women challenged the notion that respectability was tied to marriage and instead questioned the respectability of women who remained with adulterous husbands.

Over the course of her first marriage, Deborá's husband's infidelity, a form of disrespect, was the source of embodied suffering. She described sleepless nights, chronic headaches, and a general sense of malaise that permeated her day-to-day life. At the end of her marriage she exhibited depressive symptoms and was prescribed a *calmante* (tranquilizer). Deborá's suffering was both the product of marital conflict and dissolution as well as a socially mediated response to divorce that indexed Deborá as a respectable person. Embodying these symptoms allowed Deborá to express her unhappiness and receive the emotional support she needed from her community, while mitigating the loss of respectability associated with marriage dissolution. Deborá's case reveals how women experienced a double bind in which divorce was a necessary process for women to maintain their respectability if their husbands were disrespectful (i.e., were abusive or unfaithful), yet they had to demonstrate distress due to their divorce to remain respectable. Although divorce was becoming more accepted and increasingly necessary for women who wanted to maintain their self-respect, there were social repercussions for women who ended their marriages without a "good reason" and did not grieve their divorces. I asked Deborá if women felt they needed to demonstrate grief over their marriages dissolving, and she responded, "Yes. Only because people want this, that you have to pass through this [suffering]. I don't agree with it. I think you should do what is best for you. Here people don't think like that. They think you have to live for society, for people like a neighbor or a friend." Deborá's narrative demonstrates how the social perceptions of divorced women dictated a certain gendered performance of suffering in order for women to maintain some level of respectability. However, Deborá and other women also critiqued that notion and argued that women needed to live for themselves and respect themselves, rather than "live for society." In many cases, the women who waged this critique did not recognize that their beliefs surrounding the necessity of women ending marriages to maintain their respectability also reflected efforts to satisfy emerging social expectations.

Whereas in the past suffering through an unhappy marriage and remaining in the marriage was a way for women to claim respectability (cf. Mayblin 2010), women in Brogodó demonstrated suffering to avoid the potential stigma of having divorced their husbands without good reason (cf. Fonseca 2001). The discourse of suffering and somatic symptoms of distress were a means for women to maintain respectability by demonstrating the negative effects of their marriages and the grief they experienced over their divorces. Deborá described how people in town gossiped and the public opinion of women who did not suffer at the end of their marriages:

> Yes they are going to talk. Sometimes women separate because of the fact that their husbands have cheated on them. So then a woman will look for . . . after a time separated . . . for a boyfriend. People will talk more about the woman. Instead of talking about the man, they talk more about the woman. Because the woman found a boyfriend, because she is out with a friend in public. Sometimes she's not even out with a boyfriend but she wants to go out and have fun, go to the dance club, go to a bar and have a beer, and people already speak poorly of her. . . . . They will say, "She said she liked her husband so much, but she is already out." They say this, you can be certain of that.

Divorced women had to navigate a social obstacle course of public scrutiny that demanded a performance of specific emotions and behaviors. Social acceptance and respectability were as easily rescinded as they were granted.

Opting Out of Remarriage

The narratives of divorced women in Brogodó highlight the reasons women opted out of remarriage irrespective of norms linking marriage to respectability, and even if it meant relinquishing the fantasy of intimacy that marriage grounded in the ideal of romantic love promised but so often failed to provide. Roberta's decision not to remarry was informed by her past marriage experiences, which held more weight in her decision making over remarriage than conventional notions of respectability did. Although I had met her five years earlier as a guest in her bed and breakfast, it was not until we sat down for her first interview that I learned about the challenging circumstances surrounding Roberta's marriage and divorce. Roberta was thirty-five years old when she met her husband while caring for a sick relative in the city of Salvador. Roberta acknowledged that she got married at an older age than is typical in Brazil: "When I got married I was old and I knew what I wanted. The only thing I didn't want was to separate [divorce]." Roberta and her husband moved to Brogodó with his two-year-old daughter. She opened a three-room bed and breakfast, and he worked as a freelance hiking guide. However, according to Roberta it was not long before the marriage became a source of distress. Her husband became addicted to crack cocaine and stole from her bed and breakfast guests. His behavior was erratic and Roberta also suspected that he was unfaithful, which was an additional source of distress. An Evangelical Christian, Roberta professed religious beliefs that dissuaded her from ending her marriage: "People say that I kept going until I couldn't tolerate it anymore. Because I didn't want that. In my head marriage is only a onetime thing. You don't get married, get divorced, get married again then separate, get married. I don't think this." Ultimately Roberta's husband's drug addiction, criminal activities, and imprisonment led her to terminate their marriage.

Contrary to the conventional norms of respectability, Roberta told me she did not feel judged for ending her marriage, even within the Evangelical community, because her husband was not only unfaithful but a criminal and addict. Instead, she explained, "The people who know me and like me wanted me to divorce him. They all wanted it. Because it was a lot of things. It was a lot suffering. The people who liked me, really, didn't want me to stay in this relationship." Roberta suggests that people who truly cared about her and "liked" her accepted and even encouraged her divorce. This indicates that perhaps commentaries surrounding the respectability of a divorced woman in Brogodó would be more likely to come from community members who were not socially close to the woman and/or were more likely to come from people who did not believe that there was a strong enough justification for the divorce. This indicates that the notion that respectability was inherently tied to marriage was not hegemonic. Roberta also believed that people's impressions of her "changed for the better. People started to think that I didn't respect myself to be in that situation and not do something about it So the people who knew my situation became happy" when she ended it. Here, in an evolving redefinition, respectability is tied to women's self-respect and autonomy, rather than the simple fact of marriage per se.

Roberta's thoughts about whether or not to remarry were heavily influenced by her experiences in her first marriage, in which she suffered and her self-respect was questioned. She explained that "when you were in a relationship and you weren't well, you were sad, you weren't happy and everything went wrong, you need to give time for yourself." She also noted that as an Evangelical Christian, "I have to follow the rules of the church. And so I can't live with a man without getting married. I will have to get married again because I don't want to leave the church." And yet, she told me,

> When I remember this marriage, I don't want to have a relationship with anyone. I want to be on my own for a while. . . . I want to spend time with my daughter because she also suffered with her father. . . . Because I don't know, sometimes you find people who really like you, and sometimes you find someone who is jealous, acting in self-interest, something like that. . . . So I know that in my mind, at this moment I don't want [to remarry]. I want to be well, be at peace, take care of my inn, take care of myself. . . . Bad relationships, even good relationships, are not worth it. So I don't want one.

Roberta's desires to be "at peace" and "take care of herself" demonstrate a preference for prioritizing her own well-being rather conventional norms surrounding remarriage. Furthermore, whereas women who were financially dependent on men might have continued to rely on marriage for respectability, women who were financially independent might have been able to achieve respectability on their own (cf. Hautzinger 2007). In deciding not to remarry women eschewed respectability tied to marriage and instead advocated for notions of womanhood grounded in independence and self-respect.

Alternatives to Remarriage

As an alternative to remarriage, divorced women in Brogodó cultivated forms of intimate relationships that gave them some of the benefits of a marriage while mitigating some of the risks. To examine these nonmartial relationships, I give an overview of some of the most commonly used relationship terms in Brogodó and the ways that women described and distinguished between them.

Prior to twentieth-century shifts in courtship practices, Brazilian scholars studying kinship did not recognize a distinction between the terms *namoro* (courtship) and *noivado* (engagement) (Azevedo 1986). This was largely due to the brevity of the period of courtship preceding an engagement that had been arranged or sanctioned by the couple's family. When changes in courtship practices extended the length of courtship, as couples discovered whether they in fact liked one another and wanted get married, the relationship category of *namorado/a* (boyfriend/girlfriend) emerged in Brazil.

In Brogodó during my fieldwork, there was a spectrum of flexible and fluid terms and labels to describe the courtship between men and women. Flirting, *paquerar*, was an activity enjoyed by both men and women. While historically women had been discouraged from flirting, discreet flirting had become more acceptable, except for married and recently divorced women who were required to mourn the dissolution of their marriages in order to maintain some semblance of respectability. Men flirted more openly than women and often continued to do so after they were married. This was often a source of marital discord because people viewed flirting as the precursor to other forms of courtship, like *ficar*. While the literal translation of *ficar* is "to stay," it became a euphemism for a variety of intimate physical interactions, from kissing someone once at a bar or dance party to—less commonly—having sexual intercourse with someone with little to no intention of ever dating them seriously. To *ficar juntos* (stay together) indicated that a couple engaged in physical intimacy repeatedly, but without any form of commitment.

Women in Brogodó explained to me that a couple began to *namorar*, to date and identify themselves as being in a relationship, when they decided to be monogamous. A namorado (boyfriend) was not expected to contribute to his girlfriend's household or assist with child care if a woman's child was not his own. The main expectation women had of their boyfriends was that they be *fiel* (faithful), be respectful, and decrease the amount of time they spent going out at night to drink with friends because they might be tempted to be intimate with other women. After a period of time, or if the woman became pregnant, a couple might decide to get married, through a civil ceremony, through a church ceremony, or by moving in together, after which they were considered to be *casado* (married). I asked Karolina to explain to me the difference between a namorado and a *marido* (husband). She stated that the marido "has responsibility. You know he has a *comprimiso* [commitment]. A *namorado* [boyfriend] also has a comprimiso but it's not that thing of responsibility, to help you [financially or with the children] and to share everything with you. A husband shares, a boyfriend does not. A boyfriend has to be faithful, but they don't have the commitment or responsibility to share things. A boyfriend doesn't owe me anything, he doesn't have to do anything for me, and I don't have to do anything for him, aside from being faithful to each other and being conscientious with one another." The main difference between boyfriend and husband relationships, according to Karolina, was the responsibility of material support, not just of the husband for his wife, but also the wife for her husband in the form of domestic and reproductive labor. This distinction is important to consider since many of the divorced women I met expressed a preference for a boyfriend rather than a husband and all the responsibilities a marriage entailed.

Thirty-two-year-old Cesaria was one of those women. For Cesaria, a boyfriend offered her freedom and autonomy that a marriage did not afford: "These days I feel very well, because my boyfriend doesn't restrict me, because he also doesn't have a reason to restrict me. . . . I don't want to remarry. I want my *biju* [good, kind, agreeable person], I'm all for that. But to arrange another husband, I don't want it. I don't want it. God help me, I don't want it, no." Thirty-year-old divorced mother of two Mariana also told me she was not interested in remarrying but would really like a boyfriend. She said that a boyfriend offered companionship and was someone to vent to. She explained that she would like someone who would come and stay (sleep over) once and awhile, but not move in permanently; someone who was not a husband. Likewise, forty-four-year-old Claudia described the benefits of having a boyfriend over a husband: "A husband is more possessive. He thinks he has a right to everything, and has the right to do . . . to every part of your life. If a boyfriend tries to do this you can tell him no, you are only a boyfriend." For Claudia, marriage required her to relinquish some of her agency, but relationships with a boyfriend enable her to maintain her autonomy.

Although boyfriends may have provided companionship, they did not reside with their girlfriends and were not responsible for providing them with any household support. Furthermore, while monogamy was expected from a boyfriend, a long-term commitment was not an expectation. Or in other words, the assumption was that a relationship with a namorado would either end or become a marriage. For divorced women in Brogodó who wanted the intimacy and independence associated with having a boyfriend, but also wanted a commitment, to cohabitate with a partner, and have them share in some of the household responsibilities—relationship characteristics associated with husbands rather than boyfriends—neither relationships with boyfriends nor marriages satisfied all of their desires.

The namorido (boyfriend-husband) relationship offered a potential solution for divorced women's quest for a relationship that offered intimacy, companionship, and support without martial suffering. For Karolina, a namorido would make a commitment to a woman and shared in more of the household responsibilities than a boyfriend did, but the relationships did not bear the weight of marriage or marital responsibilities. Roberta concurred: "They [namoridos] have to help yes. Especially a boyfriend who lives in your house. A namorido. Imagine a person living in your house and not helping you with anything." A key component of Karolina and Roberta's discussions of namoridos is the notion that a namorido entered a woman's home. It was "her" home rather than "their" home. In a matrifocal society in which women often owned homes that had belonged to their maternal kin, or constructed homes on property shared with kin, women felt a strong sense of ownership over their homes. Getting married meant relinquishing some control over the home and the household to one's husband. A namorido relationship enabled a woman to share a home with someone but maintain her autonomy and her role as head of the household.

I believe that women's expectations for relationships with namoridos were intentionally slightly vague. The fewer and more ambiguous the expectations women had of a partner, the less likely they were to suffer from the disappointment of unmet expectations. In Brogodó, women's narratives described their desire for intimacy with a man but also revealed that they did not feel they could rely on men for emotional intimacy. They denied the existence of love in conjugal relationships but aspired to receive a form of (romantic) respect that was influenced by the ideal of romantic love and demonstrated through fidelity (Medeiros 2018). They also asserted themselves as independent and relatively financially autonomous, stating that the support of a man was helpful but not essential. Thus, the ambiguity of the namorido relationship allowed women to avoid emotional and material dependence on partners who they believed would disappoint them in the future. In many ways a namorido relationship also increased women's agency. Women in Brogodó controlled the namoridos' access to the household and to physical intimacy. Furthermore, because the namorido was an emerging relationship model, it did not yet have the weight of expectations, for women or men, associated with marriage.

Years into her relationship with her namorido, and after Karolina successfully conceived and gave birth to their daughter, I asked her to once again categorize her relationship with him. This time she referred to him as her husband. When I asked her why that was, she giggled at my question and responded, "And so, what changed? . . . I think we have had more time together. At the beginning it hadn't been long enough for me to call him my husband. But after a time, he started to really live with me, he helped me with the house. He took care of my sons with me. And now he takes care of me, my children, our daughter, and my father. He's a super husband." Karolina's explanation indicates first that there is a temporal component to relationship models, and that with time and trust, women might be more likely to call namorido their husbands. But her response also reveals some subtle changes in how she perceived her partner's responsibilities to her and the household. When describing the time in their relationship when she referred to him as a namorido she mentions that he began to help her with the household responsibilities, including domestic and financial responsibilities and help her with child care. When she mentions the shift to calling him her husband, her language changes to describe him taking care of her and the children. This corresponds with Karolina's definition of a husband as someone who takes on the responsibility of the household. Over the course of my fieldwork, one other woman, thirty-three-year-old Viviane, transitioned from calling her partner her namorido to calling him her husband. When I asked her what changed, she said, "We had a child. Now he is my husband because of the child." Conventional notions of respectability required children to be born in wedlock, therefore making marriage a necessity for maintaining a pregnant woman's respectability, at least at the start of the child's life. Women who might have questioned the need for remarrying for respectability were still apt to remarry if they became pregnant. This indicates that the relationship between having children and getting married was inextricable, but also that parenting was a critical component of marriage making. Both Karolina's and Viviane's shift in the labels they used to describe their intimate partners demonstrate that the namorido relationship, like the namorado, may be impermanent or a stepping stone to the type of marriage women strove for before their divorces.

Women's decisions not to remarry combined with their desire for intimacy and companionship led some women to prefer namorados to husbands, and other women to engage with the namorido relationship model, which absolved their male partners and themselves of some, although not all, of the expectations of a marriage. However, I argue that the difference between a husband and a namorido was a symbolic one—by rejecting remarriage women protected themselves from marital dynamics that did not serve them. The category of namorido allowed them to dictate the terms of new relationships, in which they held equal or even more authority than their male partners. Women tended to have namorido relationships with men who were ten to fifteen years younger than them. I suspect, but admittedly have not yet collected the data to support my hypothesis, that younger men were willing to acquiesce some of their gendered authority to older and more established women. As I discuss elsewhere, women's employment and high rates of men's unemployment challenged men's authority in the household, which for many men compromised their ability to perform normative masculinity (Medeiros 2022). For younger men who have not yet married and taken on the role of primary breadwinner and patriarch, the namorido relationship might also give them permission to perform masculinity in ways that differ from previous generations (Medeiros 2022). Potentially, women's decisions to prioritize self-respect and opt out of remarriage and its concomitant suffering were also influencing men's gender roles and performance. In this sense, as youthful boyfriend-partners to older women, men are opting out of marriage as well.

Conclusion

Evidence from interviews with divorced women in Brogodó complicates the notion that divorced women lose their respectability and can regain it only through remarriage. While interviewees described the assumptions made about divorced women's respectability, they also revealed that as a result of sociocultural and political economic change, remaining in a marriage with an abusive or adulterous, and therefore disrespectful, husband puts women's respectability into question and induces profound suffering. Divorce was a way for women who were being disrespected by their husbands to regain their sense self-respect and their respectability. However, women had to navigate a complex system of social expectations in which they were less worthy of social respect if they remained married to an abusive, unreliable, or unfaithful husband, but were also deemed unworthy of respectability if they took their experience of divorce too lightly. For divorced women, earning respectability via the demonstration of self-respect required a gendered performance of suffering that justified divorce. A divorced woman then had to navigate perceptions that she was more sexually available and thus not respectable. Thus, social expectations for divorced women's behavior continued to reinforce patriarchal notions surrounding women's sexuality, and in particular Black women's hypersexuality. For some, these perceptions of divorced women influenced decision making surrounding remarriage. However, the majority of women I encountered asserted that the potential benefits of marriage did not outweigh the risks associated with remarriage. These women preferred to remain single, date, or in some cases adopt the hybrid relationship model of the namorido. This latter option provided women and men with new forms of relationship freedoms that also challenged gender norms.

Resisting remarriage is especially remarkable in light of the historical legacy of social marginalization experienced by working-class Black women in Brazil, who unlike white women must prove their respectability. Marriage, an institution associated with white respectability, affords Black women the respectability normally reserved for white women in Brazil. In Brazil, the ideal of romantic love and companionate marriage is also associated with whiteness and with being moderno. Women in Brogodó's aspirations for marriages reflecting values associated with romantic love, such as fidelity, were wrapped up in a larger identity project to be moderna and achieve the social equality and respectability that are linked to whiteness and the privilege it affords (Medeiros 2018). These women, by refusing to accept infidelity and divorcing their husbands, made a statement that they too were worthy of the respect afforded white women. Furthermore, by opting out of remarriage, Black women in Brogodó rejected the conventional notion of respectability, which as Black women had always been difficult to achieve, and instead aspired to an alternative formulation of self-respect and independence.

Acknowledgments

Excerpts from the author's book *Marriage, Divorce, and Distress in Northeast Brazil: Black Women's Perspectives on Love, Respect, and Kinship* have been published in this chapter with the permission of Rutgers University Press.

NOTES

1. It also led many to affirm the ways in which they could receive emotional intimacy and companionship from women in their families, rather than from husbands (Medeiros 2018; cf. Freeman, Hannaford, this volume).

2. I conducted life history interviews and semistructured interviews with sixty women ranging in age from eighteen to ninety-three years old.

7

The Upward Mobility of Matrifocality and the Enigma of Bajan Marriage

CARLA FREEMAN

> Marriage is regarded with a certain amount of reverence . . . yet many prefer to admire it from afar. To Caribbean women, in particular, its benefits seem dubious.
>
> —Hodge (2002)

It was by accident that I turned to the question of marriage some twenty years ago in Barbados and even more of an unexpected turn when I stumbled upon the evocative divorce stories of white Barbadian women, the focus of my chapter. As sometimes happens in fieldwork that stretches from years to decades, patterns I described as novel and transformative in the early 2000s began to show visible fault lines if not outright rupture a decade later. At the start of that period, in a study of an emerging entrepreneurial middle class, I was surprised to find that a striking percentage of the entrepreneurs I came to know (Black and white, men and women, alike) were, by national standards, disproportionately married. These higher rates of marriage were accompanied by a shifting set of dreams and expectations for these relationships and for the more general self—fashioning themselves as businesspeople and members of families and communities—and in their own self-understandings. Among women, especially, most striking was their bold, often passionate, articulation of a desire to forge new forms of marriage, new modes of motherhood, and new ways of relating to family and friends that featured emotional expressivity, romance, and intimacy. Often their testimonies drew explicit contrasts with the relationships of their mothers and grandmothers. Even where they saw love and affection in generations past, they were intent to make clear that the modes in which such sentiments were expressed were very different than what they sought. These women readily named their desires as very "non-Barbadian" in that they departed from the "stiff upper lip, tough love, grin and bear" culture in which they were raised. Also striking was that as self-employed entrepreneurs, these women were gaining economic independence as well as visibility in the public sphere. This combination also bolstered their capacity and inclination to bargain for new intimate relationships and aim for new modes of self-actualization more generally.

As part of a newly burgeoning affective culture that I detail elsewhere (Freeman 2014, 2020), I came to see not only the desire for a newly imagined marital intimacy but also its structural obverse—the *upward mobility of the matrifocal form*. As entrepreneurial women gain the economic wherewithal to realize their ambitions, they are pursuing their dreams along two tracks. They seek a new form of emotional-partnership marriage that intervenes at an interpersonal level, sharing not just the practical rhythms and stresses of their work days but their fears and vulnerabilities. Their vision of an intimate marriage pointedly challenges the traditions of gender-segregated social life as well as a deeply entrenched emotional culture of reserve. Here, they entreat husbands away from the male dominated homosocial spaces such as rum shops and sports bars and toward couple-oriented wine bars, seaside restaurants, boardwalks, and galleries, introducing "date nights" and shared leisure time. Today, public recognition of "the couple" and even the emergence of (secular and religiously oriented) couples therapists to bolster this social form are part of a new sensibility in this society where "the bottle and the pew" have formerly reigned as the dominant outlets for distress, longing, and sociality. Moreover, thanks to a lively entrepreneurial landscape of new and appealing gathering places, women can safely enjoy public spaces alone or in the company of others where once the church, home, and "yard" would have circumscribed their respectable whereabouts. As entrepreneurs, many of these women have forged successful new enterprises catering precisely to customers like themselves and in so doing often blur the boundaries between home and work, client and friend, and bolster their economic and their emotional security.

Over the years, the optimism I heard among married women began to falter. Like the young Brazilian women described by Melanie Medeiros (this volume) who also sought new modes of emotional connection in marriage, their aspirational efforts to forge new forms of romantic intimacy as a self-conscious departure from love as expressed solely through material "support" reached their breaking points. In several dramatic instances, the revelation of husbands' infidelity and "outside" children led to tumultuous divorces. In other cases, subtle resentments by husbands toward their wives' entrepreneurial success coupled with their unwillingness to pitch in and take on a heavier share of the domestic responsibilities led women to "opt out." While I never heard women use "matrifocality" in self-referential terms, their admiration for the strong and autonomous figure of the Afro-Barbadian household head and the ubiquitous reliance on extended kin networks were frequent points of cultural pride. It became more and more striking to me that their own domestic circumstances, kinship, and relationship to work—the pressure to work longer hours and multiple jobs, and their increasing reliance upon extended family or fictive kin—now resembles the Afro-Barbadian matrifocal majority.[1]

These observations put into stark relief the profound cultural specificities attached to marriage and matrifocality as both institutional structures and affective relations. In the United States and many other parts of the world, the growing impulse to "opt out" of marriage presents a radical threat to both custom and the social order. By contrast, in the Caribbean case I describe, despite its powerful weight as a conjugal ideal, the historical *marginality* of marriage and the norm of matrifocality and extended kin network provide a valuable ideological, emotional, and practical bolster for an unexpected sector of Barbadian society. I began this chapter with the words of Trinidadian writer Merle Hodge, who summarized marriage as an idealized but fraught institution in the Caribbean (2002). For privileged white women, poor Black women, and middle-class women of all racial and ethnic identifications, marriage is steeped in a history of ambivalence, an aspiration signifying respectability and economic security more than affective harmony or intimate union. Matrifocality, on the other hand, in the anthropological parlance of Afro-Caribbean studies, was coined primarily to denote the predominance of woman-headed households in which *mothers* come to occupy the pivotal relationship.[2] Many scholars have emphasized that matrifocality, long understood as an expression of Black Caribbean women's economic grit and ingenuity in the wake of plantation slavery, is neither consigned to the poor classes nor an expression of creole dysfunctionality (Smith 1988; Barrow 1996). How these forms operate as household structures, modes of conjugality, social institutions, and self-identifications has been anchored in what many scholars have explored (and critiqued) under the rubric of "reputation" and "respectability" (Wilson 1973).

As a nation Barbados is often characterized as more orderly and more concerned with the values and markers of "respectability" than its regional counterparts. This stereotype is both caricature and source of envy. In the jovial repertoire of island comparisons, if Trinidadians and Jamaicans are known for their spirit of carnival and fun, Barbadians are portrayed as somewhat uptight and "Afro-Saxon." This stereotype is attributed to two historical phenomena: under colonial rule, throughout the centuries of plantation slavery, Barbados remained steadfastly British, whereas the other territories changed hands among the Spanish, French, Dutch, and English and, in so doing, established traditions of cultural and demographic mixture among European, African, East Indian, and other groups. Unlike Jamaica and other Caribbean territories whose white planters were often absentee—extracting sugar wealth from the comfortable distance of the motherland—in Barbados white indentured laborers and planters remained in residence and became an established minority throughout the colonial and postindependence eras. Today, self-identified white Barbadians represent roughly 3 percent of the population. Though a few hundred descendants of white indentured laborers continue to eke out a living on the island's rugged east coast and others occupy middling strata as small shopkeepers, service professionals, and the like, it is commonly (if erroneously) believed that white Barbadians are a monolithic and economically powerful corporate elite minority. Indeed, postcolonial white Bajans tend to be glossed (in both popular parlance and in what little scholarship has focused upon them) as a single clannish, economically dominant, politically and socially conservative bloc. While some research has attempted to document the economic power wielded by the white minority (Karch 1981; Karch and Carter 1997), there is almost no such effort to document white Barbadians in more quotidian terms.[3] For historians and novelists of plantation life, the ubiquity of white men's infidelities and their "outside" children is part and parcel of this brutal institution's racialized, sexualized logic. How their wives and children tolerated these simple truths of masculine power and sexual prowess is a more minor subplot (Jones 2007). White Barbadian women, in particular, occupy an especially shadowy place in the public imaginary. In relation to the institution of marriage, their powerful but ghostlike significance is especially profound, for it is white (middle-class and elite) women who are assumed to be both the symbols and guardians of the powerful and elusive value complex of respectability (Bush 1981; Douglass 1992; see also Medeiros, this volume).

Many have argued that in formerly slave-based plantation societies of the Caribbean marriage was largely rejected or made impossible for enslaved men and women, giving rise to looser, consensual, and often nonresidential unions for the Afro-Caribbean majority populations in the region (Reddock 1988; Green 2006; Bush 1981). As a social form, formal marriage remained an institution closely associated with Europeanness and steeped in the moral order and structural parameters of (white) plantation respectability. Changes to the most recent census (1980 and 1990) reveal that efforts to capture household and relationship flexibility are ongoing. The *visiting union* continues to be commonplace—a formal household category denoting consensual sexual but nonresidential conjugal unions. In 1981, the Barbados Family Law Act conferred all rights of formal marriage (including inheritance after separation) to "common law" unions of coresiding couples of at least five years. Indeed, at the dawn of the twenty-first century, regionwide, between 60 and 85 percent of all children continued to be born outside of legal marriage (Green 2006, 6). Only 23.8 percent of the adult population is married, whereas 47.5 percent of all households are female-headed, the fourth highest in the world. According to Barrow, "Marriage may be the norm in the middle and upper classes but, to the chagrin of local moral authorities, most Barbadians seem to prefer to 'live in sin' in common law or visiting unions" (2019, 238). And when marriage *does* occur among the Afro-Barbadian majority, it has often been late in a couple's life, *after* the children are reared and a stable house and savings are secured. In other words, marriage as an early adult rite of passage, the locus of romance, sexuality, parenthood, and a shared residential, coupled-social structure remains an idealized modern European model that operates as a powerful aspirational referent in Caribbean life but one that is realized by a small and largely middle-class minority.

For centuries, patriarchal marriage and the matrifocal household have been figured relationally, seemingly opposing sides of the gendered and racialized household/conjugal coin. As the value orientation of one side changes (i.e., what can be expected of marriage beyond the patriarchal order), so too is the other being redefined (i.e., matrifocality as age-old survival structure of poor, Black women, offering possibilities for middle-class and white women as well). Evelyn Blackwood argued more than a decade ago that we must "de-center marriage and the nuclear family ideologically" in order to "account for other forms of relatedness," and she too returns to Afro-Caribbean *matrifocality* to achieve her "decentering" (2005).

My own perspective is less about "decentering" marriage and instead turning toward marriage but in a largely uncharted direction—to the group long thought to embody its very essence and act as its most ardent gatekeeper: the white, middle-class Barbadian woman. For though white women may serve as powerful guardians of marriage, their own relationships have never been held up as paragons of Hollywood- and Mills and Boon–style romance. What is fascinating about this group and this moment is that they have been an *abstract* figure—a ghostlike face of "respectability" that all Barbadians carry in their minds, but as social beings are seldom figured as agents in flesh and blood. The puzzle that interests me here is this: what do divorce and single womanhood mean for *the only group for whom formal marriage has been assumed*, the group projected as its static figurehead. Notably, in "opting out" of marriage (whether by their own or their spouse's choice), white middle-class Barbadian women are, consciously or not, *opting into* one of the island's signature cultural markers of the Black majority—matrifocality. In so doing, they are contravening the primary institution on which their gender/race/class position has hinged and they are entering into an alternative social form as it too is undergoing transformation. What, then, can matrifocality offer white middle-class women, and in turn, how are they contributing new meanings to this long-standing institution? I began to examine these questions when comments like the following started popping up in my conversations with white women: "There must be something in the water here in Barbados . . . everyone I know is having affairs or breaking up."

As wives and mothers, the women in this ethnic minority have been paradoxically invisible and emblematic. In the kinship literature, they and their formal marriages are portrayed one-dimensionally, little more than silhouettes with assumed (generally negative) qualities. Early plantation accounts cast them as "tetchy"—irritable, obsessed with social decorum and domestic order, harsh and unfeeling. They serve as both icon and arbiter of formal marriage. Notably, for Black women in the majority it is *labor*—in the cane field, in the market, or in the paid domestic arena—that has defined their strength and anchored their autonomy. By contrast, white women's labor has been hidden in the back offices of husbands' and fathers' businesses, and as stoic wives and mothers as managers of paid domestic workers. Defined by kinship—as daughters or wives—their labor is naturalized as duty, unremunerated and unrecognized. In essence, marital respectability has often excluded white women *from the recognized market economy*, whereas matrifocality has defined Black women as resourceful workers in the market and in the home (both their own and others').

The Upward Mobility and New Intimacy of Matrifocality

My discussion centers primarily around three white middle-class Barbadian women whose lives, work, marriages, and divorces I have followed over almost thirty years. When I met them in their teens and twenties, these women would have symbolized to most Barbadians some of the quintessential expressions of white femininity: Sarah was the daughter of a physician and a dutiful, stay-at-home wife-mother, whom she described as "thoroughly under the control" of her charming but conservative father. She noted that it was only after her father's death that her mother, although manager of the domestic space, was "allowed" to write a check. Sarah had recently married an English manager of a fancy hotel when we met in 1989. Lillianna was the daughter of a successful planter. Having left school at fourteen, her father worked his way up to manager and sugar estate owner; her mother was a warm, energetic mother of four, talented at flower arranging and Sunday school teaching. Lillianna had recently earned a master's degree, returning to the island from abroad to take up a teaching job at a local secondary school. Justine was a rebellious eighteen-year-old, kicked out of boarding school abroad for smoking despite her top grades and "head girl" status, partying with "beach bums" at the time we met. The youngest of five children and a member of a prominent white Barbadian business family who trace their lineage to the white indentured laborers or "redlegs" of the seventeenth century, even today she recounts her parents' divorce as a painful flashpoint in her early childhood. Now a self-educated polymath and successful businesswoman, she has divorced twice and is, by her account, "on her third and final marriage." "I was not like the other white Bajan women. I was always a bit different. When my [first] marriage . . . ended I was lucky to have my own business and thus my own independence." Restless at home with her first child and gifted with a green thumb, she began a gardening business, starting seedlings on her back patio. Within a few years Justine had become one of the largest exporters of tropical plants in the region. When a serious illness led her to the United States for treatment, she relocated with her daughter and bought a small farm in Alabama. A terrible burn accident inspired her to research and launch a line of botanical skin care products, drawing upon medicinal plants from Barbados and marketing techniques and packaging from the top U.S. manufacturers. Justine has since passed this business on to her daughter, herself a new mother with a similarly independent character, living with a partner but without intentions to marry. She reflects openly about changing gender dynamics as well as about her own life and generational change in Barbados. "I've been married *three* times and I will never marry again. I think most marriages between men and women are destined to fail. We are too different; women no longer need men. My mother certainly put up with a lot. Women do . . . over and over again. I really think we will start to see a shift . . . women will start cohabitating with other women. It would make so much more sense."

Although all three of these women were raised in upper-middle-class households, studied abroad, and got married, they also challenged the conventions of white respectability from an early stage. Sarah's marriage ruptured after only two years with a "marriage swap" (and a whirlwind of island gossip) in which she "took up" with the husband of a friend, a mixed-race businessman with whom she soon had two daughters and assumed an active role as a "silent" (unpaid) business partner. Years later this marriage ended in one of the island's ugliest and most prolonged divorces, prompted by her husband's infidelity. Divorce left Sarah economically adrift and struggling to support herself and her children. Meanwhile, her friend Lilliana also entered into married life in a manner that challenged the conventions of white Bajan society. Like Justine, she was already several months pregnant when she married a mixed-race Jamaican whom she had met as a graduate student in Canada. After twenty tumultuous years of economic insecurity, periods of separation and long-distance work, and mounting tensions surrounding her husband's drinking, the final straw in their marriage came with the revelation of his infidelity (a woman half his age) and news of his "outside child." By her own account, the fact of the affair was far from new within Barbadian life, as she said, "*even* within our white Barbadian milieu." As most histories and novels of the region make plain, the infidelities and "outside families" forged by white men are a staple of plantation life. Indeed, Lillianna and Justine are each independently researching the history of their grandfathers' "outside child" whose existence has only recently come to light. What is new in this story is that more white wives are choosing to *opt out* of such marriages, in contrast to the women of their mothers' generation who were expected to "grin and bear." As Lillianna observed,

> You know, I am seeing more women, professional women, that are choosing to be single, because they are finding that it's so difficult to have faithful partners or people that are their intellectual equal. . . . As women become more empowered and work, they don't have to put up with [the outside women and children]. . . . More and more women across the Caribbean are single, either they are choosing it or they just find they cannot find a mate. And if they are divorced, they are not remarrying . . . because they don't want to put up with the shit. . . . There were affairs in my parents' generation too, it was rampant . . . but among the men . . . those happened under the carpet . . . with women *not* in the same social milieu. They didn't lead to divorce.

As Lisa Douglass (1992) notes in her study of the white Jamaican elite, marriage has been so central to women's identity and security that they put up with all of these indignities rather than opt out of this signature institution.

Lillianna sheds further light on the stigma of divorce throughout her upbringing: "My parents always conveyed 'you wouldn't want to go with someone from a broken family.' That's a sentiment people feel less now, but the idea was . . .

it suggested an insecurity. And if you're going to connect with somebody, the *whole thing about marriage is security.*" By contrast, in the Black lower-class tradition, as Sarah recounts, a woman's *independence* is prized and fostered. She tells Lillianna and me that recently she has gotten to know an old woman: "Gran is her name. She's in her eighties. . . . She cut cane most of her life. Gran always told her children: 'Always have your own house; he can visit, but he cannot stay.' If you go into his house, he can always kick you out. But if you have your own house, he cannot."

Lillianna concurs. The charming house she lives in sits on former plantation land that has been in her family's possession for more than four generations. She pays rent to her brother, and her home doubles as the site of her consulting business; she also benefits from the close physical proximity of her brother, sister-in-law, and parents, all of whom live on the same property.

> The extended family certainly makes my life bearable. . . . Jesus, if I was divorced and living like you [motioning to me] in Atlanta, and my family was dispersed, it would have been extremely difficult. Impossible! I get an enormous amount of support from my huge extended family. That has made a huge difference. I would also say I have enjoyed time alone, but I also hit a road bump, and [referring to a recent accident] that fall . . . that really hit me for a loop; it really drove home the point that it's hard when you live on your own and you're ill and there's nobody to bring you a glass of water if you can't walk up the stairs. I found that really difficult and I think, shit, I will more than likely be on my own for the rest of my life . . . because it's very hard to meet people here, and . . . not that I want to get married again, but it would be nice to have intimacy with someone, to be able to have conversations with someone. . . . But [and here, her voice becomes strong and resolute] it's also good to have quality friendships and quality relationships and I think we have been sold the idea that the most important love is romantic love, but there are other loves that can be also fulfilling, friendships and family, and love of your work, and love of ideas and love of a dog and love of nature . . . those are things that can also be very fulfilling. Doing exercise, or walking, or yoga, where you have a sense of who you are, I think these are important things; but all of the films and novels, and so on, [social media] platforms. . . . Romantic love is the most important love and if you don't have it you feel that you are not fully human.

The timbre in her voice vacillates from stoic and confident to emotionally vulnerable and a little sad. "I don't have it, which means I don't have it quite right, I'm not as complete, I haven't been able to do it properly, you know, I've failed . . . , why can't I get that one thing to work out?"

The stigma surrounding divorce among her family's social class has not disappeared entirely, and this stigma is particularly acute for women. As Lisa Douglass noted, "The social lives of women are hurt most by divorce." Indeed, so stigmatizing is divorce for Jamaican elite women, many "move abroad . . . to escape the social embarrassment and discomfort. . . . There is really no place in the small world of Jamaican upper-class society for the divorced woman. She becomes a social misfit who makes married women feel uncomfortable. . . . They may be pitied as spinsters or disparaged because they are presumed to be lesbian" (1992, 197). On this topic, Sarah chimed in to describe what she dreads most in her divorced status: "It's all the events and celebrations that are supposed to be happy family gatherings—the graduations and the weddings [she anticipates for her daughters]—those will be pure torture."

For Lillianna, her gendered social shame centered around a more mundane space:

> I found *the supermarket* the most difficult place to go when I was divorced or recently separated, because the supermarket is a space for families . . . it's about eating meals together, a lot of the *packaging* is about families; I found the supermarket very difficult. I hated going to the f-ing supermarket. . . . I think emotionally I found it difficult because the way that you are supposed to function in the society is as a married unit in the class that I come from . . . and so there was an enormous amount of shame and a sense of failure that you couldn't even keep your f-ing marriage together. So, emotionally, I found that very, very difficult. And then, of course, if there is *another person* involved, [the "outside woman"] that . . . was a very humiliating thing; there was a lot of shame around that . . . and . . . [she] was a much younger person and there was a whole other layer of shame on that. . . . I think the shame of that, of course brings in issues of desirability . . . you're no longer desirable, no one will ever be interested . . . so that's a whole other thing to process. . . . It was humiliating. It felt like if you were divorced, that people *knew something*. That's a very private thing to go through [the infidelity]. But the fact that you were divorced was information that is now public. . . . I don't know what people would say because they would never say it to your face, but there would be *something* . . . and that's humiliating.

I found Lilliana's emphasis on the qualitative distinction between the *private* humiliation of her husband's infidelity, and the *public* shame wrought by her divorce, of particular significance.[4] Women across class and racial boundaries have faced infidelities and "outside children" throughout Barbadian history. What they will tolerate today and how they respond in meeting their own social, sexual, and emotional needs is, as one of my earlier interlocutors put it, "a work in progress." These brief snapshots of white Barbadian women "opting out" offer an important vantage from which to explore marriage and divorce in a society that has never held marriage to be the practical norm except in relation to *their minority group*. Where they had once occupied the idealized place of public exception, they now join the majority of Bajan women in their household headship and matrifocal status. Like many Black Barbadian women who end relationships—whether formal marriages, common-law marriages, or more flexible unions—and/or remain single,

Lilliana and Sarah find their current states of entrepreneurial autonomy (both in an economic sense and in terms of their own self-actualization) desirable but also challenging. The economic vulnerability they face with divorce, along with the loneliness and social marginality they sometimes feel, sharpens their reliance upon and appreciation for their extended networks of kin and female friends. They highlight the inextricable sense of threat and possibility, shame and pride that others all over the world are noting when analyzing divorced and single women. Both Lilliana and Sarah discuss their desires for an intimate sexual relationship with a new partner, but agree that their prospects on this small island are very few. Sarah even laughingly recounted "doing the math" with her daughter and agreeing that if they were to limit their scope to white Bajan men their options were both unappealing and "ridiculously few," and among Black Barbadians or visitors to the island, much more attractive but unlikely given their advancing middle age. A shared realization that their futures may well remain uncoupled seems to deepen their mutual care and support for one other and for their other close friends and family. Indeed, observing their closeness anchored in a friendship going back to their schoolgirl days shed unexpected light on an unexplored relationship—the friendship among women. In a region whose anthropological staple has been the study of kinship, and where a rich tradition of linguistic, socio-logical, and cultural analyses of male "crews" sheds light on class, politics, and creole social life, relationships *among women* tend to be painted in one (or both) of two simple ways: as duty-bound kin ties that demand reciprocal support for basic survival or as rivalries riddled with jealousy and strife.

No idiom has more powerfully captured this dynamic among Caribbean women than the region's well-known expression "crab antics." Like so many clever West Indian glosses for social mores and the subtleties of human behavior, this one conjures the twinned dynamics of eager determination, like crabs in a barrel, to climb to freedom and a better life, and ruthless (even if unselfconscious) competition, yanking down others just above. Women are believed to be especially prone to this dynamic. They are seen as cunning and conniving, determined to steal another's man and usurp her rival's position. The extended kin network notwithstanding, intimate, emotionally close, and trusted friendship among women has not figured prominently in Caribbean social analysis. By contrast, the manner in which both Sarah and Lillianna relate to each other and describe their other close female friendships suggests a significant transformation. Opting out of marriage has focused their quest for support of all forms, from the practical and material to the affective and intimate.

"Cutting and contriving," they piece together a livelihood for themselves and their children, exhibiting the economic grit and fierce independence that have defined matrifocal Caribbean womanhood for centuries. With the support of an extended kin network and a growing array of new venues and services, they also find ways to forge new modes of sociality and intimacy. In "opting out" of marriage, they are *opting for* a new matrifocality. Where previous generations of white women benefited from but were ultimately confined by a racialized class privilege conferred and secured through marriage, today, in adopting matrifocality and joining the majority of Afro-Caribbean (working) women, entrepreneurial middle-class white women too may claim autonomy and are intent to imbue this new independence with the added valence of emotional intimacy forged among their women friends. As new kinship studies increasingly recognize relationships beyond blood and marriage, this matrifocal intimacy suggests a rich new frontier. Caribbean feminists have offered a more nuanced interpretation of matrifocality that transcends earlier structural-functional portraits of "mothers who also father children" (Clarke 1957) and accounts of the "missing men" of the household (Miller 1991), by highlighting women's personal and economic autonomy and, concomitantly, their relative lack of emotional, social, and economic dependence on male partners.

Notably, in Lilliana's and Sarah's testimonies, their reliance upon their extensive kin networks and circle of female friends points to the deepening of emotional bonds and a conscious desire for intimate friendship and connection. In these relationships with other women, they not only derive support in the form of meals and in-kind exchanges of provisions and services so well documented in portrayals of matrifocal households (Gonzalez 1970; Greenfield 1973; Massiah 1983; Smith 1996), but also take pleasure in sharing a wide range of leisure activities—going out to lunch or to the beach, ordering takeout dinners, watching movies, attending lectures or art openings together—celebrating special occasions, and offering a therapeutic ear on a dark day. As Sarah remarks, *the family* was the center of social life in her parents' day: "Certainly my mother and her generation didn't have female friends to have tea or lunch with; she and Daddy went to cocktails or they stayed home. . . . But in my generation I go out with my [women] friends."[5] In Lilliana's life, a large and close-knit family has anchored her adventurous and unconventional life. Whereas she and all her siblings followed the convention of marrying within a familiar circle (fellow white Bajans, other white West Indians, or British), her interracial marriage and later her husband's infidelity, outside child, and divorce, along with her lifestyle of travel, overseas education and work, and what they deem her "radical" feminist and racial politics all set her somewhat apart. Nonetheless, the closeness and support they show Lilliana and her children suggest no hint of rejection. Much like lower-class women in tight-knit village life who benefit from the care and close proximity of kin, she appreciates the emotional and physical safety net of her parents and siblings. In hurricane season and the pandemic lockdowns, she can be assured that family members will be checking on her security; after a hard work week, a Saturday morning's walk with her sister-in-law through their fields and meadows offers both emotional salve and physical exercise; when her mother's ill health calls for frequent clinic visits, her siblings take turns driving and providing soothing company and meals. Birthdays, anniversaries, and holidays are always large, multigenerational family affairs—the most recent being the birth of the first great-grandchild. Today, in addition to this rich and ritualized kin-based social life, both Sarah and Lilliana enjoy other friendships and modes of sociality that take them outside the white Barbadian cocoon. Their household headship makes these forays and relationships easier to forge.

Many years ago when we were discussing the hectic rhythm of working motherhood, Lilliana told me she would "sooner give up her husband than her maid." At the time, I took this remark in jest. In the intervening decade, however, its seriousness became clearer. Even in her current straitened circumstances, Lilliana employs part-time domestic help. With her ex-husband gone she is spared the rancor and frustrations of married life. Having "launched" her children, she is free to manage her own time and household rhythms, devoting time and energy not only to her professional work but to grassroots political issues—the environment, social justice, LGBTQ and feminist activism, and a new movement for racial justice.

Moreover, her intimate circle of women—sisters, sisters-in-law, and friends—provides another vital nexus of intellectual, political, social, and emotional exchange that she and many of the other women I interviewed over the years sought unsuccessfully in marriage. Like the female household heads many others have portrayed in the literature, they make no bones about the fact that a loyal and loving life partner with whom they could share the trials and celebrations in life would be a welcome addition to their lives. They have (mostly jokingly) discussed using Tinder to see who turned up. However, there is a notable resignation in their voices as they fantasize about finding the kind of companionate intimacy they most desire. They express the widely held belief that, given the limitations of "your typical Bajan man," this would be possible only with "a foreigner," and even then, Lilliana stated plainly, "I have no patience for a relationship with a man now . . . they are so unevolved. I don't know where the men are that are our equal. Men have just not caught up with the progress women have made. It would be nice to have sex again, but I don't have to put my energy there." As Justine related to me recently, "It's not that I don't like men, I do. I just don't like having them around me all the time. Sometimes I feel like taking [my best friend] up on her offer of going home to be her wife!"

My discussions with these women were full of animated social critiques as well as painful personal disclosures. The manner in which they share their intimate lives, worries, hopes, and dreams with close kin and female friends—punctuated with thoughtful pauses and peppered with good natured humor—illustrates a new degree of emotional openness and expressivity and offers a new dimension to the matrifocal figure as a tough, stoic, autonomous woman. On one hand, these white women opting out of marriage resemble their hardworking Black Bajan counterparts—their workdays begin at daybreak and end long after sunset, and they are the sole providers for their households. Moreover, they remain responsible for all the traditional domestic duties (in Lilliana's case, paying for some part-time help) and in a fashion that has intensified in both quantity and quality. Motherhood is a central part of their identities, as is codified by West Indian norms of

FIGURE 7.1 Marching for women's rights in Barbados.
Photo by Anonymous.

femininity for all women, but their relationships with their children also show emotional transformation. For both Sarah and Lilliana, it is clear that their grown children not only confer upon them a critical dimension of their womanhood but are equally important to the fabric of their emotional lives. Like all other Caribbean women, they take pride in their children's educational accomplishments and travel, enabled by their own sacrifices and ingenuity.[6] When they share their worries about their children's jobs, relationships, health, and futures, and as they recount their recent conversations, their musings reflect a closeness and emotional intimacy that, at their own admission, is on a whole new level.

These white Barbadian women eschew the pressures of social convention that required previous generations to "put up with the lash, the outside woman, the drinking, verbal abuse and emotional remoteness" as one of my informants described the common elements of the patriarchal marriage form. Their struggles as well as the structural contours of their support systems closely resemble generations of poor Black households in their simultaneously patriarchal and matrifocal society (Gonzalez 1970; Massiah 1983; Smith 1996). That white Bajan women are living much like Black Bajan women should not surprise us in a small, densely populated island where people have always lived "cheek by jowl." I state this observation plainly because public perception still upholds an air of mystique around the white women in this society and that imagines them apart from mainstream culture by virtue of their class and racial privilege.[7] Their capacity to benefit from a long tradition of matrifocality and the extended kin network and to foster the kinds of rich emotional relationships within that age-old structure gives new dimensions of matrifocal life.

For these women, matrifocality, more than marriage, offers the tools for an enriched emotional, social, and political life. They can now challenge many of the gender-segregated social spheres that have long marginalized women from mainstream public discourse; they may occupy new public spaces, experiment with new modes of leisure, and claim a public voice in matters of local and global politics, including politics surrounding abortion and LGBTQ civil unions / marriage, all the while giving expression to emotional desires and connection that were previously foreclosed.

When they speak out against white privilege and march with the local Black Lives Matter movement, for women's rights, and in the gay pride parade, they challenge the normativity of white respectability, and its pinnacle institution of patriarchal marriage with an extraordinary visual power. In so doing, they highlight the convergent political and affective forces of this particular historical moment in which both marriage and matrifocality are being reexamined and transformed. Through their close friendships with other women, more expressive and emotional motherhood/kin relationships, innovative entrepreneurial projects, and new modes of embodied "self-care" and self-discovery, matrifocality may offer a more flexible medium by which to piece together a livelihood as it has long done for the majority of poor Black Barbadians, but for all Barbadian women it may offer a medium for forging both domestic organization and social reproduction, expressive intimacy and bold public engagement, creative self-discovery and sociopolitical transformation.

NOTES

1. There has been a great deal of debate over distinctions between "matrifocal" vs. "woman-headed / female-headed" households (i.e., the degree to which mothers and/or women occupy the central kin relation and/or retain economic and political *power* within kin groups) and the degree to which men are "missing" or "marginal" to such households, a debate I do not return to here (Smith 1988; Blackwood 2004; Barrow 1998). One aspect of this discussion that is seldom examined in the Barbadian context relates to same-sex relations among women who head their own households. Gloria Wekker's discussion of "mati work" vs. marriage among the working-class Afro-Surinamese diaspora provides a useful wedge for examining matrifocality, the extended kin network among women, and lesbian relationships (2006).

2. Biological motherhood, preferably, but fostering other children, usually nieces, nephews, and grandchildren, is also common and highly valued.

3. Thirty years ago, Connie Sutton urged me to study white Barbadians, observing this group to be more complex than the available literature revealed and seeing few inroads for an ethnographer to gain access to these communities. I am grateful for this urging and am indebted to the generous friends and family who have allowed me the privileged (if sometimes confusing) relationship convergences of close friend/family/fieldworker over more than thirty years.

4. In her study of Jamaica, Foster (2013) notes that most women deal with infidelity privately rather than through gestures of public shaming or even sharing this knowledge with others for fear of gossip and damage to their own pride as well as their partner's reputation.

5. Bianca Williams's (2018) discussion of African American women's pleasure and happiness derived through "Girlfriend Tours" to Jamaica offers a rich window into the listening, recognition, and affirmation these women offer one another to redress their invisibility and reckoning with racism, sexism, and ageism in the United States.

6. Stories of maternal (biological or otherwise) sacrifice on behalf of children's education and opportunities for a better life are the bread and butter of Caribbean fiction (Zobel 1980); so too are accounts of the particular severity and admonishing style of West Indian mothering (Kincaid 1985; Bellot 2019).

7. The perception that white Barbadians, and women in particular, live radically different lives was brought home to me once in the context of a trip to the supermarket with two Bajan women friends of mine who had not previously met. Both were educated abroad and were now back working on the island. Shopping for ingredients to make dinner together, my Black Barbadian friend was shocked to discover that my white Barbadian friend chose fresh pumpkin and other local vegetables and didn't purchase only imported foods. We all had a good laugh about her assumption, but it illustrated the "mystique" I allude to about white Bajan women's shadowy place in the popular imaginary.

8

Messing with Remarriage

The Problem of Widows in Guinea-Bissau

JOANNA DAVIDSON

In the Jola villages of Guinea-Bissau, the residents of more than a third of the houses are what you and I would call widows. These houses are called *kungomaku* (sing. *hungomahu*), but there is no word in the Jola language for widow. This chapter explores the problem of widows in a place where they are many, but they are neither named nor recognized as a social category. I consider how the dynamics of widowhood present problems for Jola society, where a dramatic decline in the rice-based economy is severing the knot between production and reproduction. These shifts open up unexpected—and perhaps unspeakable—possibilities for new social formations outside the normative bounds of gender and marriage. The absence of a Jola term for widow speaks volumes about the fragility of social relations. By opting out of remarriage, the very existence of Jola widows suggests that current configurations of marriage and masculinity are outmoded.[1]

Perhaps there is no word for widow because kungomaku and the women who reside in them have proliferated only recently.[2] Before the increase in kungomaku, reproductive-age widows were typically remarried to one of their deceased husband's agnates, a practice that Jola call *butunorabu*. But such an explanation fails to account for a range of dynamics involving women who live in kungomaku, who do not see themselves as part of a category into which most women eventually enter, as well as their Jola neighbors and kin, who seem not to see these women at all.

I have been intrigued, perplexed, and troubled by widows since I began ethnographic research among Jola villagers in Guinea-Bissau in 2001. My initial fieldwork focused on Jola responses to the substantial changes under way in the region that made it increasingly difficult for villagers to lead a life embedded in the rice-based agrarian economy they had developed—and still clung to dearly— over many centuries (Davidson 2016). As my research documented and analyzed these transformations, widows kept cropping up in other things I was writing about—like secrecy, work, and development—but they often appeared as a poignant illustration, an extreme case, or an abstruse exception to whatever else I was talking about. I found myself stymied again and again when I tried to make sense of widowhood itself, or to be more precise, the increase in widowhood along with its seeming invisibility and unspeakability. My attempts over the years to "solve the problem of widows" were thwarted by contradictory statements among Jola themselves, or they came up short when I subjected them to my own critical scrutiny. I eventually found it helpful to engage in a kind of negative dialectics (Adorno 1966/2007), both emphasizing the limits of knowledge itself and opening up the possibility that the outcome of the dialectical process—still valuable as an explanatory mode—may not be inexorably positive. In this case, the dialectical approach has highlighted the sense of elusiveness and social opacity that characterizes Jola (and perhaps all) lifeworlds.

Lost in Translation

When I first moved to Esana,[3] a village of about two thousand mostly Jola residents, I kept getting lost. As I wandered around the village, I began to notice small houses that looked a bit different from those I had already become accustomed to as "typical" Jola houses. Typical Jola houses were rectangular, with small window openings, a front and back door, and a heavily thatched roof. The atypical houses had all these elements, but they were smaller, shabbier, not quite the same. I was told that these houses were kungomaku.

Shortly after these initial wanderings, I began to conduct a village-wide household survey. I learned from the various companions who walked around with me as I jotted down the names of each house's occupants that the inhabitants of these kungomaku were *solteiras*. *Solteira* is a Portuguese and Guinean Kriyol word used to designate unmarried female status: a single woman. I was curious about why there were so many single women living in their own houses, especially when I started to meet some of them and realized that they ranged in age and that many of them had young children. A few conversations cleared this up when it became evident that these were, of course, widows' houses and their occupants were the widows, and often children, of a deceased man from that compound's lineage.

That the Jola language has no word for "widow" is not so uncommon across Africa, and perhaps elsewhere. What a widow is called tends to reflect local understandings of life and death (see Kirwen 1979; Potash 1986b). Among Jola, women whose husbands have died, and men whose wives have died, were referred to in the same way as other women and men their age, relative to who was addressing them. Sometimes widows and widowers were described as *apañorol akem*, meaning "his or her spouse died," but this was not used as a title or designation so much as a description.

The lack of a word for "widow" does not reflect a general paucity of marriage-related vocabulary in the Jola language; indeed, a plethora of Jola words refer to a range of marital, nonmarital, and postmarital states. Elsewhere in Guinea-Bissau, Kriyol speakers used the word *viuva*—a more precise match for the English word

FIGURE 8.1 A *hungomahu* in Guinea-Bissau, March 2016.
Photo by Joanna Davidson.

"widow." But when Kriyol speakers in Jola-land referred to the inhabitants of kungomaku, they called them solteiras, not viuvas. Perhaps because viuva has no corresponding word in Jola, they opted for solteira as a recognizable "unmarried female" term. Or perhaps—I thought, as I began to get a sense of the circumstances of widows' lives—they were signaling some aspects of a widow's experience, since solteira derives from root words that mean "single" and "alone."

So that is what I had so far: no Jola word for "widow," but a word for their houses. The Jola word for a typical house is *elupay* (pl. *silupasu*), which also means family. Building an elupay represents a young man's most concrete move toward adult status, whether or not he has been ritually initiated. That the words for "family" and "house" are the same reveals the extent to which the two are inextricably tied as relatively autonomous units for producing, consuming, and decision making. Designating a widow's house as hungomahu emphasizes its difference and distance from the family-based elupay. When a man dies, his elupay is torn down about a year after his death and his widow's hungomahu is built in her virilocal neighborhood, often adjacent to where the destroyed elupay once stood. In some cases, if she has no kin to help her, she builds her own hungomahu—a task that, even for men, is a collective activity.

Not only is a dead man's house torn down, but his land is incorporated back into his lineage and redistributed among his agnatic kin. In Jola land-tenure practices, a woman has access to land only through her husband, and once he dies, she is no longer entitled to work in his forest grove or rice paddies. Once the husband's rice paddies have been reabsorbed into his lineage, his widow must borrow unused paddies from her own kin, a fragile and tenuous arrangement at best. If she has sons, they will inherit their share of their patrilineal land when they come of age. If she does not have grown sons or benevolent uncles who will hoe the paddy for her, she will wield the heavy fulcrum shovel herself and perform what is considered quintessentially male labor. If she cannot borrow paddy, she begs for rice. Sometimes a widow's grown children provide her with a small quantity of rice; sometimes neighbors send over some rice. One widow with several young children told me that she regularly did not eat all day. As with other women in kungomaku I came to know, her main efforts were to *kuji-kuji*—that is, to produce or acquire any small quantity of goods (palm oil, chili peppers, eggs) that she could trade or sell for rice to feed the smallest children in her household.

After I completed the household survey, I was surprised to find that of the Jola households in each traditional neighborhood, an average of 34 percent were kungomaku.[4] Again, like the lack of a specific word for "widow," this proportion of widows, I found out later, was quite common across rural Africa (Cattell 2003; Mutongi 2007; Potash 1986a). At the time, however, I did not know that this was common, so my initial questions focused on why such a seemingly significant proportion of Jola houses were kungomaku. Were women simply outliving men? Was this a new phenomenon, or was the proportion of kungomaku as compared to silupasu the same as it had been for many years? And how were Jola reconciling what seemed like the extreme poverty of women who lived in kungomaku with their generalized claims about economic parity across all households? In posing these questions, I immediately cast widows as a problem.

And, at first, my most trusted interlocutors in Esana seemed to agree. For example, when I commented on the surprising number of kungomaku to my friend Tegilosso, he explained it as a consequence of recently eroded butunorabu practices of remarriage. "Now there are more kungomaku than before," he said. "Before, if a man died, a woman would be obliged to marry again. . . . But now, women refuse to remarry, so there are more kungomaku than before." When I discussed the matter with other residents in Esana, some agreed that now, "women refuse to remarry." Others pointed to the current economic impossibility of a man taking on a second wife and her children: "When you cannot put rice in your own children's mouths, how can you bring others into your elupay?" But whatever my interlocutors identified as the primary reason for eroding butunorabu practices—be it women's or men's refusal, changing attitudes and norms around gender and marriage, or Jolas' increasing poverty and decreasing ability to sustain their families—everyone seemed surprised that there were so many kungomaku. They clearly did not know about either the quantity or the intensity of widows' predicament.

This reaction motivated and textured my ongoing preoccupation with women who lived in kungomaku during the earlier phases of my fieldwork. Observing that my household survey data were a surprise to Esana's residents, I cast my role in Freirian terms; surely, once others realized the magnitude and intensity of the problem, they would come up with culturally appropriate ways to resolve it. After all, as Tegilosso had pointed out, this was not an endemic problem per se. Such was my first take on "the problem of widows." I continued to gather information, conduct many frustrating and seemingly fruitless interviews with women who lived in kungomaku, and jot down anything I heard from anyone else talking about a particular woman whose husband had died or about kungomaku residents in general (although such talk, because no one recognized them as an actual category, was exceedingly rare and usually a consequence of my prompting). All this led to my first explanation of the problem of widows, which went something like this: Widows were an extremely vulnerable and numerically significant segment of the population, yet one that Jola still did not recognize as such. Their numbers were growing because of increasing general poverty and eroding butunorabu practices. The increase in kungomaku appeared to result from uneven change. Butunorabu practices had eroded without concurrent shifts in linked customs, such as breaking down a man's elupay, reclaiming his agricultural landholdings, and redistributing them only to married sons with their own households. If the increase in kungomaku was seen and understood as an unwitting negative consequence of economic and cultural plate tectonics, people would develop new social safety nets in line with general Jola mores that emphasize a rough economic equality.

But calling attention to these women and their severe circumstances did not yield the reactions and responses I expected. And the longer I stayed, and especially over subsequent years and periodic visits, what I was hearing and gathering just did not add up.

For example, when I increasingly brought up the topic of women who lived in kungomaku to my friends and neighbors in casual conversations, they often responded with a comment or anecdote about a particular woman whose husband had died, but they almost never talked about widow*hood*. My interlocutors had no problem recognizing the extreme poverty of the women I mentioned, but they did not recognize that they themselves (or their mothers, sisters, or wives) were or could be in the same situation. The number of kungomaku, even when exposed, did not change this atomized view of the women whom my interlocutors continued to either call solteiras or refer to by their personal names.

Women who lived in kungomaku even viewed themselves in this light. After getting to know several of them and becoming increasingly aware of and concerned about their austere conditions, I asked one woman with several young children in her hungomahu whether she spoke to other women in kungomaku about their shared situation. Her response was unequivocal: "We do not talk about such things. . . . For us, it is a secret." "Poverty is a secret?" I asked. "Yes," she responded. "For you to tell someone, 'Today I don't have this or that,' he'll listen to you, but won't give you anything. That's why, in this sense, I stay alone with this poverty. That's why I don't tell anyone." In many subsequent discussions with women who lived in kungomaku, they stressed to me that they did not talk with others, even other kungomaku dwellers, about their hardships and struggles to survive.

In one neighborhood there was an entire cluster of kungomaku: five small houses whose residents were within earshot of each other. But what I initially saw as a widow's neighborhood ripe for collective action, or at least mutual assistance, Jola literally did not see. I counted them and showed the results to widows themselves and their married neighbors, and they were impressed: "Huh! We never noticed."

It is important to note that widows' poverty was, in fact, an extreme form of a general problem. Most families in Esana were involved in the same kind of day-to-day struggle to survive as were women who lived in kungomaku. Even households with healthy adults, access to abundant land, and combined male and female labor power rarely produced enough rice to feed their members throughout the year. A middle-aged man in Esana once told me, "Solteiras [referring to women who lived in kungomaku] have an even better life than us, because they have a special way of economizing. Rice that won't last more than a day in my house will last a solteira several days, because they have a special manner of stretching such things out." I initially dismissed this statement as perverse, but later came to see how much it reflected Jola reasoning (Davidson 2020).

For now, though, it seemed that the women you and I would call widows refused to be categorized or even named as such and that other Esana residents increasingly emphasized (or at least hinted at) other dimensions—like work ethic and a "special way of economizing"—over and above eroding butunorabu practices. My efforts to understand—let alone solve—the problem of widows had reached their limit, and I was stumped.

Widows Elsewhere

In "Belief and the Problem of Women," Edwin Ardener (1989a, 73, 75) laments that the anthropological study of women is tantamount to "mere bird-watching," and that women appear in fieldnotes "in the same way as . . . Nuer's cows, who were observed but did not speak." The problem, he said, is with anthropologists—even female anthropologists—who cannot overcome their own attachment to a vision of society bounded from nature. Women, Ardener (1989a, 74) argues, provide models of society that "are not of the kind acceptable at first sight to men or to ethnographers. . . . To put it more simply: they will not necessarily provide a model of society as a unit that will contain both men and themselves." Male models of society, on the other hand, fit better with what ethnographers are trained to look for, or even—as he asserts in a follow-up essay—what women ethnographers understand based on their own mutedness within their native "world-structures" (Ardener 1989b, 128–130).

Ardener's short but powerful essay kept coming to mind as I puzzled over the problem of widows. Putting aside the more obviously outdated and essentialist aspects of the essay, the overall implication of Ardener's perspective is still quite radical and not fully realized. Ardener (1989a, 72) insists in the first line of his essay that "the problem of women has not been solved by social anthropologists. . . . Indeed the problem itself has been often examined only to be put aside again for want of a solution, for its intractability is genuine." In my various efforts to solve the "problem of widows," they have appeared on my pages in precisely the way Ardener decried. And after developing but remaining dissatisfied with various explanations, I put widows aside, just as Ardener predicted.

But they continued to haunt me, so I belatedly turned my attention to other scholarship on widows for help. With the exception of India, where scholarly and policy preoccupations with widows have been extensive, the general literature on widowhood is rather scant, and more often than not a specialized concern within gerontology (e.g., Jenkins 2003; Williams, Sawyer, and Allman 2012). There is, however, a rich literature on the extremes of widowhood, sati being the most highlighted and contested case, but also child widows, AIDS widows, controversial celebrity widows, war widows, and refugees (e.g., Cattell 2003; Cohen 1992; Das 2006; Green 1999; Haram 2001; Hawley 1994; Mani 1998; Mojola 2014; Nandi 1990; Rhine 2016; Stamp 1991; Yang 1989; Zia 2016).

Since the 1970s, scholarly literature on widows themselves has fallen roughly into two camps. The first documents how widowhood produces harsh social and economic penalties, generally portraying widows as dejected victims subject to "customary injustice" (Ewelukwa 2002; see also Iwobi 2008; Owen 1996; Sossou 2002). They are wretched and abject, often cast as witches. As vulnerable charity cases, they are sometimes dangerous and often pathetic. In this literature, there is an oft-repeated refrain that widows "suffer from a variety of controls and restrictions" (Tovar 1998, 232; see also Van de Walle 2013).

Partially as a corrective to this "widow as victim" trope, feminist scholarship in the 1980s took a more widow-centered approach that emphasized the increased autonomy of widows and showcased widows as agents with choices, often being "freer" than wives. Even in societies that heavily restrict wives, widows were shown to have relatively more autonomy. The various case studies in Potash's (1986a) volume, for example, pushed back on the dominant negative casting of widows.

Characterizing widows as either abject victims or autonomous agents, however, caricatures their status by flattening what are often complicated, multidimensional facets of widowhood. Moreover, it fails to distinguish the range of widows' experiences even within a given society depending on such factors as class, caste, age, and whether they have children. Sarah Lamb (1999, 2000, 2001) has done the most to differentiate accounts of widowhood in India across the life course, countering both the monolithic representation of widows and the tendency to portray them as "either oppressed victims of 'patriarchy' or compliant followers of Hindu 'tradition'" (Lamb 2001, 22). Lamb has instead avoided "classifying widows as a unitary group, scrutinizing the profoundly different consequences of widowhood" for young women, childless women, mothers, and senior women

(Lamb 1999, 558–559; for similar insights in Africa, see Nyanzi, Emodu-Walakira, and Serwaniko 2009; Obbo 1986).

Not surprisingly, though, some common themes emerge across the literature on widows, even in markedly different contexts. There is, for example, a general emphasis on self-reliance as a defining feature of widows' experiences (Cattell 2003; Davison 1996; Lopata 1987, 1996; Mojola 2014; Potash 1986a). There is also an elaboration of how particular attitudes and practices concerning widows reflect general social anxieties around sex and death. Widows are often seen as contaminated by their husbands' death, and the range of ritual practices in the bereavement period (or sometimes much longer) speaks to the perceived pollution attached to widows (Whyte 1990). In some cases, widows are implicated in their husbands' death and cast as "poison brides" (Lamb 1999, 550). Jane Guyer (1986, 204) relates a mid-nineteenth-century version of this among Beti-speaking people in colonial Cameroon: "If the husband had been an important headman, one or more of his widows were executed on the grounds of having caused his death, and it was not clear in advance who this would be." A more recent iteration of these anxieties emerged in the era of HIV/AIDS, as widows have been imagined both as victims and perpetrators of their husbands' death based on sexual transmission (Haram 2001). Sex, more generally, is a major preoccupation undergirding perceptions and practices concerning widows, especially younger ones. There has been significant scholarly attention to the "moral panic" arising from widows' uncontained sexuality, with detailed accounts of myriad ways to desexualize or constrain them, whether through proscribed dress and diet, restrictions on sociality, ritual cleansing, or forced remarriage (Bremmer and van den Bosch 1995; Lamb 2000; Nyanzi, Emodu-Walakira, and Serwaniko 2009). Some cases note an easy slippage between words and perceptions that conflate widows and prostitutes (Lamb 2001, 29; Nyanzi, Emodu-Walakira, and Serwaniko 2009; Walters, this volume). As we will see, this concern about widows as unmoored sexual agents subtly seeps into the Jola case as well.

What Do Widows Really Want?

In her foreword to Betty Potash's (1986a) landmark volume on widows in Africa, Mariam Slater (1986, xxii) asserts that "a kind of marriage-ism has dulled our lens for studying single women." Jaqueline Solway (1989, 804) picks up on this claim in her review of the volume and suggests that "by questioning whether widowhood constitutes a phase or a long-term status, the volume returns to the more fundamental question . . . of whether marriage itself should be considered a permanent status or just a phase. Thus the 'naturalness' of the conjugal state for adult women is challenged. The data suggest that in many African societies marriage is the ephemeral institution and it is Westerners' biases based on our own conjugally structured society that has contributed to the stereotype of the widow as marginal."

Prompted by this perspective, as well as by my ongoing reflection on what Jola women who lived in kungomaku and their neighbors were telling me, I began to consider yet another way to consider widowhood. This had to do with what might be called the fantasy—or at least the attractions—of widowhood. When Jola women who lived in kungomaku told me they preferred to "stay alone with their poverty," and when Jola men made cryptic remarks about solteiras who "refused to remarry" and were "better off than we are," perhaps that is exactly what they meant. When seen from a certain perspective, not only the "naturalness" of marriage might be challenged but also its very desirability over the long term. Maybe it was not widows but marriage, or at least remarriage, that was the problem.

In its most obvious form such a claim might be bolstered by the relative freedom (sexual, economic, social) of widows compared with wives.[5] But what if these more underneath, unacknowledged attractions of being a widow were really the heart of the matter? Put starkly, who really needs a husband, especially after having children? Maybe therein lies the real danger: that widowhood is not aberrant but attractive. Perhaps the scholarship that emphasizes the "harsh social and economic consequences" of widowhood, casting widows as abject victims, missed the opportunity to see these consequences as disincentives to what might be a state to which women aspire (or at least fantasize about). "Better to stay alone than to marry another man": so said a Jola woman when I asked her how she managed to provide for her four children and three grandchildren, all of whom resided with her in her hungomahu. "Another man just makes for more work," she added. On another occasion, when I asked a woman I had known for over fifteen years, whose husband had died the previous year, whether she considered getting remarried, she whispered to me, "You sit and suffer under the punishment of your husband. When he dies, why would you go get punished by another man?"

Once it occurred to me that widowhood might, in some circumstances, be desirable, I was reminded of a conversation I had in Esana several years earlier with Lamine and Ernesto, two Guinean representatives of the only national NGO active in this isolated northwestern corner of Guinea-Bissau. At the time I was still stuck in my limited understanding of widows as primarily a humanitarian problem, and I was trying to engage these two agents of social change in considering the "problem of widows." I asked them if they knew how many women were living in kungomaku in Esana, and when they looked puzzled, I summarized my household survey data. At first, they responded much as the local Catholic mission leaders had, suggesting that it was something the World Food Program, which was beginning to develop projects in the area, could address as a special-needs case. I countered that while that might be a productive approach in the short term, this seemed like a problem rooted in Jolas' structural inability to provide for a significant segment of their population. The problem would only get worse, I submitted, given increased male mortality because of AIDS, involvement in military campaigns, and high-risk productive activities, such as increased palm wine tapping. The problem, I continued, could not be solved with food aid, which was a highly erratic commodity as it was, and surely just a stopgap. They nodded in agreement, and Lamine (who was not Jola) became very thoughtful, murmuring that such a predicament required immediate attention. Perhaps, he brainstormed aloud, they could set up a kind of pension fund for kungomaku residents that could be generated by a collective contribution from all villagers. Ernesto (who was Baiote—a neighboring "cousin" ethnic group to the Jola) quickly shook his head, dismissing the idea. He insisted that if wives perceived that women who lived in kungomaku were getting a good deal, they would start killing their husbands. Ernesto recounted an example of such a practice in Ziguinchor, just across the Senegalese border. Several years earlier, there was an announcement that women whose husbands were performing national military service would receive full pensions, in perpetuity, if their husbands died. Supposedly, women started poisoning their husbands in droves. According to Ernesto, when the problem became too obvious to ignore, state authorities were forced to change the pension stipulations so that a widow would receive pensions for only three months after her husband's death. Only when women began to perceive that they might gain in the short term, but would be worse off in the long term, did they stop killing their husbands.[6]

At the time I was still steadfast in my efforts to help solve the widow problem, so I saw Ernesto's point only as a further challenge to addressing widows' poverty because it would increase rather than diminish the overall population of widows. But, perhaps, from widows' perspectives (and as reflected in men's anxieties) this was precisely the point.

The image of superfluous husbands provokes, at first glance, an amusing and surprising jolt, in part because of the deeply ingrained dependent status often attached to wives. But if we take this possibility seriously, beyond the obvious question of what husbands are really for, perhaps we can pivot to a new perspective— one that gives us insight into how particular people experience and navigate their positions within the bounds of marital expectations. We might also be able to reconsider other moments of dramatic economic and political transformation that shake up business-as-usual gender and conjugal relations, often resulting in a sometimes comical, sometimes violent reassertion of patriarchy in the form of reining in women's sexuality and shoring up husbands' fragile and fleeting relevance (e.g., Allman 1996; Auslander 1993; Das 2006; Hodgson and McCurdy 2001; Schroeder 1996).

Most scholarship about widows has focused on the "harsh social and economic penalties" produced by widowhood, and these penalties can indeed be severe and unfair and require our attention and concern. But perhaps we can also productively interrogate the provenance of these penalties. Why are there so many disincentives to remaining an unattached adult woman? Why is so much social and cultural effort put into making it less desirable for widows to remain single than to remarry? Why would it be readily acknowledged (not just by Lamine and Ernesto, but by many other men and women) that a widow's pension fund would be enough incentive for women to murder their husbands?

Writing around Widows: A Kaleidoscopic Approach

The long process of thinking and writing about women who live in kungomaku has required me to rub up against and reconsider several treasured anthropological tenets. One of the animating impulses of anthropology, especially feminist anthropology, is to draw attention to the otherwise invisibilized members of a given population. This did not work, and it should not have been the presumed ethical or justifiable orientation. Yes, women who lived in kungomaku could speak, but they usually chose not to. After many futile attempts to probe deeper, to push these women to talk more frankly about their situation, I felt increasingly awkward and uncomfortable pursuing them. It felt like badgering. Of course, all ethnography is a form of badgering, but this was of a different order. They did not want to call attention to themselves; they wanted to be left alone. So I did. And this left me to pursue a technique more common in other humanistic and narratively attentive disciplines: the write-around, asking and listening to what other Jola villagers said about women who lived in kungomaku. This was not just a matter of politeness or feasibility, although it was partly that. It also made more sense in relation to an effort that had shifted from documenting widows' lives to, instead, trying to understand why this significant segment of the population was simultaneously visible and invisible—there being no word for "widow" but a word for their houses. But even my write-around approach could not circumvent the ultimate ethno-graphic conundrum; by broaching the topic of widows, I had to name something that might not emically exist. I have tried to avoid this—in both fieldwork and writing—by not even using the word "widow," instead referring to "women who live in kungomaku." But not only is this cumbersome, it does not resolve the conceptual problem.

In my effort to account for the increase in kungomaku by writing around their occupants, I found myself accumulating a growing list of cryptic comments and asymptotic explanations from various nonwidowed Jola villagers that tended to deepen my confusion rather than my understanding. But as the answers and years accumulated, I began to see these responses not so much as thwarting my effort to get to the bottom of the issue, but as prismatic chips in a kaleidoscope, each offering a partial but linked glimpse of various Jola views on what you or I would call widowhood.

Some Jola hinted at the spectral presence of HIV/AIDS and other STDs on women's remarriage prospects. For instance, a middle-aged man obliquely proffered, "Before, if your husband died, one of his brothers would seek you out for remarriage. But now he thinks, 'I don't really know why my brother died, and maybe if I marry his wife, I'll get whatever he had that killed him.'" When I responded, "You mean like AIDS?" he nodded, then changed the subject to widows' sexual lives: "Some women say they don't want to remarry but then go have affairs with much younger men, so maybe that's their reason to stay in kungomaku."

Some Jola women pointed to changes in men themselves. "Before, men behaved better," Nha Buinem told me. "But now *prasandai* [city ways] entered in men and they don't treat women as well as they used to." Other villagers, though, continued to emphasize the general decline in economic wherewithal, which underlay both men's resistance to fulfill their obligation to marry their dead brothers' wives and women's reluctance to subject themselves and their children to second-class status in the changing economic and household structures. As one of my closest companions spelled out for me,

> The problem is, your husband dies. His brother wants to inherit you. But you refuse because you know that you and your children won't be treated right in his house. He has children of his own, a wife of his own. He will always favor them. Your children will be upset and always get into conflicts with him and his children. So you prefer to stay in your own hungomahu and with your own children and your own suffering. But your refusal to marry your husband's brother makes him mad. This rejection turns to bitterness. That's why he doesn't help you or your children. That's why he takes all his brother's land back. Because you refused.

When I asked why women used to accept butunorabu, some women simply shrugged and said, "Because we didn't know better then." But Nho Keboral went a step further and made explicit the link between the increase in kungomaku and the declining rice economy:

> Because now is not like before. The rain doesn't fall, and children don't stay here to cultivate with their father and his brothers. They didn't used to scatter like they do now. Now each kid costs more money. You are going to have to look around to pay for their food, pay for school, send them rice, send them money. . . . So, if you go to butunorabu, your kids won't get fair treatment. That's why, today, women whose husbands have died refuse butunorabu. That's why there are so many kungomaku. Because the rain doesn't fall and children have scattered. Before, they stayed put, and it was the same for them whether they ate in their mother's house or in their paternal uncles' houses, because they would all cultivate together. [My sons] used to eat sometimes here, sometimes at [their father's brother's cowives'] houses. Because they would all cultivate in each other's paddies.

Paddy Power

Certainly these explanations help elucidate the decrease in butunorabu practices and increase in kungomaku in terms of men's and women's motivations, but they do not quite get at what made it possible for women to reject their husbands' brothers' proposals. It used to be (most Jola agreed) that once their husbands had died, women were *obliged* to get remarried, regardless of their concerns for their own autonomy or their children's treatment. So how has their current refusal come to be exercised? To get at this, we need to reinsert questions about the increase in kungomaku back into the Jola rice complex. With the changing environmental conditions and, as a consequence, declining viability of a rice-based economy, there has been a significant—although barely perceptible—shift in gender-based power. Put simply, men once truly had the upper hand and could quite readily oblige widows to remarry. But because the wet-rice paddies have decreased in productivity, men's power over women has eroded somewhat. In the gendered system of rice production, men are more associated with the paddies (*butonda*) and women with the forest (*butat*). Women do not exactly own the forest, but they have relative dominion over its use and products, except for palm wine. Given the decrease in paddy use, women increasingly use the forest to plant upland rice. Women and men work in both places, so it is more a matter of from where each gender derives a sense of potency and power. But a particular kind of Jola power that is not only rice-based but subtly exercised. Men's decreasing capacity to command the butonda has spilled over, in some ways, to their decreasing capacity to command women. Whereas before a widowed woman would have been forcibly remarried, that kind of force is no longer easily exerted—although all this in unstated, indirect, and very Jola ways. The decrease in men's paddy power introduced a hairline fracture into the monolith of patriarchy. And women who lived in kungomaku were silently slipping out of a system based on marriage, in which they produced and reproduced largely for men.

Widowhood is always inextricably connected to other aspects of marriage systems, which, in turn, are "implicated in the politics of resource control" (Guyer 1986, 218). As Jane Guyer (1986, 219) has noted, "The central theoretical problems in interpreting the history of kinship lie in relating such apparently cumulative processes to the political structures that only partially control and direct them, and the 'practice' through which people continue to redefine their situation under shifting conditions." In this case, the practice in question is that of Jola women whose husbands have died and who choose (although that, of course, is a fraught and inadequate word in this context) poverty over remarriage, preferring to "economize in their special way" rather than sign up to be wives again. Part of what is so interesting about this practice is that it both exposes marriage as a form of economic entrapment for women and shows that women can make (very limited) decisions about whether or not to participate.

It might be tempting to read this as a kind of feminism; it might look as if widows are giving the middle finger to male power. But it would be a mistake to cast Jola women who live in kungomaku as heretofore unrecognized feminists. Their decisions do not really express or manifest a feminist politics, nor do they seem to be about resistance or even refusal (McGranahan 2016). They are, rather, a kind of quiet opting out of the system. Women who live in kungomaku are not so much transgressive as they are digressive. They wander out of the marriage plot.

They guard their privacy—and maybe even fortify their invisibility—in a world otherwise full of men trying to convince women to bear their children, farm their fields, and keep their houses. Circling back to Ardener, we might say that if widows are a problem for the social order, perhaps the social order is not quite the same problem for them. And this might be precisely what is at stake when Jola widows are not (in their own language) named as such, and rebuff (by their own silence) efforts to problematize them as a category.

A Haunting of Marriage

My aim in this chapter has been to consider the "problem of widows" on two registers: as a problem posed within a specific ethnographic context and as a problem for anthropology. The effort to do full justice to people who have been, as Ardener would put it, muted or marginalized—whether in their own societies or in anthropological discourse—is connected to the wider issue of anthropology's avoidance of areas of human experience that both ethnographers' concepts and local concepts fail to cover because they are existential rather than normative; that is, they are ways of being rather than ways of knowing.

But ways of knowing are still crucial for understanding why it is that Jola women who live in kungomaku remain unnamed and perhaps even unspeakable. For Jola, these women are problematic because they are outside the fundamental functioning unit of the household's gendered division of labor. On the one hand, they risk becoming non-self-sustaining dependents. On the other hand, in their efforts to become productive and self-sustaining, they contravene gendered categories of work and knowledge. By assuming male roles (like tilling fields or building houses), women who live in kungomaku occupy a murky spot on the threshold between masculine and feminine. As Nha Ceyo, a young woman whose husband had died, told me when I visited her in her hungomahu, "The way you see me here, it's me who is both husband and wife, both man and woman." Perhaps because of this disordering position, these women are rendered unnamed and invisible, left alone and isolated in their poverty. What could express this more aptly than the unmarked woman in her hungomahu: the absence of the person in the place where she lives.

Yet the absence of a Jola term for "widow" reveals even more about the fragility of social relations. The shifts that make it possible for women whose husbands have died to opt out of remarriage suggest a rupture between production and reproduction within a system that has, for many centuries, held tightly to practices and values—such as butunorabu and a pronatalist ethic—that harness women's labor in a male-dominated regime of rice agriculture. Production and reproduction have come apart for a range of reasons—some economic, some ecological. Given the decline in paddy-based rice agriculture and the introduction of modest development schemes, women now have more access to means of self-reliance. Not surprisingly, such changes are affecting marriage practices and gender relations.

Women who live in kungomaku, then, represent the kernel of a new system of production and reproduction, but one that does not fit into current—although rapidly transforming—norms. They cannot be named or even seen because they are, in a sense, an offense to the past. These women suggest a haunting of marriage because they embody the prospect of a new material formation that is working outside it. Seeing them, *really* seeing them, would make what is happening to marriage manifest, so there is a certain embarrassment in their visibility ("Huh, we never noticed!"). Of course, Jola know this is happening, but this is a form of cognition without recognition. A word for "widow"—this unfixed sexual actor who operates outside ordinary social circles and in between normative gender roles— would turn the hairline fracture into a perhaps irreparably fragmented reality. To one last time invoke Ardener's essay, a real inclusion of widows' models may spell the end of, if not men themselves, at least a version of marriage and masculinity that requires a particular relationship between production and reproduction to remain intact. The outcome of exposing this is a chilling prospect: not the feminist realization of women's power but the apprehension that fully acknowledging this open secret—that women in kungomaku manage, albeit precariously, as free economic and sexual actors, making husbands superfluous—would mean that the system is not just unfair but unnecessary.

Acknowledgments

This chapter is a revised version of Davidson (2020).

NOTES

1. Given its nonexistence as a word and social category among Jola, I try to avoid using the word "widow" throughout this chapter and instead refer to "women whose husbands have died" or "women who live in kungomaku." But where it is impossible or undesirable to avoid the word "widow," the reader should add imaginary scare quotes to it.

2. Until recently, there was generally only one *hungomahu*—or, at the most, two *kungomaku*— in each village neighborhood, occupied by a post-reproductive-age woman. I have been unable to glean any further meaning or etymological information about the word *hungomahu*. Currently, Jola use the word to refer to any house lived in by a woman whose husband has died and who has not remarried. Each time I return to the region—most recently in 2019—I count the *kungomaku*, and each time there is a significant increase in them.

3. The name of the village is a pseudonym, as are all personal names in this chapter.

4. The number of *kungomaku* is not the same as the total number of what we would call widows. Some widows enter *karoŋaku*, where they live with a married son. Others—especially cowives—live together, and still others live with another family member. But typically once her dead husband's house was broken, if she did not remarry, a woman moved into a *hungomahu*. During the time I lived in Esana, there was only one widow*er*; he lived alone.

5. This was, of course, also the case for Euro-American widows up until the nineteenth century, at least those with some independent means: sexual freedom, because

virginity was not at stake, as well as economic, public, and sometimes even political freedom.

6. In some ways, this story—I was never able to determine the extent to which it was imagined or real—is an interesting twist on the "poison bride" trope in widowhood literature. For an account that brings to the fore the perception of women's interest in men's wealth, and thus their motivation to kill their husbands, see Nyanzi, Emodu-Walakira, and Serwaniko (2009).

PART THREE

Within Marriage

9

Extramarital Intimacy

Juggling Femininity, Marriage, and Commercial Sex in Contemporary Japan

AKIKO TAKEYAMA

The fact that my womanhood ends soon makes me shiver. I must go for it, if necessary, before my womanhood expires. It is meaningless to be born female unless fulfilled sexually. I have to make up my mind for extramarital sex.

−Chieko (2009, 3–4)

In her 2009 autobiographical novel *Deribarī Hosuto* (Delivery Host), Chieko, a forty-one-year-old wife and mother, describes living a life that many Japanese women could only dream of: she resides in an affluent Tokyo neighborhood, the stay-at-home wife of an elite surgeon who runs a family-owned hospital, and mother to their teenage daughter, a student of a prestigious private school.[1] She maintains her beauty and model-like body and perfects her house chores. Her enviable lifestyle has been featured in Japanese tabloids and fashion magazines. Behind her flawless public façade, however, she suffers from a sexless marriage that has lasted more than fifteen years. Her husband no longer touches her or looks at her as a woman. He only wishes her to be a good mother for their child.

The couple maintains a façade of a happy, intact marriage. By the same token, its modality, especially in the area of intimacy and emotional bonding, changes over time. Chieko's frustration about her dissatisfaction peaks when her gynecologist points out signs of premature menopause, which the doctor claims is most likely due to her sexual inactivity. Chieko writes, "The fact that the clock of *onna no shōmikigen* [expiration date of womanhood] is ticking has made me desperate to revive womanliness one more time even if it's a transient joy" (Chieko 2009, 178). She resorts to bold action in bed, grabbing her husband's hand to direct it to her private parts. He quickly shakes off this advance, turning his back to her. His reaction completely shatters her hopes for sexual intimacy in marriage.

Chieko's problem is not uncommon in Japan, where almost one out of two married couples are reportedly sexless.[2] The Japan Society of Sexual Sciences officially defined *sekkusuresu* in 1994 as a social problem whereby a healthy couple has no sexual activities for more than a month (Moriki 2017). This discourse emerged against the backdrop of the so-called "1.57 shock" in 1989, the lowest fertility rate in post–World War II Japan and far below the 2.1 replacement rate needed to maintain the current population. The fertility rate dropped further to 1.26, the record low, in 2005 amid Japan's rapidly aging society. The causes are largely understood as men's lack of time and energy—too *tsukareteiru* (tired) to have sex—and women's reluctance—too *mendōkusai* (too much hassle) to fulfill their partners' sexual needs (Tsuji 2018, 1).

Married men and women are, by no means, disinterested in sex at large. Japan's sex industry has a long and thriving history of catering to men. It is expanding today to include women as customers. This is the sociohistorical and demographic background when Chieko makes up her mind to seek commercial sex with a professional lover, called a "delivery host," which becomes the subject of her book. Men and women expect different things from sex, however. As Chieko's opening quote illuminates and I further detail in this chapter, women expect extramarital sex to assure them of their worthiness and sense of self as a woman both within and outside marriage.

Marriage as an institution has long been criticized as a system through which women are trafficked from one man (the father) to another (the husband), subordinated to their counterparts, and turned into domestic slaves (Engels 1884; Rubin 1975; Pateman 1988). While this kind of critique sheds light on the patriarchal form and function of heteronormative marriage as an enabler of men's control over women's bodies, sexuality, and labor,[3] such a view often overlooks the affective dimensions of marriage underneath the façade. Like gender, marriage is neither static nor fixed. It is constantly negotiated on the ground into a livable modality. In other words, as essays in this edited volume demonstrate, marriage is malleable and its meaning changes over time.

To delve deeper into the affective dimensions and changing modalities of conjugal relationships in contemporary Japan, I employ what I call affective ethnography (Takeyama 2016, 19), an ethnographic method and account of often-invisible elements—feelings, emotions, and intimate relationships—of lived experiences. Drawing from Japanese married women's experiences in my in-depth interviews, Chieko's autographic novel, and other popular accounts on sexless marriage, this chapter portrays Japanese women who are in sexless marriages and are pursuing extramarital intimacy in exchange for money. I ask the following questions: How do they manage to juggle their "affairs," marriage, and femininity simultaneously? How do they make sense of the apparently masculine act of paying for sexual pleasure, which requires them to transgress such cultural norms as women's sexual passivity and maternal responsibility? What does marriage mean to them? By posing these questions, I examine the changing meanings and modality of marriage in contemporary Japan. Despite the exterior appearance that patriarchal marriage stays intact as an institution, I argue that changes in married women's emotional needs and sexual intimacy are indicative of transformations of intimacy within and beyond the boundaries of marriage in contemporary Japan.

My findings illuminate that although these women may not overtly fight for specific goals such as gender equality and sexual liberation, they do not simply subject themselves to patriarchal sex roles and norms either. In the fine-grained portrayal of married women I provide, transformations in sexual intimacy are symptomatic of the ways that they chip away at male-centered gender and sexual systems. Where the politics of sexual intimacy, emotional fulfillment, and ideal womanhood—at the heart of the affective realm of marriage—are concerned, I contend that such non-teleological negotiations in everyday life contribute to challenging how marriage is lived and negotiated in subtle yet significant ways.

New Sexual Subjectivity as Consumer Citizenship

Japanese society has witnessed a series of sociodemographic changes since the 1990s: increasing numbers of women entering the workforce, divorce cases, sexless couples, and an aging population in inverse proportion to a declining national economy, birth rate, and familial bonds (Alexy 2020; Allison 2013; Brinton 2011; Danely 2014; Heinrich and Galan 2018; Lukacs 2019; Manzenreiter and Holthus 2017). Over this period, large numbers of single young women have been hired as "office ladies" in emerging financial, information, and service industries. With their newfound disposable incomes, they were the first generation of Japanese middle-class women expected to self-fashion their lifestyles through consumption. This generation of women, feminist scholar Yamashita Etsuko pointed out, deviates from the conventional image of Japanese mothers as self-sacrificing and devoted to their children and husband (1996, 40). Many have avoided the confines of the marriage and family system in order to pursue *jibun no jinsei* (a "life of their own," not for others). Such a collective attitude has led to postponing marriage, declining birthrates, and increasing divorce rates in Japan (see Nelson's and Jones's chapters in this volume for similar trends in South Korea and Indonesia).

Shying away from traditional marital and family expectations, this new generation of women has been drawn into market discourses of a "life of one's own" in postindustrial consumer capitalism. In the consumer market, the individual, rather than the nuclear family, became the iconic unit of consumption, and heterosexual romance, rather than marriage, was illuminated as the ideal avenue for the expression of new womanhood (Takeyama 2005). Valentine's Day, Christmas Eve, and birthdays were all promoted as special events for couples' romantic outings, luxurious dining, and gift giving. In these market discourses, new women were celebrated as novel—self-centered, pleasure seeking, and free spending— consumer citizens (Takeyama 2016, 30). By the same token, they are the target of a torrent of advertising for antiaging beauty products and wellness programs that will help stop wrinkles, frizzled hair, and chronic fatigue. Free from the conventional marriage and family system wherein frugal, "self-sacrificing" women from previous generations were in charge of taking care of the family, however, they have been increasingly pressured to care about the self in consumer capitalism.

Sexual commerce for women's wellness is a market niche in this socioeconomic context. Its content varies from intimate conversation and companionship to flirtation and sexual advances, largely depending upon their needs and financial capacity. While a middle-class part-time worker can afford only so much to satisfy her moderate sexual fantasies, a wealthy stay-at-home mother like Chieko, as I will describe shortly, can expend much more time, energy, and money to explore an adventurous "affair." Regardless of class differences manifested in sexual demands, however, women who pay for sexual services commonly avoid expressing their sexual desires explicitly.

Why do women, unlike men, stress anything else but sexual pleasure itself when they narrate their sexual pursuit commercially? After reading anonymous women's essays like Chieko's and interviewing male hosts on women's sexual behaviors, I have come to realize that women's reluctance to be explicit is a particular kind of communication style. Women clients often suggestively send signals to their hosts to attain what they wish. For example, Chieko, who made up her mind to seek sex with a "delivery host," still hesitates to express her true feelings when she books the service online. She writes in her novel, *Delivery Host*, "Can I honestly say that I want sex? I can't. I wonder if it's because of my *pride* as a woman. Choosing erotic massage therapy or the like makes me feel miserable about myself like an old man desperate enough to pay for sex. . . . I cannot help clinging to my useless *pride*" (2009, 25, emphasis added). Due to her "pride," Chieko ends up booking a host who specializes in dating, not in sex per se (25). The fact that she cannot say what she really wants does not mean that she simply suppresses her desire and subjects herself to masculinist control over women's sexuality. It is rather a way for her to maintain her sexual "decency" despite her seemingly deviant sexual behavior.

Why can she not express her real feelings straightforwardly? It is perhaps partly because of her prideful personality. It is also because of gendered sexual norms. In her 1984 article "Thinking Sex," Gayle Rubin points out, "Part of the modern ideology of sex is that lust is the province of men, purity that of women" (1984, 307). As such, sexual lust is the male domain, and sex is what men do to women, not the other way around in penetrative heterosexual relations. Chieko's sexual desire and deeds are deeply embedded in this gendered sexual script. She secretly wishes that her host would sense her sexual desire and deliver it. "My goal," she writes, "is to have sex. But I need a story that my host wants me badly, not because he is paid for it" (2009, 26).

In order for women to participate in the masculine domain of sex, Rubin continues, women have to "overcome serious limitations on their social mobility, their economic resources, and their sexual freedoms" (1984, 308). To a degree, women users of sexual commerce in Japan have overcome limits on their social mobility and economic resources in the country's consumer-oriented economy. Nonetheless, many still struggle with bending their sense of sexual decency. These women must carefully navigate their way through the existing sexual double standard so that they can safely pry open what has traditionally been a male domain. In this sense, sexual ambiguity is not an embodiment of female passivity in sexual matters, but rather a tactic for women to mediate their sexual desires through strategic communication styles.

Chieko, who wishes a young, good-looking man would fall for her and lust for her, avoids requesting a companion who specializes in sex work. She instead orders a tall and handsome twenty-five-year-old "boyfriend" to rent for a date. His name is Ryuichi, the most booked host at one of the largest sex commerce dating sites for women. In her text exchange with Ryuichi, Chieko shares her frustration about her sexless marriage, expecting him to read into the hidden meanings—her sexual disappointment—beneath the fact of sexlessness. She also intentionally avoids initiating sex on their first date even though she has carefully prepared herself for the occasion, having waxed her body and made it presentable in sexy lingerie for the date. She instead enjoys intimate conversation with Ryuichi over lunch at a fancy hotel. Stepping out of the restaurant after the meal, Chieko receives a gentle kiss on her lips from him. That kiss soon evolves into a deep kiss. At this point, she goes to the front desk to book a hotel room where she ends up having sex.

Underneath the appearance of a woman buying sex, affective dimensions of sexual intimacy are more nuanced. At least, women's expression of their sexual experience is nuanced. It is depicted as more about emotional satisfaction than physical pleasure itself, though those two are inseparable. Chieko's detailed depiction of her experience with Ryuichi illuminates that: "Once we entered the hotel room, he immediately undressed me while kissing me passionately. Putting me down on the bed, he started touching me. . . . His head gradually descended to my private parts to provide what I had longed for so badly, but my husband had never given me. Reaching out to and holding Ryuichi's erect penis in my hand, I was happily assured that he acknowledged me as a woman. I am a woman! Such a young handsome man is sexually aroused by my body" (2009, 47). It is Ryuichi, in her mind, who has made sexual advances. In this way, Chieko resolves the dilemma she faces between her sexual desire and a cultural code of lust. She also finds a story that she needs: he has lusted for her, not for her money. With the second-order logic, her sexual interaction becomes more meaningful, as a vehicle to fill her void—the lack of sexual intimacy, emotional bond, and assurance as a woman—in marriage, than transient pleasure.

Despite the pleasure she feels, indeed Chieko cannot reach orgasm. But she is fully satisfied. She writes that Ryuichi, who sensed her frustration, gently holds her from behind and promises that he will help her experience an orgasm one day. "This is what I have wanted most—this sense of warmth, comfort, and security!" (2009, 49). This realization leads her to the ultimate understanding of what she has been looking for: a "man who sincerely listens to [her] and provides comfort" (50). She concludes that her lust for sex was about soul-searching.

If technologies of the self, as Foucault defines the term, involve individuals working on their own bodies, actions, and ways of being so as to "transform themselves [and] attain a certain state of happiness" (1988, 18), sexual intimacy with hosts functions for Chieko as a technology of the self—specifically, a means to attain self-fulfillment by transforming herself into a woman who, as she sees it, is sexually desirable to the kind of man whom she also desires. However, sexual intimacy, as a technology of the self, is gendered. Drawing from Nietzsche, Simone de Beauvoir asserts, "Men might be passionate lovers at certain moments of their experience, but there is not one who could be defined as 'a man in love'" (1974, 683). In contrast, "a woman in love" not only serves as a technology of the self but also provides an existential reason. Along with the gendered script of love, sex, and the care of self, sexual intimacy, as a technology, compels women to make necessary changes and celebrate their consumer citizenship. Such a technology of women's desirable selves, which is on the edge of conventional marriage, is made commercially available in Japan's consumer capitalism.

Buying Ideal Femininity in the Marketplace

Over the past two decades, the sex industry (*fūzoku*) has increasingly targeted women. "Delivery hosts," "rental boyfriends," and "erotic massage therapists" are all available today. Although there are no statistics or systematic studies, primary users of these services are allegedly women in their mid-thirties and forties (Hara 2018; Suzuki 2019). Why this demographic of women? They fall in the crack of compartmentalized female sexuality and womanhood in Japan.

Womanhood and sexuality, as I have argued elsewhere, have long been closely intertwined with the reproduction of marriage and family systems. Womanhood in Japan is "conceptualized as a mere transition period from sexually sealed girlhood to desexualized motherhood" (Takeyama 2016, 132; also see Robertson 1998, 66). This model provides a narrow window for young women to get married and involve themselves in reproductive sex. Years later they are trapped in limbo. Once celebrated as "new women," women in their thirties and forties with children are largely desexualized as mothers. Once their children start school, these women find more time to reflect on their life choices. Some women with disposable incomes and/or some savings—like Chieko—are compelled to do something about their sexual dissatisfaction. In other words, they seek sexual intimacy, not sex for procreation, to prolong narrowly defined womanhood and sexuality beyond the boundaries of marriage.

One option for that is sexual commerce for women who are sexually unfulfilled. Nonfiction writer Hara Sho reveals that sexless marriages and spousal infidelity are the two most common reasons women become interested in sexual commerce (2018, 158). According to Hara, a heartbroken woman can heal her wounds only when she finds a man who acknowledges her as attractive and holds her tightly in his arms (190). A woman like Chieko, who suffers from a sexless marriage, seeks sexual intimacy in exchange for money.

But what exactly are these women paying for? The reason that women buy sex aligns with Chieko's example. Based on her tryouts of a wide range of sexual services for women—an erotic massage, a "rental boyfriend," a "delivery host," and a host club visit—Suzuki Seiko, a forty-year-old counselor who is fifteen years into a sexless marriage, succinctly summarizes that "buying" a man is actually about buying "the self who is romantically excited" (2019). The majority of women I have interviewed at host clubs are also seeking *tokimeki*—romantic excitement (Takeyama 2005). Most women told me that their encounters with desirable partners help them feel beautifully radiant about themselves; as a result, they experience increased self-esteem and a thriving sense of their own womanhood. In this sense, as Suzuki points out, paying for sexual commerce is an act of purchasing a technology of the self, that is, self-investment.

In the narratives of sexual commerce for women, however, sexual desires are subsumed under the discourse of emotional fulfillment. Megumi, a middle-aged wife of a carpenter and mother of three, was seeking some sort of "spice" in her life when I first met her in 2003. Like Chieko, she had been sexless for many years after giving birth to three children, although she had a love marriage with her high school sweetheart. Once married, she told me that her priority had shifted from her own needs to her partner's and then to her children's. However, she had not even noticed her lack of self-care because she was preoccupied with childrearing. Meanwhile her husband and children alike called her "Mother." After her youngest son started school, she began noticing that she felt as if she had lost her identity as an individual woman. Megumi confessed that her emotional and sexual void grew inside her. Her host clubbing, Megumi said, filled that void.

Visiting her host club once a week and spending at least 20,000 yen (about $200) per visit out of her own savings, Megumi flirts with her host to rebuild her self-confidence. "It's a pleasing experience for a woman to have an attractive young man look into her eyes and say, 'You are so beautiful tonight,' even if she knows it is only a performance or a lie," she said. Megumi also enjoys embracing a "time of her own" and having someone to care about her. That is what she misses in her everyday life. Filling the gap satisfies her void. "Host club dating has the kick of an energy drink, it delivers a dose of happiness and reverberates throughout my day," Megumi said.

In Japan's youth-oriented marketplace, where young single women, especially attractive ones, are highly valued, older married women are keenly aware of their age-related vulnerability in and outside marriage. Pointing out the gendered and culturally specific notion of aging in Japan, Millie Creighton states, "Women are defined as reaching 'middle-age' and 'old age' younger than their male counterparts, and younger than often conceptualized in the West" (2016, 5). Like middle-aged married women in this chapter who seek extramarital relationships commercially,

Creighton finds that others fantasize about younger Korean male stars on screen for a "different type of relationship with a possible partner, one more romantic than what their marriage and daily life offered" (6; see G'Sell, this volume, for how foreign men are idealized among South African women).

Fantasizing about a romantic relationship with a younger attractive man is one thing. Dating him is another. Yuki, in her mid-forties when I first met her at a Tokyo host club in 2004, contends that middle-aged women subconsciously feel ashamed to be "old" and "ugly." Chieko's account similarly addresses her experience of changing values of femininity: she has never naïvely believed that youth is eternal. But it never occurred to her that she would one day face the vanishing of her sense of self as a woman. Looking back on her premarriage days, "It used to be a puzzle for me," Chieko reflects, "that a whole host of men spent so much money on me to have sex" (2009, 177). She eventually found an ideal spouse—a promising surgeon and successor of his family-owned hospital—to marry. "Sex [read: youthful and beautiful femininity] was my weapon," Chieko reveals. Two decades later, she still mobilizes all sorts of technologies to combat against aging and maintain her beauty. However, she stresses, "Looking young is not the same as being young" (2009, 200).

Yuki, a mother of three, shares a similar view. "I did absolutely nothing to attract men when I was in my late teens and early twenties," she said. Like Chieko, Yuki married her ideal husband—an older, successful entrepreneur who became a wealthy business and property owner. Over twenty years later, she still maintained her ageless beauty with the money her husband provided. However, she discovered that her husband was having an affair with a much younger woman. For stress relief, she started visiting a host club. "I have learned," Yuki reflected, "[that] once aging, a woman has to make extra effort to even draw men's attention. She needs to seduce them into doing things for her."

For the middle-aged women I have met, youthful femininity remains a source of empowerment—still accessible, largely due to their class status and spending power. By the same token, it is what they fear losing most. In this sense, youthful femininity is not just a part of an evolving life cycle. It is a cultural construct through which women gain (or lose) social value. Femininity is, Beverley Skeggs contends, "something which is struggled with to gain some value and to ameliorate invalidation. It is a performance not considered to be necessary all the time. . . . [But] to not invest at all in femininity is seen to jeopardize others' investments" (1997, 108). As Yuki, Megumi, and Chieko exemplify, femininity is something that women can summon to enhance their social value and gain access to what they usually do not have—money, political power, and equal social standing with men, for example. Their display of femininity in a flirtatious and manipulative manner is therefore not an innate female trait. It is an acquired skill used to appeal to those who are in power and leverage their interests in a male-centered society.

Women's use of sexual commerce, as a technology of the self, uniquely shapes the cultural politics at the intersection of gender, sexuality, age, and class within a masculinist market and patriarchal marriage. Japanese women's erotic pursuits in exchange for money seem to transgress the conventionally masculine domain of lust and paid sex. Fed up with their sexless lives within marriage these women pursue sexual and emotional fulfillment outside marriage. Nonetheless, they do so secretively. As Megumi and Chieko, among other women, demonstrate, they carefully navigate the existing gender and sex systems by employing the market discourse of a "life of one's own" and foregrounding the cultural script of a "woman in love." In this way, they create a smokescreen to cover their transgressive acts as if their commercial, sexual pursuits were for their self-transformation, not out of their sexual perversion.

These Japanese women's strategic exercise of their agency echoes women's negotiation in opting in and out of particular kinds, or aspects, of marriage in this volume, even if there is a symbolic risk involved. If some women in South Africa, who see foreign migrant workers as ideal husbands risk being labeled greedy prostitutes (G'Sell, this volume), Japanese married women, who fantasize about professional lovers, risk being seen as sexual deviants. Even so, women in these different countries do not easily give up. Women I met strategically maneuver gendered scripts of sexuality and aging to make their lives livable and meaningful. At the same time, their strategic move itself is circumscribed by the very same masculinist, youth-oriented market logic. In the youth-oriented marketplace, middle-aged married women's femininity is vulnerable to start with, and aging is inevitable no matter how much spending power they have. As such, there is no way to win the capitalist game.

Negotiating Femininity, Marriage, and Family

Like the capitalist market that shapes an ambivalent power relation in women's sexual subjectivity and aging femininity, social institutions of marriage and family often play a dual role in these women's strategic negotiations too. Those who experience disappointment in marriage and commercially pursue extramarital intimacy might paradoxically cling to a very disappointing marriage, especially when it is a source of their spending power, psychological security, and maternal respectability. Similarly, women who feel guilty about their extramarital pursuits channel their guilt into perfecting their roles as wives and mothers.

Chieko confesses that she married for the privileges—economic wealth, social status, and opportunities to travel abroad. Although she felt her husband was sexually selfish before marriage, she says, "I naïvely wished that a perfect marriage would magically fix everything" (2009, 14–17). She still thinks that her life is blessed overall and intends to maintain what she has in marriage while compensating for what is missing through commercial sex. Similarly, Yuki told me that she prioritized financial wealth and security in her marriage. Leaving the northern island of Hokkaido for Tokyo by herself as a teenager, she needed someone who could financially provide for her. A man's generous spending, as she saw it, was a barometer of his love. "Many can say sweet words to please you," Yuki says, "but not so many actually do things for you. Once you reach economic stability, you secure a peace of mind. It's a form of happiness and wellness."

With financial stability and spending power, wealthy, stay-at-home wives and mothers like Chieko and Yuki can devote themselves to being good, supportive mothers who fulfill their primary role to send their children to prestigious private schools and gain social respect. Besides their maternal role, they can now perform being superwomen as good mothers and dutiful wives who also remain sexually vivacious and desirable. Going to host clubs is a way of making themselves sexier for themselves and sometimes for their husbands. "Men are proud of their beautiful wives," Yuki claims, "because society gives them credit for that. So, my effort to maintain youthful beauty is ultimately for my husband." Yuki's remarks indicate that, like mothers who earn credit for their children's success in education, husbands receive social recognition for their wives' success in beauty. In the patriarchal family and, by extension, social systems, men are the head of household and symbolic proprietor of familial assets, including their wives' and children's achievements.

In this material-based perspective, along with the male-centered symbolic matrix, married women's pursuit of commercial sex falls in a catch-22 situation. They are unhappy about sexual intimacy with their husbands, yet they cannot lose them as financial providers and familial foundations. They are disturbed by their vanishing femininity, but they cannot let go of it without risking the security and stability essential to their sense of what it means to be respectful mothers. Although the marketplace and marriage/family system seem to generate an unresolvable tension between youthful femininity and respectable motherhood, I argue that they are essentially two sides of the same coin.

Youthful femininity and respectable motherhood coexist in these women's lived experiences even as they might appear mutually exclusive and contradictory in the eyes of others. Women I introduced in this chapter conform to normative marriage, family, and motherhood to secure their wealth, privilege, and stability. They also deviate from what they appear to conform to when they participate in commercial sex. Thus, their compliance and disobedience are manifested in context-specific ways. In such a discursive construction of meanings, the meaning of resistance is also circumscribed by the context. Women's pursuit of commercial sex is a form of resistance, if not unconscious revolt, against the institutional norms that conventionally oppressed women's sexual subjectivity. When women, desexualized as mothers in the eyes of others, including their husbands, take advantage of commercial sex to resexualize themselves, they bend the gendered cultural code of female sexuality. They are in a position to adopt ideal femininity and sexual services, defined and provided by the capitalist market, so as to see their desirable selves through the eyes of their male counterparts. If the social institutions of marriage and family used to define maternal citizenship and discipline for women, the economic institution of postindustrial consumerism substitutes for that apparatus on the macro level.

These findings should not be taken as the endpoint of such analyses of women's lives. Rather, they are an entry point into more nuanced understandings of the micropolitics of sexual intimacy—at the heart of the care of the self—that cut across both social and economic institutions. Married women's juggling of femininity, marriage, and extramarital romance is indicative of their context-specific agency and multilayered negotiations that potentially mess with and transform the macro status quo.

Nonetheless, this is not a linear, progressive transformation. It is messy and contradictory at times. Chieko, who is afraid of attracting trouble by finding an anonymous sexual partner through online dating sites, chooses to hire a professional "boyfriend" from a business establishment. She states, "As a mother, I prioritize the protection of my daughter and family foremost. I cannot take any risk such as stalking and blackmail. For this reason, I have no other choice but a delivery host" (2009, 21). Yuki agreed. "I have never dated laymen who might end up too involved to control themselves. I don't want to destroy my family." Both Chieko and Yuki, among other clients I interviewed, keep their confidentiality, revealing only their first names and cell phone numbers to their hosts. In their minds, it is a tactic to protect their families as well as themselves from trouble. In other words, it is a form of risk management and damage control.

Even if these women succeed in managing risk to ethically engage in sexual commerce while maintaining their marriages, they still need to reconcile their own sense of guilt about "buying" a man and enjoying sexual intimacy outside marriage. To avoid this feeling, women I have studied trivialize the fact that they pay for commercial sex by downplaying the sexual nature of their extramarital intimacy. After her first date with Ryuichi, Chieko writes, "It was painful to accept the fact that I just purchased a man and paid for sex" (2009, 51). She then swiftly reinterprets her act of paying as if equivalent to other kinds of shopping: "Just like paying cosmetic surgeons, I paid Ryuichi because I needed someone to help me. Falling in love with him was an accident" (2009, 51–52). If her consumer logic eases her sense of guilt, her tautology of "falling in love," which is always accidental anyway, frees her from the burden of her responsibility.

Her guilt trip, which troubles her, also empowers her to perfect her house chores. Before going out for the night, she always prepares dinner for her family and comes back home by dawn, so she can make breakfast and see her daughter off to school. Yuki and Megumi also do the same and fulfill their maternal duties without fail. As such, they remain good mothers. Yuki said, "It is important for a woman to have a space where she can relieve her everyday stress so that she makes a fresh start at home and does a better job." Megumi similarly described the positive effect of host clubbing. Admitting that she feels tired, worn, and haggard the morning after her host club partying, she also insists, "In my mind, I feel full of positive energy that makes my life more joyful and meaningful" (Takeyama 2016, 108). These women manage to turn their sense of guilt into positive energy for the sake of their own lives as well as their families.

Despite the appearance of participating in transgressive acts, the way these women narrate their experiences puts their primary role as mothers (and wives) above their secondary one as desiring and desirable women. They draw from a logic that dictates gendered divisions of labor in marriage to strategically trivialize their extramarital activities as a necessary outlet that enables them to more dutifully fulfill their primary role. In this way, their primary and secondary roles are not mutually exclusive but rather mutually constitutive. On the one hand, these women's narratives discursively maintain the status quo of the marriage-and-family institution—no matter how sexless, insufficient, and dysfunctional that system may be—for such specific reasons as financial, psychological, and familial stability in the long run. On the other hand, they carve out a space for their extramarital intimacy to supplement what is missing in marriage.

Even without sex, the majority of women maintain a bond with their spouses for financial reasons, love of children, or simply comradery. Yuki succinctly summarizes what she attains from her host and her husband (and family). "Hosts do all sorts of things to please you insofar as you pay them. It is, after all, my husband and family I can really rely on when I'm in trouble."

What Yuki expects from her conjugal relationship echoes the notion of familial love that Suzuki Seiko, a counselor who also partakes in commercial sexual relationships, describes. "Being with my partner over 20 years," Suzuki asserts, "'betrayal' means that one walks away when the other half is in deep trouble. I no longer feel that an affair is betrayal" (2019). From this perspective, she argues that women's careful pursuit of extramarital intimacy manifests a form of familial love in Japan where many couples are in sexless marriages (2019). Japanese women's pursuit of extramarital adventures is, in this respect, a paradoxical manifestation of their deep commitment to their marriages and families.

Such a paradoxical commitment to marriage is not unique to Japanese society. Hannaford (this volume) similarly points out that women in Senegal, whose husbands live overseas as migrant workers and often fail to provide financially and emotionally, cling to marriage for their social status and manage to secure necessary support outside the marriage, usually through their friend and kin networks. Thus, women's needs root in and derive from what is missing in their everyday lives. As such, their needs are embedded in specific sociohistorical contexts, and their wishful pursuit is nested in what has become available at a particular historical juncture. Japanese women's pursuit of extramarital intimacy is, therefore, symptomatic of a historical shift in ideal femininity from the desexualized maternal figure to the self-sexualizing model. Neither desexualization in traditional family-oriented motherhood nor resexualization in today's individual-centered model leads women to a total, self-defined sexuality or a life independent from the gendered expectation of sex roles. Nonetheless, women's everyday negotiations end up maintaining what is useful and meaningful to them, while letting go of what disappoints them. In other words, their collective modality discursively reshapes the content of the marriage and family systems as social institutions.

Conclusion: Of Gender Politics and Feminist Agency

Despite their seemingly transgressive act of seeking extramarital intimacy in exchange for money, these married women are hardly regarded as feminist subjects in Japan. Nor is their agency acknowledged in feminist scholarship. Ueno Chizuko referred to historical transformations in women's sexual subjectivity in Japan as *nashikuzushi kakumei* (revolution without a spectacle) as a result of women's postponing marriage and sometimes opting out of it (2009, 29–30). This is because feminism, as Saba Mahmood argues, is often understood as a movement to fight against male domination and achieve gender equality (2001, 205). Indeed, the women featured in this chapter were seeking neither gender equality nor freedom from male domination in their use of sexual commerce. Rather, using sexual commerce to revive their womanliness and transform themselves, they reinforced gender difference. Committing to their marriages and families, they maintain the status quo. There seems no overt resistance.

Nonetheless, the lived experiences of married women subtly reveal the affective dimensions of marriage—sexual intimacy, emotional bonds, and self-identity—underneath the patriarchal façade of marriage and consumerism. Middle-aged women's negotiation with their aging femininity and sexless marriages reinforces and also complicates poststructuralist gender politics. Japanese women's practice of womanhood as something one attains, maintains, and must regain, if lost, echoes Judith Butler's (1990) claim that there is no gender before or without *doing* it. Emphasizing gender as a repetitive performance of masculinity and femininity within regulatory heterosexual norms, Butler has theorized the subversive possibility in the doing of gender itself. Nonetheless, as women's accounts in this edited volume illuminate, subversion is not so clear-cut in everyday life. Womanhood is, for example, embodied not only through visible identity politics but also through often-invisible efforts, feelings, and performances. The process is not always congruent. It is messy, paradoxical, and contradictory.

How do we understand the multiple paradoxes that these women live—seeking extramarital intimacy while sticking with marriage, transgressing cultural codes of sexual lust while reinforcing a sense of womanhood, and clinging to youthful femininity while knowing aging is inevitable, to name a few? One approach is to employ a more context-specific feminist analysis of *which* aspects of a particular act are transgressive and normative, and to *whom*. Another method is to see things from the "native's point of view" by examining how they make sense of the discrepancy between their transgressive actions and their normative descriptions. These approaches allow us to trace women's lived experiences of the marriage-and-family institution and produce a grounded theory of gender and sexual politics. And yet another approach I propose is to look into the affective dimensions of the marriage-and-family institution, which is deeply embedded in gender and sex systems but is often invisible (see Davidson, this volume). This approach entails two important tasks: the first is to delve into contradictory aspects of human lives underneath seemingly nonconfrontational movements; the second is to put into question such a presumption that feminism requires resistance, subversion, and dismantlement (Mahmood 2001, 205). Without such a nuanced and reflexive interrogation, our preconceived notions cast analytical limitations on the messy, often contradictory activities at the heart of women's everyday lives.

Affective ethnography demonstrates that Japanese women's use of sexual commerce hinges upon a series of nonconfrontational negotiations and minor changes. I argue that these negotiations and changes should be considered mundane feminist activism. A gender and sexual system is, as Gayle Rubin states, "not a monolithic, omnipotent structure" that one simply subjects oneself to or resists (Rubin 1984, 294). It is, rather, created and re-created within a specific context. As a result, the values and virtues that shape sexual behavior can change. If conventional sexual norms are defined to be heterosexual, marital, monogamous, reproductive, and noncommercial (Rubin 1984, 280), women I introduced in this chapter undermine what counts as "good" and "normal" sex. They do so while secretly engaging in non-monogamous, nonreproductive, and commercial sex with much younger men.

Perfecting their motherhood roles and fulfilling their domestic duties without fail, these women create a smokescreen for their secret pursuit of extramarital relations. By the same token, they play the role of men's favorite "girls" at the host club to finesse their interests. Such maneuvers are an integral part of a negotiation process in which socially marginalized women attempt to improve their living conditions without losing face. Married women's host clubbing reveals their attempts to carve out a narrow path through seemingly confining notions of normal sex and womanhood within the patriarchal marriage-and-family systems.

This kind of unorganized, non-teleological movement does not look like typical goal-oriented feminist activism. Their secretive transgressions may seem a mere side effect of their mundane negotiations to make their lives more vibrant and meaningful. Even so, these negotiations have the potential to bend the normative definition of "good" sex and render compartmentalization a tool through which women might seek more livable lives, rather than it being simply a hallmark of repression. Making extramarital intimacy acceptable as a woman's technology of the self is, I contend, symptomatic of non-teleological feminist activism.

Acknowledgments

My multiyear fieldwork and writing have been supported by the following agents and grants: Wenner-Gren Hunt Postdoctoral Fellowship, SSRC-JSPS (Japan Society for the Promotion of Science), Japan Foundation Doctoral Fellowship, National Science Foundation Ethnographic Research Training, Freeman Student Fellowship for Personalized Learning in Asia, as well as the University of Kansas General Research Grants. I am grateful to Sherrie Tucker for her support and feedback during my revision process. I would also like to thank Joanna Davidson and Dinah Hannaford for their helpful comments.

NOTES

1. All informants' names in this chapter are pseudonyms.
2. The Japan Family Planning Association survey (Kitamura 2015, cited in Tsuji 2018, 1). The number of married couples is based on the 2015 National Census; 635,156 marriage couples are living in Japan (Statistics Bureau of Japan 2015, 4).
3. The marriage contract, Carole Pateman has argued, for example, establishes legitimate access of men to the sexual property of women, that is, men's sexual control over women (Pateman 1988, 168).

10

"What's Wrong with These Mens?"

Reworking Relationships and Finding Foreign Love in the New South Africa

BRADY G'SELL

Zandi was in the midst of a difficult visit home. She had returned to her rural township to tell her parents that while away at university in the city, she had become pregnant. The pregnancy was an issue, but more so the context. Zandi's father had ignored the warnings of his neighbors who said that education in the city only led to trouble. Then there was the issue of the boy. This was not just any boy. Zandi met Toussaint in 2009 while working together at a beachfront restaurant. Their coworkers mistreated him because he was Burundian. In response, Zandi befriended him. To Zandi's relief, her father did not rebuke her for having a relationship with "a foreigner." Instead, he asked that Toussaint offer *inhlawulo*—a payment made by a man to a woman's family to restore honor for impregnating an unmarried woman. Toussaint swiftly agreed, eager to begin marriage negotiations.

The relative ease of her father's acceptance, however, was unusual. During the same visit, an old friend came by to see Zandi. "Hawu!" her friend said, "Are you not scared if this guy can make you pregnant and then leave you with the children and run away to his country?" Her scorn revealed her underlying judgment. Zandi replied quietly, "No, I am not scared of that." Her friend continued to scold Zandi for consorting with unreliable men such as "foreigners from Africa" as they are called. After a pause, Zandi asked her own question:

"Isn't it you have a baby?"

"Yes."

"How old is the baby?"

"Two years."

"And where is the father?" Zandi landed the question pointedly.

THE ANSWER CAME MUCH QUIETER NOW, "I don't know." In the retelling of the interaction, Zandi continued, "[Her] boyfriend stays there, you can see the house where we are sitting," she pointed out an imaginary window, "but he can't come and support [the baby]. . . . [sigh] People they make people pregnant and run away. . . . So if it happened to me, it won't be new. It is what is happening here, even now."

Here Zandi offers a pointed commentary on the landscape of intimate relationships in South Africa today. In the span of a generation, rates of marriage have dropped dramatically to the point that marriage is now the highly prized exception rather than the norm (Budlender and Lund 2011; see also Solway's and Pauli's chapters in this volume for other Southern African examples).[1] Among black Africans, marriages are formalized through *ilobola* (*ilobolo* n.) or bride wealth exchange in addition to other gifts.[2] The collapse of the wage labor system and neoliberal economic restructuring have left many families unable to amass bridewealth resources. Though now quite rare, the symbolic—if not also the economic—import of ilobolo payments and married status remains paramount (Yarbrough 2017). Finding a man who will ilobola is equivalent to winning the social lottery (Hunter 2006). This investment signifies the groom's self-sacrifice and commitment, the social value of the woman, and the good work her family did in raising her. By marrying, women gain the status of moral adult personhood, meet a primary kin obligation as daughter and sister, legitimize future claims to support for herself and her children, and become the envy of their peers. Like Solway's interlocutors in Botswana, the inaccessibility of marriage in South Africa tempers the deep-seated ambivalence many women have about the gendered and generational inequalities that marriage often entails (this volume).[3] In this context, some women are willing to gamble on marriage to a lobolo-paying foreigner.

This chapter draws from my research with women trying to raise children in the context of widespread unemployment and infrequent marriage. As with many of the women featured in this volume, the women I know were wary of the gendered subordination that marriage inevitably brought. However, unlike the women described by Pauli or Medeiros, my interlocutors preferred conjugal hardships to the challenges of single motherhood they experienced (this volume). Though fertility has declined in South Africa, children are cherished (see chapters by Solway and Pauli, this volume). Childbearing outside of marriage is a stigmatized, if ubiquitous practice. A child born without lobolo is seen by elders as a disrespectful detaching of reproduction from its crucial role in upholding kin relations—hence Zandi's father's request that Toussaint pay for the "damages" her pregnancy wrought upon patriarchal authority (Erlank 2004; Rice 2015).[4] Many young couples I know fervently hoped that the relationships that bore extramarital children would eventually become nuptial unions. However, the challenges of poverty and practices of infidelity often lead to separation. Unemployed men who could not ilobola also struggled to send money to support their children overwhelmingly raised by their mothers. Thus, as Zandi notes, the idea that a man could "make you pregnant and then leave you with the children and run away" was not an imagined nightmare, but, for many, a lived reality.

Fed up with what they see as the irresponsibility of South African men and the undesirability of singlehood, some South African women have opted for an unexpected arrangement that affords them many of the benefits of marriage while avoiding some of the institution's most pernicious drawbacks. Here I outline the experience of a small number of South African women who chose to marry African immigrants. The choice to opt into foreign marriages had high stakes. Though the majority of immigrants are from the African continent, relationships between foreign African men and South African women are rare and subject to intense criticism.[5] Thuli, a Zulu-speaking woman also married to a Burundian man, described her initial doubts: "When he asked me out, I was scared of dating foreigners because . . . people used to say terrible things about foreigners, that they are selling drugs or criminals. . . . Local people also say bad things about you when you are dating a foreigner. Things like you are a bitch, you are dirty, you like money, you are a prostitute. So, I was afraid of being seen with him." These everyday forms of discrimination also had violent counterparts. As we are seeing across the globe, in South Africa foreigners have become the scapegoat for the economic and political ills of the country, with everything from crime to a lack of public services blamed on them (Warren 2015). African immigrants are regularly beaten and harassed, their papers torn up, their shops burned, and their communities rounded up for deportation (Amit and Kriger 2014). Spates of xenophobic violence in 2008 and 2015 resulted in injuries and deaths for hundreds of immigrants and those who sought to defend them.

Here I consider why women are willing to tolerate derision and submit their intimate lives to the threats of violence to enter into these binational marriages. I argue that through marriage to an African national, women are opting out of unsatisfactory relationships with local men and opting into unions that offer key nuptial benefits. Through these marriages, women meet many of their kinship obligations to their natal family—the receipt of ilobolo and the legitimacy of their children—and achieve the revered status of married woman. Further, because they are South African citizens and their husbands are undesired others, these women hold forms of power that they can use to mitigate the inequities marriage usually entails. In other words, they can leverage their status as an indigene to reorder gendered expectations to more satisfying ends. These benefits do not erase the discrimination or the insecurity to which these marriages are subject; but for the women I know, such challenges are the price of a reworked union.

Point Partnerships

The group of twenty black South African women whose experiences frame this chapter called themselves the "Muslim Sisterhood," making light of a shared religious commitment that is unusual in the Zulu and Xhosa ethnic groups from which they hail. They married their Burundian and Tanzanian husbands both through customary ilobolo and an Islamic Nikah ceremony and converted to their husband's religion. The Sisters met their husbands because they lived in the unusually heterogenous Point neighborhood of Durban, South Africa's third largest city.

South Africa offers African immigrants not only relative economic and political stability but some of the most progressive asylum laws in the world (Warren 2015). Whereas in other countries refugees are forced into overcrowded camps, in South Africa asylum applicants can live and work anywhere in the country until their refugee status is finalized. Like most immigrants around the world, foreigners in South Africa are often employed in more precarious, lower-paying, and hazardous jobs that locals are unwilling to perform. However, in South Africa, quite unusually, foreigners have a significantly *higher* employment rate than local counterparts (Budlender and Fauvelle-Aymar 2012).[6] This relative economic success gives immigrants a contradictory social position. They occupy low-status jobs but enjoy greater wealth and the prestige of employment (Tafira 2014). Furthermore, foreigner men also choose to use their earnings to formalize marriages, occasionally with South African women.

In their marriages to foreign men, Zulu and Xhosa women held a unique form of power in the conjugal relationship by virtue of their ties to South Africa. Binational unions were often criticized by outsiders as being driven both by women's greed and foreign men's desire for residency status. The privileges of residency were certainly important, however the process of obtaining it took upward of a decade, suggesting other motivations. As citizens, the women had access to state support in the form of child support grants or resources such as food parcels or waivers for school fees. These tempered their otherwise pronounced economic dependence on their husbands. Socially, the women were more secure than their husbands. African immigrants were widely despised and did not have abundant choice in marriage partners or many local allies. Though they had relative economic security, these foreign men were far more socially and politically vulnerable than their wives. That they had found a South African woman willing to marry them was a great privilege of which many of the foreign husbands were well aware. Though women might fear abandonment by foreign men, many had the support of natal kin should they decide to dissolve the relationship and halt his residency application process. Natal kin were less likely to resist such actions because they would not be asked to return bridewealth monies to the husband's kin, as they would in a local union. Further, in the event of marital discord, numerous persons or institutions were ready and willing to assist these women in disciplining an errant man through physical violence, indefinite imprisonment, or deportment. Such positioning allowed these women to shift the gender hierarchies of their marriage more in their favor and forge conjugal relationships imbued with greater respect, economic support, and fidelity.

Disappointing Domestic Couplings

Among Zulu and Xhosa people, marriage marks a critical part of the social transition from adolescence to fully recognized adulthood with the accompanying forms of respect and responsibility (Cook 1931). By creating an *umuzi* or separate household, men become *umnumzana*, the head of household, a man of worth and status, and women become *inkosikazi* (lady/woman/wife) (Hunter 2010).[7] Zulu and Xhosa marriages are patrilocal, and especially in rural areas, women are expected to spend a period of time, *ukukotiza*, proving their value to their in-laws through domestic labor and adherence to *hlonipha* (respect) practices of speech and conduct (Rudwick and Shange 2006).[8] Such periods are arduous and infuse women's relationships with in-laws with tension and mistrust.

Marriage ideals have changed in recent years. Under the migrant labor system, marriage was a "patriarchal bargain" whereby as long as a man remitted sufficiently, women would tolerate his absence and care for children and aging in-laws so both could enjoy marital status (Moodie 1994). In contrast, women now seek a companionate, monogamous marriage that retains normative gender roles of male economic providership and female domestic care but also involves shared decision making (Ashforth 1999; Hunter 2010). As is occurring elsewhere, South African women maintain that marriages centered on romantic love and sexual intimacy have more egalitarian gender relations (Hirsch and Wardlow 2006; Sronk 2009; Thomas and Cole 2009). They seek a softening of gender hierarchies wherein women can expect men to be less sexually—and by extension financially—promiscuous, to assist with household tasks, to spend less time and money drinking with other men, and overall to respect their wives as social equals (Rice 2017; for other parts of Africa, see Spronk 2009 and Smith 2009). However, the lived reality is quite different.

Many black women currently raise children as single mothers or in serial short-term relationships (G'Sell 2020). While marriage remains the desired childbearing context, life without children is pitiable. As Pauli discusses in Namibia, motherhood is mandatory (this volume). Children are valued both for the joy they bring to a household and as a continuation of the family line. Childbearing also enables young people to achieve a qualified adult status more accessible than marriage. However, men are often both physically and financially absent from children's lives.[9] Cohabiting without an initiation of bridewealth is viewed as dishonoring the couple's families and their ancestors by forming an unrecognized union (Posel and Rudwick 2013; Hunter 2016). Black women also do not wish to live with, perform domestic labor for, or financially support an unemployed man who has not demonstrated commitment through ilobola (Posel and Rudwick 2014b).[10] Without ilobolo or an inhlawulo payment, women also cannot claim support from the father's kin. Further, women's disproportionate unemployment levels make them financially dependent on men. Many women and their children end up shifting between living with family, with female friends, or with a string of boyfriends qua aspirational husbands. It is no surprise, then, that the black South African women I know are overwhelmingly disappointed and disillusioned with their domestic partnerships.

Finding Foreign Love and Reworking Gendered Expectations

On a cool but sunny afternoon, I gathered with a group of five women from the self-titled Muslim Sisterhood in the apartment of Zandi and her husband Toussaint. We sat on the floor sipping tea because Zandi's living room furniture had been taken away to be repaired. Such seating arrangements posed no hardship. These now very urban women all came from rural households where sitting on the floor with guests was a regular practice. With the men away hauling furniture, the women were free to enjoy the most spacious front room and the most optimal patches of sunlight that streamed through the windows. The women removed their headscarves, and we unwrapped the babies—my own daughter among them—allowing the children to explore the room and the next welcoming lap. Gossip and tea flowed freely, and quickly the conversation shifted to how the Sisterhood had come to be. Not surprisingly, their stories began with an outpouring of frustration and criticism of the local men they had dated.

Zodwa, frequently the most vocal of the group, loudly exclaimed, "Hey, these *eMzanzi* men are running away from responsibility. They want no strings attached."[11] The circle chorused, "Ehe!" Phindi, threw up her hands in frustration. "I don't know what is wrong with these mens," she said, meaning local men, "how can a man be able to take a plate of food and eat and they don't know what their child is eating?" To eat for oneself is a criticism that cuts to the heart of moral personhood in South Africa. Hoarding resources or stinginess is seen as not only selfish and rude but a refusal to participate in the relationships of support that make one fully human. Phindi saw this selfishness of men as a violation of the sanctity of fatherhood. "You can be responsible and you don't have the money," she said, particularly concerned with her elder daughter's sadness over her father's lack of contact. "At least he should show his children that they have a father."

Their narrations of their own experiences aligned closely with tropes of the absent black father that are widespread in South Africa and are used to justify everything from new crackdowns on child support defaulters to enhanced liquor laws (G'Sell 2016). These portrayals castigate black African men as irresponsible, sexually rapacious, and the cause of the nation's moral degeneracy (Posel 2005). And, indeed, many of the Muslim Sisterhood had friends or family who had children by multiple fathers who did not offer support. They had experienced or seen the emotional pain induced when every refusal of payment was felt as another rejection. They also knew well the anger, frustration, and desperation of mothers trying to keep children fed, clothed, and in school without support. In addition to describing their own experiences, these women also used these discourses of absentee fatherhood to mark a distinction between local, problematic men and their upstanding foreigner husbands.

They argued that their foreign husbands' different orientations to family were a key advantage to these unusual marriages. Thuli was one of the women who had been quite reluctant to date a foreigner out of fear for her reputation. However, her experiences with local men prompted her to reconsider: "The benefit [to marrying a foreigner] is that we are able to stay together as a family. What I saw different about him from other South African mens is that his children always come first. Other South African mens make their children a last priority. With him I know whatever happens his children will always be number one." For Thuli, the lack of support from local men bred discord and forged separation. In contrast, her foreign husband's willingness to financially invest in his marital and parental relationships allowed them to "stay together" both physically and economically. Unlike many South African men, foreign husbands were willing and eager to take on the role of social fatherhood to children born of other men. They did not insist that children by other fathers be sent to natal kin, but instead incorporated them into the household (see also Solway, this volume).

The integrity of the family was also preserved because, as the women explained, their foreign husbands were "clean." This cleanliness stood in opposition to stereotypes both that foreigners physically smelled and that they were morally impure, earning their money through illicit means. Though none of the women were even middle class, they enjoyed unusual economic privilege—such as the ability to not only buy but also repair lounge furniture—that provoked resentful commentary. They were quick to defend their relative prosperity as being the result of their husbands' initiative and work ethic in contrast to local men's laziness and desire for *impilo elula*, an easy life.[12] The Sisterhood defended their husbands' frugality and integrity, noting that they did not drink alcohol or patronize the neighborhood clubs—practices that drew resources and attention away from the family.

Relatedly, women contrasted their husbands' faithfulness with South African men's sexual proclivities. They were concerned on the one hand with affective and sexual loyalty, anxieties heightened by a high HIV infection rate. Also at stake was financial fidelity, arising from the close link between sharing sexual pleasures and exchanging economic resources (G'Sell 2016). If men were with other women, it meant some of their money was going elsewhere. Many women had been in relationships broken up by such conflicts, but, they noted, foreign men were different. "We do fight," Maya said, "but never one day do we fight about a lady. If he is cheating, [laughter] he is doing it so nicely that I can't see anything, ever." Whether due to his social undesirability or discretion, Maya's "clean" husband brought his earnings home.

Such actions, the women argued, showed their foreign husbands' commitment to the relationship and their *inhlonipho*, respect, for their wives. A critical demonstration was their husbands' willingness to honor their wives' family and culture through the payment of inhlawulo and, ultimately, ilobolo. While the exact amounts of these payments, figured symbolically as cows, are negotiated between families, they are purposely sizeable, many times the monthly income of even the most successful of the foreign husbands (Hunter 2010).[13] For example, monthly rent for Zandi's two-bedroom apartment cost about R4500 in 2014. The inhlawulo payment for her first child was R6000. This payment had to be completed before negotiations over ilobolo could begin and the total amount eventually fell in the range of R50,000 to R70,000.[14] Assembling such resources is understood by many women as a test of their husband's character and willingness to meet kin obligations (Hunter 2009b; Yarbrough 2017). This symbolic meaning was only heightened in this binational context.

Foreign men's allocation of money was not simply important economically but was also critical for its indication of emotional commitment. In South Africa, two competing ideologies operate simultaneously in regard to the relationship between love and money (Thomas and Cole 2009). The first envisions love and money as existing in "hostile worlds" wherein the presence of one negates the possibilities of the other (Zelizer 2005). This was evident in Thuli's anxieties about being accused of being a prostitute for dating a foreigner. Her emotional engagement was rendered suspect by the financial gain she enjoyed. In the second paradigm, money or economic support is an important, constitutive part of love. Invoking this, many African women argue that though ilobolo creates barriers to marriage, it is absolutely critical to both the demonstration and creation of love. Unless they paid ilobolo, women claimed, how could they know that men truly loved them and how could they be inspired to reciprocate love (Yarbrough 2017)? Using this second set of logics, the women I know argued that how their foreigner husbands spent money—on bridewealth, on food, on the children—demonstrated the "provider love" they had for their wives and family and brought about greater love from the women in return (Hunter 2009b).

For the women, their husbands' investment in ilobolo was also an indication of the greater equality in their binational marriages. Many of the women spoke of their conversion to Islam as arising both out of personal desire and out of a cultural obligation for women to "follow their husbands." However, their conversion had high stakes. By converting and choosing to wear hijab, the women sacrificed ready recognition of themselves as South African. In Durban, black Muslims were viewed either as foreigners themselves or as South Africans masquerading as Muslims to seek aid, provoking sneers on the sidewalk, remarks from rude shopkeepers, or derisive comments made in Zulu, which of course they understood. An Islamic Nikah ceremony was sufficient to legitimize their marriage in the eyes of the husband and his kin. Yet, these foreign men also goba-ed or bent (ukugoba v. "to bend") to their wives' culture in ways that were unexpected for most men. The men had not only amassed the substantial bridewealth resources but also taken the time and care to bring together uncles and elder South African friends to facilitate the ilobola process. The women I know gained a sense of dignity and community recognition from following cultural expectations (Nilsson 2004; Rudwick and Posel 2015). The ilobolo payment legitimized the union—and the children borne from it—in the eyes of the women's kin and their amadlozi (ancestors). When the women visited home, they were greeted as inkosikazi and their married status was held up as an indication that they had been raised well and had conducted themselves with dignity in their life. Extended family rejoiced that the children had now been incorporated into a paternal line and the whole family would be less vulnerable to punishment from disgruntled *amadlozi*. Due to their noteworthy "bending," the foreign men were frequently, though not always, accepted and welcomed by the wife's family.

The women's use of the term *inhlonipho*, or respect, to describe their foreign husbands reflected an important cultural shift in gendered expectations (Finlayson 2002). *Hlonipho* is a critical concept of Zulu and Xhosa moral personhood (Whooley 1975; Mayer 1972). Historically used to indicate acts of deference that upheld gendered and generational hierarchies, this precolonial concept became linked to specifically female sexual purity through Christian missionary influence (Hunter 2010). As inextricably tied to marriage, *ukuhlonipha* regulates the power dynamics between Zulu women and her affines both in the ilobola process—which marks the transfer of women's guardianship from father to husband—and most prominently in the deferential conduct expected of *umakoti* among her husband and in-laws (Rudwick and Posel 2015). Notably, the Muslim Sisterhood used it to indicate a male commitment to marital equality in both conduct and communication. One woman, Maya, explained, "I went with him because I saw his qualities, the way he treated me. Because in previous relationships that I was in, the people I was with, either they would cheat or did not treat me right. With him I saw that he was not the type that liked women and he respected me. When we had a problem, he knew how to talk with me without fighting me. He knew how to humble himself and apologize." Here, critically, it was men who demonstrated deference and sensitivity and, notably foreign men. Though the idea that inhlonipho should be reciprocal within a marriage is not entirely new, it is widely held that the man, as the one who has paid ilobolo, should be the predominant recipient (Rudwick and Posel 2015). Notably, the women took up codes of conduct befitting a morally upstanding Zulu or Xhosa woman and laminated them onto their foreign husbands. I see this as part of a renegotiation of marital meaning that has taken place more broadly as companionate marriage and spousal choice have been knit together with so-called traditional marriage forms (Hirsch 2003; Hirsch and Wardlow 2006; Thomas and Cole 2009).

Explanations such as the above that explain women's marital choice through appeals to moral ideas such as fidelity, cultural obligation, or respect must also be understood as political acts. The women I know were constantly asked to justify their controversial marriage choice to a host of questioners, myself included. Thus, their answers were well-rehearsed and anticipated the accompanying judgments. Thuli described how her family had responded to her relationship, "They were saying . . . that he wants to marry me because he wants to get an identity document and he wants to stay in the country, or he could just leave me, all those things." Sithembile noted that her motivations were also questioned: "When people hear you are with a foreigner they always assume you with him cause you after his money and also that you had no other choice." Given that the instrumentality of immigrant marriage is viewed as undermining its emotional content, descriptions of honesty, fidelity, and mutual support and respect help legitimize the women's decisions.

Negotiating Natal Kinship and Generational Hierarchies

As with marriages across the African continent, in Zulu and Xhosa marriages the union of the bride and groom is widely understood to begin the process of joining two families, both living and dead (Evans-Pritchard 1931; Steyn and Rip 1968; Ansell 2001; Rudwick and Posel 2014). In their marriage to foreign men, the South African women I know not only reworked gendered hierarchies within their conjugal unit but also renegotiated hierarchical relationships with extended kin. This involved a careful negotiation of what obligations different family members had to one another in a context in which they were separated by not only culture but oftentimes large geographic distance.

In the case of Sithembile, this reworking began early, with an unusually fast ilobolo negotiation. Sithembile spent considerable effort gently guiding her father and uncle as to how to smooth the cross-cultural interaction. Her intended was from Burundi and traveled out to her family home in rural Zululand with only his uncle and an old Zulu man he had befriended to act as familial representatives. Usually, the groom's family would come bearing alcohol, gifts, and a goat to be enjoyed at a feast following the oftentimes multiday negotiation process. In this case, they brought only the goat. The groom had no family in the area, so both the negotiations and the celebration that followed took place in the same day, allowing him to travel back and forth from Durban. The groom would not normally be allowed to be present during negotiations, but in this case, he was able to sit in and act as a translator between his uncle and the Zulu elder who had accompanied them. The back-and-forth bartering that often took place during such negotiation was curtailed in favor of a quick and amicable agreement. Because the groom was Muslim, the celebrations did not involve the traditional Zulu beer. Instead, everyone enjoyed tea, coffee, and soda from the local shop. When the happy couple departed to return to Durban, the goat was still left standing in the yard and the bride's family were left wondering to whom they had just been linked and what their responsibilities were.[15]

Ilobolo negotiations were only the beginning of marital reworking. In Zulu and Xhosa marriages, patrilocality is key to forging durable linkages between families. Even among couples who don't live with the husband's kin, the ukukotiza trial period in early marriage helps transform the umakoti from stranger into recognized kin. However, the migrant marriages were unwittingly matrilocal. "I have never seen most of his family members, but we do communicate through the phone," Sithembile said. "His mother, father and his brothers all stay in Burundi." As a new bride, Sithembile didn't struggle to prove herself to her new family. Not only was she not required to perform labor for her in-laws, she did not live with the fear that her *ilobolo* might need to be returned and that her family would be shamed. Her phone conversations with her husband's family laws were carefully choreographed and dutifully scheduled. But when the call was over, her inhlonipho obligations to them also concluded. Instead, she was mostly free to voice her own opinions in her marital household and could expect that they would be listened to by her husband. In short, as Solway discusses for Tswana women, Muslim Sisters were able to exert more control over their kin ties and the terms for their marriage (this volume).

Though they were rarely his parents, the foreign husbands often had family in South Africa who also impacted the marital relationship. Beyond the requirements of hospitality when these family visited their home, the Muslim Sisters did not have extensive labor obligations to these kin. However, they were important sources of support that could dramatically shape a woman's experience of her marriage. The women's decision to convert to Islam brought new dress requirements, dietary changes, prayer practices, and ritual expectations. Their conversion infused the inevitable conflicts that arise between spouses with new complexity. In these moments, the husband's family could be a critical resource. Sithembile noted, "We visit them often. When there are problems either in my house or their house, we go. We support each other and for me being the only Muslim in my family they are the ones who support me when there are problems, as they understand my religion more than my family." Extended family often served as important mediators in the couple's adjustment to a cross-cultural relationship. All of the women were hit by their husbands, though they did not necessarily call the interaction domestic violence. In the case of Zandi, when she desired to stop such practices, she called on Toussaint's nearby aunt and uncle to intercede. This was all the more important when involving a South African ally could quickly slip into far harsher punishment than the women often desired. In contrast, Zodwa lacked such forms of soft power. Her own family had disowned her due in part to her spousal choice, and she had no affinal kin in South Africa. She felt trapped between the difficult choice of continuing to endure physical violence or losing important economic support for herself and her children.

Reworked relations with in-laws had an inverse effect on women's relationships with natal kin. As described by Pauli and Solway, in other parts of Southern Africa, it is expected that as brides become more integrated into their affinal household, their ties to their natal kin weaken (this volume). Often this weakening is evidenced in married women's inability to care for their aging parents because of their labor obligations to in-laws (Hunter 2016; see also Nelson, this volume). Importantly, the women I know were unfettered by such demands and had not relocated so far away that they could not visit home often. This allowed those women with amicable family relationships to retain close ties to their natal kin. When they did return—to care for sick family members or to help with a household project—their labors were often celebrated and praised as exceptionally caring.

For many of the women, their relationship with their natal kin was counterintuitively strengthened by their marriage. Because they had undertaken ilobola, the women had met a key social and cultural obligation and had smoothed their relationship with the *amadlozi*, ancestors. This created space for the women to build relationships with their own family from the position of an adult woman which translated to both emotional connections and ongoing support, especially with mothers (see Pauli, this volume; Hannaford, this volume). Sithembile, who lived especially close, was able to visit her family every other weekend, taking the children to play with their cousins and allowing her husband to work double shifts. Oftentimes children of the Sisterhood would spend school holidays with their maternal grandparents "on the farm," deepening their relationships with extended family and occasionally affording the marital couple precious time together without the demands of parenting. In part because their natal family was closer attuned to the daily ebbs and flows of their lives, many women received critical support large and small—a new pair of shoes for one of the children, a favorite meal sent home after a visit, or help purchasing a car—that they may not have seen in a local marriage. The in-laws were not present to take issue with the actions of natal kin that might otherwise have been viewed as an overreach or a backhanded criticism. Instead the Muslim Sisterhood could enjoy the social benefits of being a part of a new family without losing their connection to their family of birth.

However, even the closest relationships with women's natal kin were not always smooth. Zodwa was one of three who were effectively disowned. For the others, they went to great lengths to reeducate their families about the new cultural expectations, especially around their conversion to Islam. Zandi long dreaded the conversation about differences in burial rights. For her Xhosa family, it was expected that upon her death, Zandi's body would return home and her extended family would gather to mourn and connect her spirit with the ancestors before burying her near her umbilical cord (Lee 2012). This was at odds with the Islamic practice of same-day burial. Numerous times, Zandi began a conversation about it with her mother over the phone, only to shift to other topics out of fear of hurting this beloved elder. Finally, Toussaint scheduled a visit to Zandi's family on the pretense of talking to her father about a business deal and he broached the topic of how he would be buried, opening a space for Zandi to express her preferences. Though her family was displeased, Zandi was able to draw upon both the Xhosa tradition of a wife adopting the practices of her husband as well as a strong and well-informed relationship with her parents to help facilitate the conversation. Her parents accepted her decision in ways they would have been hard pressed to do when she was still single. The respect that they showed Zandi and Toussaint was in many ways a mirror of the inhlonipho the couple demonstrated through the inhlawulo and ilobola process.

Conclusion

The landscape of intimate relationships in South Africa today affords black African women few satisfying options. Most men can neither afford to begin ilobolo nor regularly support the children they father. Even when marriages do occur, women are well aware that such relationships involve profound power inequities. Married women are expected to perform extensive domestic labor for their husband and in-laws and to consistently defer to their decisions and desires. In addition, obligations to affinal kin often impede desired relationships with natal family or extrafamilial friends.

Like the other women in this volume, a small number of South African women have chosen a different path that enables them to rework the gendered and generational hierarchies often entailed in marriage. The choice to marry a socially reviled foreigner can be understood as a practice of "judicious opportunism"—an adaptive response to the constraints and opportunities of the present moment (Johnson-Hanks 2005, 370; Pauli, this volume). These choices are borne out of political economic histories of settler colonialism, land disenfranchisement, labor migration, and neoliberal economic restructuring that affects both local men's earning potential and foreign men's migration patterns. It is in this context that Zandi can reply to her friend's question, "aren't you scared?" that marrying a foreigner is no more terrifying than current circumstances and, just possibly, more beneficial. The women of the Muslim Sisterhood took that chance.

The South African women I know have desires that mirror many of those detailed across this volume: to be mothers, to maintain relationships with natal family and female friends, and to have intimate relationships in which their ideas and desires have weight. Many in this volume were able to pursue these because of relative economic security. The case of the Muslim Sisterhood offers an example of leveraging a notably different form of privilege. While they remain deeply economically dependent on the men in their lives, these women had stronger social and political ties to South Africa. Amid pervasive xenophobia, their foreign husbands relied on their wives to access state resources and to tether the family to the nation. Women could wield some of this power, though not totalizing, to shape the terms of conduct within their relationship to be more in line with the companionate ideal they desired. At the same time, their marriage to a foreigner and conversion to Islam also ostracized them from many local friends and family. For the Muslim Sisterhood, this made the group's female friendships all the more important. These are particularities in what this volume reveals is a far larger phenomenon of women making judicious use of the options available to them to negotiate more fulfilling lives inside, outside, and sometimes in spite of marriage.

NOTES

1. The processual nature of black African marriages complicates statistical measurements of marriage rates, so scholars often couple census data with qualitative data (Hosegood, McGrath, and Moultrie 2009; Posel and Rudwick 2014b).

2. South African racial terminology is complex, and terms such as "black" have referred to varying groups of people at different historical periods. I use the terms "African" and "black African" to refer to those people who identify themselves as culturally belonging to an indigenous ethnic group and whose lineage, language usage, and/or phenotype lead others to assume they would be members of one of those groups. I do not capitalize the term black because the particular history of the term in South Africa does not imbue capitalization with antiracist politics as it does in, say, the United States.

3. Among black African women, there have long been those who have rejected the institution of marriage altogether, often citing a dislike of conjugal gender inequities (Ndinda et al. 2007; Preston-Whyte 1981; Preston-Whyte and Zondi 1989), though for most black women, marriage is highly valued (Rudwick and Posel 2015).

4. The stigma against unwed parenthood did not center on sex per se. Historically, vigorous, yet discreet, engagement in sex was encouraged among many black South Africans as long as it did not result in children (e.g., Mayer 1972). Nonreproductive sexuality was historically sustained through nonpenetrative practices such as *ukuhlobongo* or "thigh sex" in isiZulu *ukumetsha* in isiXhosa (Hunter 2010). However, missionaries' condemnation of such practices led to an increase in extramarital childbearing (Delius and Glaser 2002).

5. The 2011 census found that 2,199,871 documented immigrants were living in South Africa, with 71 percent of those from the African continent (Statistics South Africa 2012; UNHCR 2012). An exact number of undocumented immigrants is not known, but a conservative estimate is 500,000 in 2011 (Warren 2015).

6. This statistic is all the more surprising because it accounts for features of "immigrant advantage." Budlender and Fauvelle-Aymar found that "a foreign-born migrant with the same age, gender, and level of education, belonging to the same population group and residing in the same place as a South African, has a higher probability of being employed than a South African non-migrant. In most developed countries where data are available, the rate of employment for foreign-born migrants is significantly lower than for local workers" (2012).

7. Although married women enjoy heightened status relative to their unmarried counterparts, this does not, at least in the early years of marriage, result in greater freedom or autonomy (Hunter 1936/1961). Whereas unmarried women can often move about a village freely or dip in and out of their chores, young wives are expected to stay close to the *umuzi* and continue their labors until released by a superior.

8. *Ukuhlonoipha* involves both the linguistic avoidance of certain terms and refraining from voicing one's opinions as well as behavioral prescriptions such as the wearing of long dresses instead of pants or not crossing a path in front of an elder. Though practices have changed over time, ukuhlonoipha has remained remarkably culturally salient (Fandrych 2012).

9. In 2012, 69 percent of black children lived without their fathers (Hall, Meintjes, and Sambu 2014).

10. The payment of some portion of ilobolo offers the couple distinct social legitimization that is neither that of marriage or illegitimate cohabitation (Hunter 2016).

11. A Zulu term that literally translates to "in the South," *eMzanzi* colloquially refers to South Africa in general.

12. Discourses about black African men as lazy or "work shy" feature in the (written) archives since the early nineteenth century, often deployed by white settlers to criticize the refusal of black African laborers to submit to Eurocentric labor logics. Over the intervening century and a half these discourses have been mobilized to argue for changes in welfare, housing policy, segregation, and many other policies preserving the racial hierarchy (Atkins 1993; Tallie 2019).

13. Ilobola predates colonialism, however the currently accepted value of the equivalent of ten cows (and an eleventh for the bride's mother) derives from an early colonial law seeking to make marriage more accessible to families without large herds (Sheik 2014). There is no official cash equivalent for a cow, but negotiated amounts are frequently quite high and out of reach for most men (Yarbrough 2015). While many families

acknowledge that higher ilobolo costs are a barrier formalizing marriage, they resist lowering the cash-to-cow equivalent (Hunter 2016). Instead, some families will accept a lesser number of higher-priced cows as initial ilobola to partially legitimize the union.

14. This bridewealth payment is not unidirectional but part of a many-year exchange between the families (Comaroff 1980; Hunter 2016). However, in this context where the husband's extended family were from a different culture and resided in another country, the exchange between the extended kin was less robust.

15. For example, following the ilobolo negotiation, the bride's family is responsible for hosting an *umbordo* ceremony, which involves buying extensive gifts, mostly bulk food, for the entire family of the groom as well as special recognitions for the *abakhongi* (roughly the *ilobolo* negotiators) and their immediate family (Rudwick and Posel 2015). Many families of the Muslim Sisters had tremendous anxiety that migrant marriage provided no clear means to reciprocate ilobolo and solidify their bonds with the groom's family.

11

The Appeal of Absent Husbands in Contemporary Senegal

DINAH HANNAFORD

A Senegalese proverb states that it is easy to say you have a camel in Mauritania ("am naa gëléem ca Gánaar yomb na wax"). For someone in Senegal, claiming to have a camel in Mauritania offers the chance to partake in the prestige and bragging rights of owning a camel without necessarily having to purchase, feed, house—or even groom—the status object. For who would be able to verify this claim?

For women in Senegal, a husband abroad is also a status object. Marriage is a critical rite of passage for achieving Senegalese adulthood. As Muslims, Senegalese believe marriage is a "divine directive" (Dial 2008, 42) and women in particular are eager to marry and have children as a means of honoring God and fulfilling their gendered duty. For women, there is an urgency around marriage as the event that can determine their individual and social destiny (Nanitelamio 1995, 278). This marital imperative can be illustrated by another Wolof proverb, which claims that "a bad husband is better than a good boyfriend" ("jekker ju bonn moo gënn faar bu baax"), emphasizing the indispensability of marriage itself above other considerations such as compatibility or even a partner's virtuousness (see Hannaford and Foley 2015).

Women in Senegal desire the status of being married. This is not to say, however, that they anticipate enjoying married life. For all its prestige and status, women look upon marriage with considerable trepidation. Marriage in Senegal is not expected to be a pleasurable experience for women, but rather a long test of a woman's ability to stoically endure whatever obstacles she encounters. Though the expectation remains that a good husband will single-handedly provide for all the household expenses, will clothe and house his wife, pay for his children's education and basic needs (Bop 1995), the reality is that more and more women take on a central role in the financing of their families (Dial 2008, 181). In the contemporary economic climate in which women are able and obligated to take on many of the traditionally male duties of marriage, particularly the financial duties, their own domestic, affective and sexual responsibilities as wives have not waned. As in so many other geographic contexts in this edited volume, the lived reality of marriage and the gendered balance of power it entails is largely unappealing to many contemporary Senegalese women. Unlike some of these other contexts, however, there is no model of socially acceptable singledom or single motherhood in this devoutly Muslim West African country.

In this chapter, I draw from my research on transnational marriages, where women in Senegal marry Senegalese migrant men who live overseas. I have previously documented that women in Senegal are marrying Senegalese migrant men because of the social status migration confers and because they think migrants are more likely to be good providers than nonmigrant men (Hannaford 2017). Here I argue that marriage to a migrant husband has additional advantages. Marriage to an absent husband can mean access to the status of wifehood—and indeed, an enhanced status as the wife of a presumably successful migrant—without taking on all the emotional, sexual, and domestic labor of daily cohabitation with a husband. In other words, migrants' wives are able to ascend to the next stage of life as a married woman, without all of what makes married life for women in Senegal a bit of a slog. Importantly, as the case studies below make clear, an absent husband can mean that Senegalese women stay more closely connected with their natal kin, whose support is far more reliable and trustworthy. As I argue below, the absence of a husband need not represent an affective lack, as it is generally intimate relationships with natal kin and female friends that fortify and sustain Senegalese women.

Wives of Distant Husbands

The fundamental understanding of marriage in Senegal, especially for women, is that it is difficult, and something to be endured, not enjoyed. Nevertheless, it remains imperative for women to marry and perform their wifely duties assiduously. In the case studies that follow, we see women who have opted to marry migrants who reside abroad. These women's transnational marriages have allowed them to attain the status of a married woman and become mothers while escaping some of the most demanding aspects of having a husband, by not cohabitating with them. Though many migrants' wives I interviewed found married life to be a difficult trial for reasons both common to all Senegalese marriage and explicitly related to marriage to a migrant (see Hannaford 2015 for examples), women who did not live with their husbands, in-laws, or cowives expressed a great deal more satisfaction in their daily life. Furthermore, as I show below, the absence of their husbands has allowed these women to maintain closer ties to natal kin. I argue that it is female friendship and the emotional and fiscal support of natal kin that anchor the affective foundation of their lives.

Daba

Daba sat happily bouncing her baby in her lap while I chatted with her sister and her aunt about their marriages to migrants.[1] Daba's apartment in the lower-class Dakar neighborhood of Fass had high ceilings and white walls that made it feel spacious and bright. It also had all the trimmings of a successful overseas migrant's home—a fancy television, speakers, a DVD player with more remotes than she knew how to use. There were two large, framed portraits of Daba on the wall, as well as a framed photograph of her with her husband, and the obligatory portrait of Serigne Touba (Cheikh Amadou Bamba), the religious leader of the Mourides, an Islamic brotherhood in Senegal. A large, gold Eiffel Tower statue sat on the glass coffee table, and next to the television stood an impressive-looking bassinet.

Absent husbands and long-distance marriage have become increasingly commonplace arrangements for couples in Senegal. In my research on transnational marriage from 2004 to 2011 in France and Italy among Senegalese migrants and in Senegal among migrants' wives, I found that many married couples opted to live separately, for reasons that spanned from financial to logistical, legal, and emotional.[2] For over forty years, migrants have played an increasingly important role in Senegalese society on national, local, and domestic levels. The World Bank reported in 2018 that 4 percent of Senegalese are officially registered as living abroad (World Bank 2018), though this number—like others[3]—is likely an underestimate, due to the complicated nature of collecting data from a transnational group of migrants whose size and shape fluctuate constantly. Estimates state that nearly half of the diaspora resides in Europe, with the other half primarily living elsewhere in Africa (MEFP 2017).

Remittances from overseas represent nearly 14 percent of Senegalese GDP (World Bank 2017), putting Senegal fifth in sub-Saharan Africa in percentage of GDP from remittances (Uzelac 2018, 3). Not only have these remittances transformed the Senegalese landscape through construction of new homes, schools, mosques, and health centers, but they have profoundly shaped the political and social landscapes of Senegal as well, upsetting older strictures of social order such as socioeconomic status, education, and caste.

In contemporary Senegal, migrants occupy a particular place of privilege in the social landscape due to Senegal's culture of migration. Migration in Senegal is "deeply ingrained into the repertoire of people's behaviors, and values associated with migration [have] become part of the community's values" (Massey et al. 1993, 452–453). International mobility itself is imbued with prestige in Senegal. This culture of migration not only encourages international mobility as a pathway to success and social status but also profoundly shapes the ambitions and behaviors of those who never leave Senegal. In a context where fulfilling masculine goals at home is no longer attainable for most men in Senegal, these ideas have profoundly altered understandings of class, prestige, and gendered value.

In Senegal, men are migrating to fulfill gendered ideals of masculinity including becoming husbands and household heads. The effects of currency devaluation, rising unemployment, and agricultural decline have combined to make providing adequately for a family unmanageable for most Senegalese men. Nonmigrant men from middle-class families find it difficult to compete with those living overseas who seem to be a safer bet for a stable financial future for women also navigating economic hardship and social pressure to marry. Men like Daba's husband, a trader who lives mostly in Switzerland, are desirable husbands.

Three weeks earlier, twenty-two-year-old Daba had given birth to her first baby, a girl. Her husband, who had returned for the birth, came in and out a few times over the course of my daylong visit to Daba's house, but mostly was out with his backpack, "doing business" ahead of his upcoming return to Switzerland. Daba's pregnant sister was visiting Daba for an undetermined amount of time, claiming to be sick but really escaping problems with her mother-in-law, she confided. Daba's aunt, who was struggling to maintain the family with disappointing remittances from her husband in Portugal, was clearly a frequent visitor to Daba's home as well. Though those two women told of the hardships of marriage to a migrant, Daba herself seemed largely content with her situation. She told me that she was "lucky" her husband's parents were dead and he had few siblings, so she rarely had to deal with her in-laws and was able to live alone in the apartment and not be beholden to anyone most of the time.

Later in the day, two of Daba's friends also came over and joined us to talk about their marriages to migrant husbands, living in France and Spain. The conversation evolved naturally over the course of a pleasant afternoon, spent mostly piled onto a mattress in the back bedroom of the apartment, punctuated by a late afternoon lunch of rice and fish eaten out of a common bowl. We chatted about wigs and clothes, skin lighteners, pregnancy, baptism parties, a local celebrity who had recently been arrested. We discussed characters in television programs and gossiped about people in the neighborhood.

This kind of gathering in Daba's house was a normal occurrence for her, and in general Daba seemed to relish playing hostess in her own space as mistress of the household. Though she is not mean-spirited, she is clearly pleased with her situation and is well aware of the envy of her friends and relatives. Moreover, it seemed that marriage to a migrant was commonplace among her friends and family and afforded membership into a kind of club. Each of these women enjoyed the solidarity of insider knowledge about the hardships and particularities of life as a migrant's wife.

I have spent many an afternoon or evening piled onto a bed full of Senegalese women, be they friends or family members. At family ceremonies like weddings and baptisms or holidays like Eid, or even just on lazy days, it is not unusual to end up in a woman's bedroom, where there is usually no other seating than a mattress or a mat on the floor. Though I also have spent much time as a guest in Senegalese living rooms, usually with the television on, I have equally as often been invited back to be with the women of the house in a bedroom. I have had my hair braided in such a setting; drunk endless cups of sugary tea or homemade juices out of communal glasses drained, refilled, and passed to the next woman; snacked on grilled peanuts, fresh beignets, or juicy mango that I tried not to drip onto the sheets. I have been advised about love, sex, marriage, childbearing, and child care in these bedrooms; gossiped about neighbors and cousins; tried on wigs and clothes and earrings; given and received gifts of cloth, jewelry, incense, and perfume. Many of my research interviews also took place on beds, as this is a setting where women's intimate confessions to one another and moments of friendship and connection take place.

Senegal is primarily a homosocial society, and women spend most of the day in the company of other women. Much of married life is about women relating to other women. This is why so many of my interlocuters, when asked about their marriages, told stories of their cowives, sisters-in-law, and mothers-in-law. Many of these women had suffered at the hands of these other women; others counted themselves lucky in marriage because of the generosity, kindness, or absence of these women who were so central to their marriages.

One of the most famous Senegalese novels about marriage, Mariama Bâ's *So Long a Letter*, can also be read as a testament to the centrality of female friendship to the lives of married Senegalese women. The epistolary novel is one woman's long letter to her friend detailing her struggles as her husband marries a second wife. Though critics and scholars often read this book as being more of a diary entry than a piece of a dialogue between two old friends, Ann McElaney-Johnson (1999) points out that to do so is to miss a crucial theme of the book: the powerful and healing bond of female friendship. The narrator, Ramatoulaye, recounts her experiences of marriage to her friend Aïssatou because she knows that Aïssatou has had similar struggles in marriage. Just like Daba and her friends and female relatives, Ramatoulaye counts on solidarity from her friend to allay her pain and strengthen her resilience as she navigates the rocky road of marriage. In several passages, Ramatoulaye explicitly elevates her bond with her friend above the kind of intimacy of romantic love:

> L'amitié a des grandeurs inconnues de l'amour. Elle se fortifie dans les difficultés, alors que les contraintes massacrent l'amour. Elle résiste au temps, qui lasse et désunit les couples. Elle a des élévations inconnues de l'amour. (Bâ 1979, 79)

> Friendship has splendors that loves knows not. It grows stronger when crossed, whereas obstacles kill love. Friendship resists time, which wearies and severs couples. It has heights unknown to love. (Bâ 1981, 54)

This Senegalese love letter to female friendship captures a reality that is often overlooked in an anthropological focus on marriage. Friendship has not received the kind of analytical attention it deserves as one of the key enduring, orienting relationships of women's lives (see also Freeman, this volume).[4] For women like

Daba, friends represented a key encouragement to marry a migrant, a source of support, solidarity, and comfort in her ups and downs in marriage, and a well of companionship and intimacy in her separation from her overseas husband.

Though most migrants' wives I interviewed would report dutifully that they missed their husbands in the most perfunctory of terms, only a few talked of their intimate emotional connection to their husbands and a kind of complicity they enjoyed with their husband. The majority did not look to their husbands for companionship, in their visits or in their absence. Like wives of nonmigrants, their daily lives were much more likely to revolve around other women. The absence of a husband does not necessarily mean loneliness, as kin and female friends naturally take up that affective and companionate space in their lives (see Pauli, this volume).

Maty

In a more middle-class neighborhood not far from Daba, I visited thirty-six-year-old Maty in her multistory family home whose exterior is covered with attractive blue tile. Maty, like Daba, met her husband Seydou when he was home on a visit from Europe, in his case Germany. Her younger sister's husband, also a migrant, had known Seydou and introduced him to Maty. Twelve years her senior, Seydou already had a German first wife and a child with whom he lived overseas. Polygyny is sanctioned by the Senegalese interpretation of Islam as well as by Senegalese law. It is a sign of wealth and status to have multiple wives, and this is true across class contexts in Senegal—for university professors, ministers of parliament, farmers, and tailors. Unlike in other Muslim contexts, in Senegal there is no clear sign that the practice is on the decline.[5]

In fact, there are multiple reasons why polygamy is strategically advantageous for migrants. Roughly a third of my female interviewees were part of polygamous marriages. There are several ways that migrants practice transnational polygamy. Some migrants, like Seydou, have wives in the host country (either Senegalese or host country nationals) as well as at home in Senegal. Others have multiple wives in Senegal, who may or may not cohabitate. It is not unusual for a migrant man to have one wife in the rural area of his origin, perhaps a relative,[6] as well as a wife in Dakar whom he met and wooed on a visit home.

As is often the case with the European and American wives of Senegalese migrants, Seydou's first wife was not aware that she was in a polygynous marriage. Though she had talked to Maty on the phone many times with perfunctory greetings, she did not know that Seydou had been married to Maty for ten years and that the couple had two children together. She believed she was talking to Seydou's sister.

Maty, however, had different expectations for sexual and emotional exclusivity. She not only knew she was marrying a man who was already married, she had grown up in a society in which polygynous marriages are common. In Senegal, there is already a model for a husband who does not spend all his time with his wife. There is a banality to a married woman who sleeps alone (or, more realistically in most Senegalese households, with her children) for part of the time, as the Islamic directive cited by Senegalese Muslims is that cowives in polygynous marriages must have an equal number of nights with their husband. In a village setting, this means that each wife has her own dwelling on a family compound, and the husband divides his time between these separate dwellings, with no room of his own. In an urban setting, this can mean separate bedrooms in the same apartment or home, or separate homes altogether. Although there are well-documented tensions and challenges in polygynous unions (see Kringelbach 2016), there are also advantages for women. One of the key advantages is the division of the domestic and reproductive labor (see Nanitelamio 1995, 280).

As for Maty, her share of the sexual and domestic labor for her husband is far from equal to that of his first wife. Seydou is able to visit Maty only for three weeks a year. Maty's in-laws live in the region of Louga, in the village of her husband's birth many hours from Dakar, but Maty lives in her mother's home in her natal city of Dakar. I asked if her husband ever expected her to join his family, to *seeyi*, as is the custom upon marriage in patrilocal Senegal, but Maty exclaimed that she refused. "They don't even have electricity there. It's a village." Several women I interviewed were compelled by their husbands and family pressure to leave Dakar to join in-laws in the village, and most resented and suffered much from this arrangement. Women who lived in homes with their own kin, like Maty, or alone with their own children, like Daba, were much more content with their situation.

Maty says she is disappointed in her marriage. She feels her husband's remittances are paltry, especially to support his two children. Maty blames her husband's wife for monopolizing all his money. She was told by Seydou that his German wife routinely empties their joint bank account after his payday, so her husband has nothing to send. Maty complains that when Seydou comes for his three-week visit each year he comes emptyhanded, with no gifts to give her. He sends his own family in the village money only occasionally, and Maty laments that they call her to complain, thinking she must be receiving all his riches. She chafes at this assumption, and it only adds to her conviction that her husband is a disappointment.

Nevertheless, despite this disillusionment, Maty leads a comfortable, middle-class Dakar lifestyle and is generally happy in her daily life. This is because she is well taken care of by her natal kin, especially her migrant sisters. Her family counts many migrants among its members, including her five siblings who reside in the United States, France, and Italy. Though her husband's remittances are disappointing, Maty never worries about a roof over her children's heads or where her meals will come from because she lives with her mother who is well taken care of by Maty's migrant siblings. She has help with housework and child care from paid domestic workers hired by her siblings. Maty's sisters pay for private school fees for her children as well as all the related expenses of new uniforms, supplies, and transportation to and from school, and for her and her children's health care expenses.

Remittances from migrant husbands rarely live up to expectations, and many migrants' wives told me that their natal families were supporting them in the absence of sufficient maintenance from their husbands. They cited siblings and parents who provided cash for household expenses, medications, and school fees. Several said that they, like Daba's sister, went home to their parents or to their siblings when they were suffering from an illness, certain they would find better care and solace with their own kin. Several also spoke of clothing and gifts from their family members working abroad that helped them maintain the appearance of being well provided for by their migrant husbands. This allowed them to embody the much-valued Senegalese virtues of *sutura* (discretion) and *sagou* (keeping up appearances and hiding unpleasantness from others), thereby protecting their husbands' and their own reputation and honor.

Maty is at ease in her mother's spacious and well-appointed house. She is able to visit friends in the neighborhood, participate in family social life and outings, and live freely, all with the solid status of a mother and a wife. Though she is frustrated at Seydou's failure to fulfill his obligations as a husband—particularly in providing financially for her and her children—her obligations as a wife are rather minimal. She has little contact with her in-laws, and she does not cook for or cater to her husband outside of his yearly visit. Instead she enjoys the financial support of her siblings, the company of her own mother, with whom she is quite close, and the security of knowing that her natal kin will always have her back.

Marriage as a Test of Endurance

One of the most important virtues in a Senegalese woman, but particularly a wife, is that she be able to *muuñ*, to be patient, to suffer, and to endure. Muuñ reflects a strong religious conviction; faith in Allah and his superior knowledge should allow you to be able to withstand whatever trials He puts you through. A woman's ability to muuñ is essential to the longevity of her marriage (see Hannaford and Foley 2015), as marriage for women is expected to be a grueling, punishing test of their strength and resilience. A good wife must remain patient, stoic, and uncomplaining as she endures the hardships of married life.

The hardships of traditional Senegalese married life include serving a husband in a self-sacrificing way. Senegalese wives are supposed to *toppatoo* (take care) of their husbands, anticipating all of their needs and making them feel catered to and adored. This is done through several means, including the domestic art of *mokk pooj*, a practice of seduction involving incense, suggestive jewelry, and sexual technique (see Gilbert 2019).

As scholars of Senegalese gender and sexuality have noted, mokk pooj is a complicated power negotiation as well, where women at once attempt to curry favor and gain influence with their husbands as well as demonstrate their ultimate docility and submissiveness to their husbands (Buggenhagen 2012, 112; Gilbert 2019; Hannaford 2017, chap. 5). Keeping a husband happy in bed is a constant preoccupation and source of pride among women in Senegal,[7] as important a wifely duty as housework or childbearing (Dial 2008, 81). Though raising children is an important feminine obligation, being your husband's champion and caretaker is even more strongly emphasized. In fact, being an attentive wife is a part of raising your children, as potential grooms look to the mothers of their brides to understand what kind of wife she will be. Not being a notoriously obliging and indulgent wife can have negative consequences for your daughters' marital prospects.

Housework and childrearing are, as elsewhere, no small feat: carrying babies on backs, washing laundry by hand, arching at the back to scrub floors, spending all day preparing the daily meals. Even though many households in Dakar employ maids or laundresses, usually rural migrant women for extremely low wages, turnover is quite frequent as the hired help quit or return to the village (Gassama 2005), so wives of the household generally do much housework and cooking either way.

Professional Senegalese women, even at the highest levels, say that though they do employ maids, they still cook dinner for and cater to their husbands instead of letting the maid take on this work. In Senegalese marital life, there is a close connection between food and sexuality. The nightly meal is seen as the beginning of the night's activities, the first in the series of her working to please him.[8] If a wife is angry at her husband, she will not cook for him, and if he is angry with her, he will not eat her cooking (Gueye 2010, 70). To toppatoo your husband means cooking his favorite dishes just the way he likes them. Wives who don't do this kind of caring labor for their husbands attentively and solicitously are said to not be *jongee*, to lack feminine skill and winsomeness.

The hit Senegalese television show *Mistress of a Married Man*, created by Kalista Sy, lays out the thanklessness of wifehood for the modern Senegalese woman explicitly. The character of Djalika embodies the punishing sacrifices of the middle-class working wife in particular. In her first scene of the first episode of the series, we meet Djalika in the chaos of her typical morning. She is struggling to get out of the house to make it to work on time. Beautifully dressed, coiffed, and made up, she rushes to feed and pack up her preschool-aged child, soothe her crying infant, and find her work laptop. When her maid calls in to say she won't be showing up, Djalika must scramble to arrange alternate care for the baby. She finally makes it out of the house and into the car with her daughters, only to find that her husband Biram—a philandering drunk who has slept soundly through her morning crisis—has left the gas tank empty in her car.

Later during a challenging day of work in which she must cover for a negligent colleague, we see Djalika call Biram, waking him although it is midday, and ask him to heat up the full lunch that she had prepared the night before for his mother, as the maid will not be there. "My mother does not eat warmed up left overs," he tells her sharply and coldly. Catering and ministering to a husband's mother is another critical element of being a good Senegalese wife. Senior women depend on the domestic labor of their daughters or daughters-in-law, and there is great moral value placed on rendering this service—or, perhaps more accurately, there is great shame and derision for those who do not fulfill it (see Gning 2017). Djalika then offers to have takeout delivered to the home, and Biram protests angrily that he doesn't have a single penny to pay a delivery man. Djalika says she will pay for everything. Biram hangs up on her as she begins to admonish him for not at least warning her that he'd left the car with no fuel.

In a later episode, we watch Djalika come home from a long day of work, clean up the home, make the bed, put away the clothes and shoes Biram has strewn about, sweep and wash the tiled floor, and begin cooking a meal for her husband and mother-in-law. Biram does not return for the dinner of *firi* (fried fish with onion sauce, salad, and French fries) that she has painstakingly prepared and laid out, and her mother-in-law refuses to eat because the dinner is served too late for her to digest before bed. The mother-in-law's cold disapproval is like a slap in the face to the exhausted Djalika, who politely nods with tears in her eyes and wishes her mother-in-law a good night, then puts her children to bed and goes out to the courtyard to scrub the laundry by hand with soap and buckets of water. Meanwhile, we see her husband enjoying cocktails with a female companion at a hotel bar. When Biram finally comes home in the middle of the night, drunk, he wakes Djalika to heat up his dinner, despite her half-hearted protests that she must wake up at five o'clock to be at work on time.

The audience comments on the Marodi TV Sénégal video of the episode are full of discussion about Djalika and her moral virtue. Male and female commenters—primarily Senegalese, judging by their handles—discuss Djalika's ability to muñ, some praising her ("une femme exemplaire!"), others arguing that there must be limits to how much a woman should take. Many ostensibly female commenters offer solidarity: "seuyou Senegal métina" (Senegalese marriage is hard), one commented. "There is nothing harder," another chimed in. "*Walaay*, it's the reality. If you haven't lived it, you don't know. It's so hard." A third wrote a lengthy post that both confirmed the reality of experiences like Djalika's but also encouraged others in her situation to continue to remain in their marriages and endure: "What Djalika is living, so many women live it in silence out of respect for their marriage which is sacred . . . *Muñ* for your children, God will repay you."

In my interviews with married Senegalese women, I heard many tell similar tales of woe to that of Djalika. Women spoke of feeling overwhelmed by their domestic duties, unappreciated by spouses and in-laws, and occasionally of bullying and even abuse at the hands of their in-laws or cowives.

Senegalese society is patrilocal—a husband and wife living together in a mother-in-law's home is an important stage of married life.[9] In this seeyi period, dreaded by and expected of most married women at some point in their marriage and lasting anywhere from months to the duration of the marriage, the bride must demonstrate that she is virtuous, obedient, modest, and pious. Not only must daughters-in-law perform domestic labor, be respectful at all times, and do their mothers-in-law's bidding, but they are also under constant scrutiny by everyone in the household. Seeyi is not meant to be easy, and a wife's role is to muuñ (to be patient, uncomplaining, and stoic) and to please her in-laws no matter the personal cost (Gueye 2010, 81). A wife must not only please her husband through her physical and domestic attentions, but also please his mother and female relatives through her domestic service, which ranges from cooking and cleaning to laundry and care for the children of others in the home. Working women are not exempted from these duties, and though they can often use their income to pay other women for some of the domestic labor, they find themselves torn between their work outside and inside of the home (see Adjamagbo, Antoine, and Dial 2004; Gning 2017).

The social pressure to endure and to perform all wifely tasks persists despite the changing realities of marriage in this economic era in which the responsibilities of a husband are in practice much reduced. Though a husband traditionally is saddled with the full weight of economic support for his family (Diop 1985), many more Senegalese women are, like Djalika, joining the formal and informal workplace, paying for their household expenses and the care and schooling of their children, not to mention their own clothing and beauty supplies (Beguy 2009, 98). Promising local men who are ready and able to shoulder the burden of being providers and family heads are few and far between (see Hannaford and Foley 2015).

The Appeal of Absent Husbands

This is one reason why women in Senegal opt to marry migrants, hoping that migration will make them good providers. Like being a migrant, marrying a migrant often disappoints financially (as in the case of Maty), in part because the expectations are so unrealistic, yet these expectations persist and continue to motivate marriage to migrants. The prestige of marrying a migrant, complicated though it is with concomitant expectations of the wife's ability to give and loan generously, also entices many to marry men abroad.

Here I highlight another advantage of having a husband who lives overseas, and that is his very absence. Migrants' wives would sometimes describe the excitement of their husbands' visits home in ways that showed the novelty of the experience. One twenty-year-old woman who had been married only one year and had yet to see her husband since the wedding shyly patted her new satin sheets that reeked of *thiouraye*, the perfumed incense Senegalese women use as one of their weapons of sexual seduction, and told us she was preparing for his first visit later that month, to uproarious laughter from the other women present. Another, older woman said that when her husband comes home for his yearly three-week visit, they get dressed up and go out on the town, eat in restaurants, and go hear live music. Her husband's visits are like a holiday. She works hard to cook his favorite dishes and shower him with love and attention. But then he goes back to Italy, and she goes back to concentrating on her children, her friends, and her own entrepreneurial activities.

Several women said they encourage their husband not to come home for too many visits, so that he may save that money for things like homebuilding projects instead. One woman complained that when her husband comes home it is exhausting and stressful because of all the extended family visitors who descend unannounced upon their household, and she finds herself just wishing he'd leave again.

A friend named Anta who accompanied me on a number of my interviews with migrants' wives had a mixed reaction to hearing their stories. Anta's husband was not a migrant, and she noted how her life differed from the women we spoke to. She said sometimes she thought, "These migrants' wives have it really good and easy. There is no one around to make meals for, no one ordering you around, watching your every move." Anta, who married at nineteen, was twenty-five years old at the time of the interviews and saddled with three young children, a difficult living situation with her in-laws, and a serially disappointing husband who got the couple into all kinds of embarrassing misadventures and a good deal of debt. Anta argued regularly about birth control with her husband and even went as far as to get a birth control implant without his permission so as to avoid having additional children while the other three were young. She eventually had it removed on his insistence and soon after our interviews bore twins. Women whose husbands lived overseas naturally had fewer children than the average Senegalese women. The fertility rate for Senegal during my interviews in 2011 was 5.04, whereas the average among my fifty-one migrants' wives was 1.90. Of course, in a culture where childbearing is a significant mark of status for women, the women who had not been able to have children at all because of their husbands' absence felt this lack as a great sorrow or shame. For those who had one to three children, their fertility limited but not impeded altogether by their husbands' visits, the number of mouths to feed remained more manageable.

Of course, Anta and I both knew from our interviews that *jabaru immigrés* often have a tough time: not enough money to make ends meet, jealous husbands and remittance-hungry relatives, in-laws watching their every move and treating them like Cinderella. But she could mostly relate to their struggles with in-laws, dealing with pains of childbirth, fears about cowives, family pressure, and so on. Where she felt envious or wistful was in evaluating what made jabaru immigrés situations unique—their absent husbands.

Again, though women would dutifully and automatically answer my questions about missing their husbands in the affirmative, their descriptions of their affective lives showed that their natal kin and female friends and even children filled the affective void (see parallels in Medeiros's and Freeman's chapters in this volume). Polygyny and homosociality mean that Senegalese husbands are not necessarily expected to be daily companions. Women usually find companionship in other women. As marriage is not supposed to be a joyous, fun-filled romp with the man of your dreams, but rather a difficult test of fulfilling your duties as a submissive and attentive servant to your husband (now with bonus obligations to earn!), the absence of a husband's presence can be as much a relief as a privation.

In a context in which divorce is not uncommon, women count on their own kin and eventually their grown children as the most secure source of support. Affinal kin in Senegal are often a source of punishing, dangerous tension, and my fieldwork is littered with stories about violent mothers-in-law, jealous sisters-in-law and the husbands who side with them over their wives. Natal kin, however, generally represent a steady source of love and material and affective support. In both Daba's situation and Maty's case, natal kin play a key role in their lives and in ways that would be unlikely if their husbands were not abroad.

Senegalese women are aware that for men, too, loyalty to natal kin is more important than loyalty to wives. A Senegalese hotel clerk I interviewed outside of Milan underlined this idea when he told me about his divorce. His wife, whom he had married from abroad, was living with his mother in Dakar and the two repeatedly came into conflict. Though he himself had no complaints about his wife or his relationship with her, his mother's dissatisfaction was grounds for him to divorce. "You know how it is in Senegal," he said to me with some resignation, "the mother is *numero uno*." His own satisfaction with his wife outside of her performance as a daughter-in-law could not outweigh his mother's unhappiness with the union.

Conclusion

Unmarried Senegalese women wish and hope to marry, not for the intimacy promised by some companionate ideal of conjugal felicity but because to be an unmarried woman is an embarrassment and a serious threat to status and identity. A woman must be married to "live as a recognized person in society" (Papadaki 2021, 82). Yet, most women would not choose to leave their natal families if they had the choice. Marriage in Senegal is necessarily asymmetrical in its power relations. Husbands are heads of the household, wives are their caretakers and helpmeets. Even in the growing number of cases of women who outearn their husbands, taking on what were traditionally male duties of financially providing for the housing, clothing, and feeding of themselves and their children, the expectation remains that the wife is responsible for not only performing all the domestic labor but also ensuring that her husband's needs are met with submissive attention and reverence.

Women who live apart from their husbands, particularly if not living among his family members, have a different, freer daily balance. For some women, like Maty, marrying a migrant means not having to leave the familial home where she is cared for and provided for by her kin. For others, such as Daba, a part-time absent husband with no relatives means that much of the time she gets to play at being a hostess and a wife but also gets breaks from some of the hard work of wifing, and shares daily intimacy with her own sister, aunt, and friends.

The chapters in this book reveal that in a myriad of places women are finding ways to innovate and shift the ground within and outside of marriage to attempt to make it more viable or worthwhile. For many, that means creating more space from the husband-wife unit and more space for solidarity and intimacy with other women, including friends and natal kin, without sacrificing the social obligation and status security of being someone's wife. Marrying a migrant who lives overseas appears to be one iteration of this phenomenon, wherein women attempt to have their camel and eat it too.

Acknowledgments

This research was supported by the Wenner-Gren Foundation and the Social Science Research Council. The author would like to thank Jennifer Cole, Lynn Thomas, and Altaïr Despres, as well as the participants in the "Power(s) of Love" workshop at the State University in Zanzibar in 2019, for their contribution to the elaboration of these ideas.

NOTES

1. All names in the chapter are pseudonyms.
2. Though Senegalese women do migrate as well, they represent only 17 percent of international emigrants (ANSD 2015). Transnational marriages between migrant women and nonmigrant men remain quite rare. See also Mbodj-Pouye and LeCourant (2017).
3. Other estimates of households with a member abroad are alternately about half (Beauchemin, Caarls, and Mazzucato 2013; Toma 2017) to 76 percent (Melly 2011, 43) in Dakar, and 10 percent nationwide (Daffé 2008).
4. And men's lives, for that matter.
5. The UN estimated in 2015 that about 35 percent of registered marriages were plural (OHCHR 2015), though clear numbers on polygamy are elusive, as not all marriages nor all divorces are recorded at city hall, especially plural marriages. Transnational marriage also complicates these data significantly. See Whitehouse (2018) for a nuanced discussion of polygyny's enduring hold in contemporary West Africa.
6. Cross-cousin marriage is still preferred in Senegal, though it is less common than it used to be.
7. As polygamy is commonplace, a real anxiety exists among married women that neglecting your husband will make him seek a second (or third or fourth) wife. Though gaining a cowife means a share of the domestic labor, it also means a loss of authority in your marriage and also a dwindling share of your husband's resources.
8. A woman in a plural marriage always cooks for her husband on the night that he sleeps with her, and rival cowives might sabotage one another by spoiling each other's cooking (Gueye 2010, 70).
9. It is likely that pre-Islamic Senegal was matrilocal, leaving wives with more protection in the face of a neglectful or abusive marriage (Gueye 2004; Kanji and Camara 2000).

12

"Not a Normal Wife"

Marrying Activism and Aberrance in Indonesia

CARLA JONES

In 2019 my dear friend, thirty-nine-year-old Dita, did something surprising. She got married. The ceremony was held at a popular hotel in downtown Yogyakarta, Indonesia. About half of the three hundred fifty guests flew in from across the country and from the world because it was the groom's first marriage and because Dita had developed a global friend community during periods of education in Europe and the United States. During their four-month engagement, Dita and Fauzi had mapped out how their marriage would work. She would spend ten days each month in his natal home in Palu, Sulawesi, where they both have jobs, another ten in a small apartment in Jakarta where they also have jobs, and the final ten in her natal home in Yogyakarta, the city where she runs a national NGO on sustainable housing and where her sixteen-year-old daughter from her first marriage lived.

This complex travel and residence schedule revealed that although Dita might appear to have been "opting in" to marriage, she was doing so in a highly unusual, geographically dispersed way. Instead of being rooted in a single home, where she could provide daily expressions of love through domestic care, theirs would be a marriage based on connections that would not require domestic service or even coresidence. Specifically, it would be based on affective intimacy achieved through a shared commitment to activism that was expressed through dual, professionalized, and demanding careers. In spite of this configuration, or perhaps because of it, her parents were optimistic about the union. Confiding to me the night before the wedding, they proudly agreed that this would work out because everyone, including Fauzi, knew that Dita would not be expected to be a "normal wife."

I take this comment, and Dita's decision to opt back into marriage, as illustrations of some of the shifting terrain around marriage that has emerged in the past two decades in Indonesia, roughly the period of Dita's adulthood. Dita's decisions, to refuse her first husband's infidelity, to then refuse to remarry over the subsequent fifteen years, and to then do so in a way that would allow her to not have to be "normal," can each be seen as a small but telling illustration of ways that some Indonesians and their families navigate an intimate public sphere that has placed the national and the conjugal in a close embrace. In what follows, I ask how reconfigurations of marriage, through the rhetoric of the "normal," have offered opportunities for women and men alike to seek alternate configurations of marital life. Building on analyses of care, Indonesian debates about domesticity and conjugality. and the affective life of activism itself, I suggest that for some Indonesian middle-class professionals, while companionate marriage may not necessarily require coresidence, it requires something else—intimacy. Dita's decision to distribute her intimate attachments across the familial, parental, political, and marital suggests that an aberrant marriage scenario might achieve what the normative could not.

Although new marriage, divorce, and nonmarriage patterns in Indonesia suggest unique contours of conjugal life, the idea of intimacy is neither new nor uniquely modern. To the contrary, mythical and national narratives across the archipelago typically emphasize the pathos of star-crossed lovers. Javanese and Balinese myths consistently focus on the trope of lovers seeking each other through extraordinary challenges. Indonesian revolutionary fiction from the 1920s to the 1950s relied on the analogy of the urban and urbane couple choosing each other as marriage partners, rather than submitting to a marriage arranged by their parents, as a metaphor for the allure of national independence from Dutch rule (Siegel 1998). Indeed, romantic love has been a consistent and compelling feature of national and nationalist representations of Indonesia for Indonesians, in conversation with a legacy in which intimacy itself was central to the colonial state (cf. Stoler 2007).

Yet it is precisely for this reason that it is therefore telling that Dita and her family's claims on the future(s) involved situating access to intimacy in and beyond the figure of the couple. By asking, with them, what forms of attachment to others—familial, national, or conjugal—can generate a good life, I see Dita's story as an evocation of how some professional couples in Indonesia, in the face of conditions that may be beyond their control, may nonetheless refuse to settle for anything other than the sort of marriage they want. Perhaps not representative, but nonetheless not sui generis, Dita's story offers a window into new possibilities, including opting out and opting in. Neither waiting without ending or a hope in intimacy that exhausts its believers (Berlant 1998), Dita and Fauzi's "pursuit of happiness" (Williams 2018) is a commitment to the idea of attachment in the face of geographic odds that might seem depleting in the narrow sense of travel, but perhaps not existentially. Their new lives suggest that at least one way of attaining that attachment rests on a unique intersection of aberrance and activism, a node through which the professionalization of activism itself allows for respectability without conventionality.

Part of what makes new forms of attachment possible are shifting political and economic conditions that, as Carla Freeman has argued (2020, 72), have introduced a register in which "feelings of possibility" situate affective attunement as a central component of romance and intimacy. Intimacy itself is therefore central to constructing a life of mutual care. Even among those who can access domestic and global travel, education, and dual careers, those privileges do not explain the particular contours of what a good life might mean. Rather, much as Freeman (this volume) describes, even those in apparently privileged social sectors can find marriage stifling if it is primarily a social form for material coexistence and reinforcing respectability and may find forms of activism to be preferable communities for intimacy. Dita and Fauzi's new, mobile marital life recalled that the root word of the Indonesian term for a social movement, *gerakan* (*gerak*, to move), implies that to be an activist is to be in constant *motion.*

Seen in this light, the intensity of romantic love itself is neither fantasy nor submission to the normative, but itself a demand of life and love that refuses disappointment. Dita's story conveys her own vision of the possible without depicting it as glamorous. Indeed, it is a mix of coping with hardships beyond one's control (see Lamb, this volume) and making active choices in the face of those hardships. The only reason to opt back in was on her terms. Dita's original act of opting out was to refuse to remain in a disrespectful marriage, which would have been expected of a middle-class woman, and to then remain unmarried for over a decade in spite of multiple proposals. From leaving her first husband to accepting familial care in raising her child while pursing professional training and a career, refusing to consider single life lonely, and ultimately marrying a partner who shares her mission for social justice, she is pursuing a life that, in spite of its hints of aberrance, might serve as a quiet but radical expression of hope.

Reversing Abandonment

Dita married her college boyfriend in 2002. An architecture student at a premiere university in the late 1990s, she married as soon as she and her sweetheart graduated. They had both been excellent students and visible, popular campus leaders. Their wedding, with nearly a thousand guests, was one of the most notable in the city that year.

A year later they were divorced. Having moved immediately to Jakarta for entry-level jobs, Dita flew back home to Yogyakarta the day after she learned, three months pregnant, that her husband was having an affair with a coworker. Upon receipt of the news, a younger brother and a team of his friends drove a van across the island and firmly told her husband to remain away from the marital apartment while they collected her possessions. Within three days they and her things were back at her natal home. Her parents swiftly filed divorce papers on her behalf. She never spoke to or saw her ex-husband again. She was awarded full custody of the daughter she delivered six months later, who has never met her biological father.

Although her family celebrated when Dita became pregnant quickly upon her marriage, neither she nor her family expected her to suffer with a philandering husband for a single day, contrary to some Javanese conceptions of masculinity that expect wives to endure infidelity. The entire family simply had a zero-tolerance policy for any adultery.

The following year, Dita moved to Europe for a master's degree in urban planning, leaving her daughter in her family's care. They video-conferenced frequently. Dita may technically have earned a graduate degree while in Europe, but she gained something deeper, which everyone in the family recognized and supported: distance from the trauma of her husband's cheating. She gained new friends from around the world, confidence in her intellectual potential, and the unexpected delights of cooking and living on her own. She insisted on speaking to her daughter exclusively in English, treating her new fluency as a tangible benefit she could transfer to her daughter in exchange for her absence.

Shifts in Marriage Patterns in Contemporary Indonesia

Considering the "not normal" requires considering the normal. Dita's story is but one in a broader set of demographic changes that are often described to the Indonesian public as bad news, as deviation from a normative ideal. Common indicators of this decline include references to demographic shifts over the past few decades. Indonesia is witnessing increasing rates of divorce among the middle classes, increasing rates of single parenting by those divorced parents, and increasing rates of lifelong singlehood. According to the 2010 census, while the age of first marriage has on average increased by three years, the percentage of never-married women in Indonesia aged thirty to thirty-nine tripled over the prior decade, to 3.8 percent, and increased to 7.18 percent across all adults (Badan Pusat Statistik 2010a, 2010b).

Generally represented as a decay of the "family" rather than of the conjugal couple, much of this rhetoric intimates that women are opting out of marriage. From the 1990s on, white-collar career work for women has been framed as competing with women's obligations and desires, away from marriage and motherhood and toward ambition and consumption. Joshua Barker, Erik Harms, and Johan Lindquist (2013) have described "figures of modernity" in Southeast Asia as salient characters who are simultaneously recognizable as figures yet not recognizable as actual individuals. As a figure, the "career woman" is, in its most severe representations, a selfish figure. Although extensive feminist activism and rhetoric about women's development celebrate women's role in national progress, the particularly negative images focus on the career woman's absence from the domestic sphere. Spending her days, and potentially nights, at the office instead of at home, developing attachments with (especially female) coworkers instead of family members, and spending income on consumer goods rather than on the family, the career woman is a potent package of progress and pathology (Jones 2014). By extension, replacing family surveillance with the anomie and pleasures of city life makes professional women responsible for their own broken marriages.

What this rhetoric elides is the fact these norms were never applied to poor, rural Indonesians, especially those who had to migrate for work. As Hildred Geertz described in 1961, poor women were expected to enter an early, arranged marriage that would likely end in divorce, leaving a woman with at least one child to raise with the help of her family and subsequent sexual partners (56–57). Divorced women from this demographic segment were only lightly stigmatized, as they and their community recognized that their partners were likely to have had to migrate for work and would inevitably disappear. If a woman sought a legal divorce ruling, abandonment was an acceptable and recognizable explanation. These expectations have changed little as migration has increased. For working-class men in particular, marriage remains an elusive privilege for the few who can afford to maintain it. Narratives about male abandonment have grown alongside increasingly regulatory and documentary techniques of citizenship (Amster and Lindquist 2005). Their experiences resonate with those of men elsewhere whose absence from formal marriage may not be by design and may challenge masculine conceptions of dignity (cf. Inhorn and Smith-Hefner 2020). These patterns suggest that although marriage remains an ideal, for some it is the aberrant social form hiding in plain sight. Indeed, Dita and her siblings were raised by a live-in domestic worker whose own life story parallels this pattern. She married young, had a daughter, and was "abandoned" by her husband when he migrated to Jakarta for work. She never pursued a formal divorce, and her daughter grew up alongside the children of the household in which she served.

By contrast, urban middle-class women have been central, almost essential, to narratives of national independence in the early twentieth century, and of national development in the latter half of the century. Public and academic conversations about normal marriage and national decline reinforce a sense that there is one "normal" way to be an Indonesian adult: married with children in a neolocal residence. These conceptions precede the postauthoritarian period, linking categories of national development that were promoted during the Suharto New Order era (1965–1998) to what feels like new, increasingly religiously inflected guidance. Building on prior cultural stigmas around divorce and attaching them to much newer anxieties about the home and its management has opposed the housewife (*ibu rumah tangga*, or "mother of the household") to the career woman. As Suzanne Brenner has described, the particular genre of public intimacy of the late New Order period concentrated general anxieties about the temptations of urban, modern life through the domestic, thereby extending the idea of the nation as a family into heightened stakes for actual families. "The affairs of the family were increasingly redefined as public rather than private matters, making the family itself the ground upon which ideological contests over the nation's future were waged" (1999, 16).

Perhaps the most formal and detailed initiatives structuring the public intimacy of national life during the New Order were the twin development programs known as Darma Wanita (Women's Duty) and Pemberdayaan Kesejahteraan

Keluarga (PKK; Familial Prosperity Enrichment). As Janice Newberry has argued, both programs treated the domestic sphere and women's labor as infinite, uncompensated resources for neighborhood qua national development through the narrative of communal harmony. PKK in particular situated this agenda in working-class neighborhoods, urging women to share food, cash, and free care for kin across households (2006). Darma Wanita framed this burden slightly differently, instead educating wives of male civil servants that their contributions to the nation were exclusively through caring for their husbands and children. Neither program encouraged women to work outside the home, even though both relied on income women earned formally or informally in order to donate time and money to national harmony and development, including through staffing nearly half of the civil service. For wives in particular, this ideal entailed childrearing and household management but also emotional care of a husband. Importantly, that care was best expressed in person, through recognizable acts of love like serving him meals or greeting him at home at the end of his workday even if the majority of the domestic labor in the home was conducted by hired help. As I and others have noted, configuring housewifery as a full-time, albeit unpaid, career produced a series of effects, including profound anxiety about conjugal care and driving some women to forfeit formal employment so as to be on site at home (Jones 2004). To not do so would be to invite a husband's philandering and lead to heartache.

Nonnormative Femininities

Dita's decision to accept familial care in raising her daughter and pursuing her career may seem aberrant in light of the ubiquitous celebration of marriage and motherhood in Indonesia. Yet Javanese households have long held expansive conceptions about shared childrearing, including caring and sharing children across kin networks. To quote Hildred Geertz once more, "A crying baby is rarely heard, mainly because no Javanese can bear to hear the sound without trying to do something about it no matter whose baby it is" (93). While an infant should be held or swaddled as much as possible, ideally by its mother, the typically large range of people in a household could step in at any point. Dita's natal family happily chipped in to provide the hands and hearts to give her a year away once her daughter was weaned. Dita knew that her daughter would be surrounded by her two grandparents, three uncles and their friends and girlfriends (and later wives), a steady stream of cousins, and two domestic workers, all of whom alternately slept with her, fed her, tickled her, and disciplined her. She was never alone.

By accessing the respectability of the extended family, Dita's family gave her the option to leave the country while her injuries were still fresh. Considering this option as normative or not calls to mind other powerful models about nonnormative marriage that also shape social control and resistance. These can serve as powerful cautionary figures to discipline expectations for marriage. They suggest that speaking out about an unhappy marriage would lead to the even worse fate of being alone. As Tom Boellstorff has argued, heteronormative pressures to embark on the "perfect path," to marry and have children, are so intense for middle-class Indonesians that gay men will marry wives so as to fulfill these expectations (1999). Similarly, Evelyn Blackwood describes how *lesbi* women either enter into marriages with men or model their relationships with women in heteronormative styles so as to maintain respectable standing with their families (2010).

For example, even though Dita has now remarried, she will always carry the stigmatized label of being a *janda*, a divorcée. Avoiding the label is ostensibly so powerful that it drives some women to endure unfaithful husbands or unrewarding marriages. As a figure who has sexual experience but no familial or marital surveillance, the janda has long been a charged character in insular Southeast Asian myths, folklore, and humor. In these accounts, she is uniquely able to use her knowledge about male sexual pleasure, combined with residual bitterness from likely having been abandoned or mistreated, to deceive and taunt men. She appears in night terrors, in popular horror films, and in whispered gossip between women. Part merry divorcée, part vengeful one, the janda remains a cautionary category for men and women alike. The janda's ongoing potency as a stigma translates long-standing sexual concerns about female pleasure into contemporary norms about respectability.

To say that Dita and her family appear to have rejected these categories does not necessarily mean that they have not been salient to them, or to debates about marriage that have unfolded over the past decade. As a number of scholars have demonstrated, new genres of Islamic expertise over the past two decades have inflected national rhetoric about marriage and family in Indonesia. This has had at least two effects. It has emphasized heteronormativity while encouraging early marriage ages. Since the end of the New Order, previously banned or marginal Islamic political parties have increased in number and visibility, making Indonesia, the largest majority-Muslim country in the world, a vibrant site for analyzing Muslim reform movements popular in the late twentieth century globally. Part of their appeal and success, as James Hoesterey has argued, has been their capacity to frame Indonesia as perpetually in moral crisis (2016). Two national laws proposed, although not passed, in 2018 and 2019 illustrate this. Both bills would have subjected gay citizens to rehabilitation and banned extramarital sex in the name of creating "family resilience." Although the bills generated substantial public protest, the fact that they were framed as a necessary response to social decay suggests that for at least some Indonesians, changes to marriage patterns are knowable only in the language of crisis, as "a rupture in the normative order of things" (Davidson and Hannaford, this volume).

Yet as many scholars of the turn toward Muslim romance and marriage have noted, this shift toward public regulation of morality has also had some unintended effects. As Nancy Smith-Hefner has argued (2019), religious romantic expertise that situates dating and marriage as one of the key foci of religious guidance may lead to shortened dating periods and both earlier and later ages for first marriage, traced to the considerable anxiety around finding the "right" partner. By contrast, when marriages fail, wives increasingly have their divorces adjudicated in religious courts, as they are likely to be able to make productive reference to heteronormative conceptions of marriage (which can also define polygyny as nonnormative) and have divorce rulings made in their favor (Rinaldo 2019; cf. Peletz 2020). Indeed, Dita and her parents made exactly this choice, filing her case in the religious court system, handling it entirely privately and with no involvement from the estranged husband or his family. Their absence during the proceedings confirmed his moral failings and formalized her return to her natal family. Although by being the first to leave the marital home it might seem that Dita risked forfeiting the legal claim of physical abandonment, she instead accessed the claim of moral abandonment.

Making Family, Making Home

"Is it true that American women freeze their eggs to ensure that they can have a child?" Dita asked me this question on a long road trip in 2007 when her daughter was five. Dita had been back from Europe for a couple years at that point and was working for two large international aid agencies, flying back and forth between an efficiency apartment in Jakarta, field sites across the country, and Yogyakarta. Her daughter was thriving in her private kindergarten, taking ballet and piano classes, and increasingly fluent in English and Javanese, the languages spoken at home. Dita had just seen a story in one of the local newspapers describing how American women were increasingly turning to new reproductive technologies to extend their chances at parenthood when their marriage options seemed slim. "Do you know about this, Carla? Do women really do this outside of marriage?" She remarked on how tragic it seemed that American women might have to resort to expensive, invasive reproductive technologies rather than face the prospect of being *sendirian* or alone. Alone, in this sense, referred to the lack of a child rather than the lack of a spouse. Although Indonesian couples regularly access reproductive technologies, it is, as with birth control, formally sanctioned in the context of marriage. Dita sighed and chuckled at how much effort it could take to accomplish something so simple as to conceive a child and then move on with life. Once a child has been achieved, it seemed self-evident that one could opt out of marriage altogether, as one would still always have natal kin along with the child. Considering that some of Dita's stigma as a janda was offset by her increased status as a mother, the question of how women elsewhere accessed that status was interesting to think through together.

The conversation then shifted to how American it was to solve a social problem through buying individual medical solutions. We all chuckled, and then her daughter and I, who were sitting next to each other in the back seat, snuggled as everyone in the car reassured her of her how happy we all were that she was a part of the family.

At this point, Dita had already turned down one marriage proposal from a friend to whom she had become close while in her MA program and would turn down two more in the years to come. Given her gregarious personality and tireless enthusiasm for her work and her family, she attracted an array of friends and colleagues, many of them male. She was also careful not to get too close to any of them. She was far from being worried about being alone, and her life had become intensely full, with demanding professional travel and graduate school. With each facet of her life, she was surrounded by friends, peers, and employees. She tried to be home with her daughter at least three nights a week, although they were not always back-to-back.

At first glance, Dita's life appeared to be a combination of aberrant types: janda, career woman, and single parent. Indeed, at that point the only moment in her life in which she had at all conformed to the norms of domestic marital life was in the brief period of her first marriage. As her work required increased travel, her apartment in Jakarta was more crash pad than domestic haven. She occasionally upgraded fixtures in her main bedroom in her natal home for her and her daughter to enjoy but investing in a single residence was not part of her mobile lifestyle. Accepting any of the subsequent marriage proposals would have entailed having to form a new nuclear family household away from the affective and material support she received and offered to her natal family.

These details are telling given the fact that Dita's professional expertise was focused on housing itself, as a basic human right for access to shelter. She received postgraduate training in the United States when her daughter was eleven and then earned a PhD focusing on the essential need for vulnerable, particularly rural, communities to have access to simple, locally appropriate housing. Her expertise became increasingly in demand by the Indonesian government and global development agencies in the wake of a series of natural disasters. Yet her own avoidance of settling down in a single residence was inspired by these rights. Rather than needing a husband through whom to be able to establish a domestic unit, her life was consistent with Southeast Asian conceptions of marriage in which spouses are equated with siblings, and to be without a sibling is a more acute form of isolation than to be without a spouse (Carsten 1997, 92–94; Cannell 1999, 54–59). Perhaps even more tellingly, her refusal to remarry over the fifteen years following her divorce hints at something deeper, what Catherine Allerton has described as the fact that because loneliness is difficult to study cross-culturally, scholars have potentially overemphasized the idea that marriage is an essential component to achieving adulthood (2017). This bias has overemphasized the impression that to be an unmarried woman is to be more deeply "alone" than to be an unmarried man.

I would argue that Dita's avoidance of domesticity and remarriage was less a rejection of those ideas than a pivot to shifting the locus of another idea associated with companionate marriage: care. In brief, rather than focus her commitment to care within the nuclear family, she associated it with a different arena, that of activism. Indeed, her brief marriage had been a fleeting entry into domestic respectability, one which brought pain, while her escape from it also enabled an escape from the normative conception that care could occur only in the context of the nuclear family. In considering Dita's options and choices in the years following her divorce, I suggest that we back up to revisit an alternate core identity that facilitated her ability to take quiet, less visible, and courageous steps in the face of heartache. Rather than see herself as an embarrassed janda, Dita's case suggests that some early and midcareer women are reconfiguring marriage outside of the rhetoric of religious piety and in ways that refuse choosing between servitude or solitude. Although approaching their forties, some women and men who became adults in the late 1990s and early 2000s seem to have different expectations for their relationships. For them, the category of "activist" is the available moral category through which to orient and describe their life choices.

Like the career woman, the activist (aktivis) is another "figure of modernity," one that carries its own array of connotations. This has become a space through which professionals who were middle class but still students during the protests against Suharto in 1998 have adopted a focus on care to the purpose of adult, employed, yet democratic goals. Indeed, care, the Indonesian word borrowed from English, exists not because it has no equivalent in Indonesian, but as a cosmopolitan loanword that signals egalitarian, dual-income, professional marriages (Jones 2004). This concept has close correlations between public and private life. While care celebrates desire over duty and choice over obligation (cf. Collier 1997), it also reanimates the parallel between romance and national revolution that Indonesian nationalists deployed in the 1920s, in the process promising to merge these apparently contrasting categories. The version of care that emerged in the late 1990s was also tied to a moment of youth activism. Dita's first marriage was a mix of middle-class conventionality and activist awakenings. Both Dita, in the late 1990s, and her parents, in the 1970s, had formative college experiences as campus activists (poignantly, against the same regime). Dita therefore built on a familial and multigenerational legacy of national organizing as an expression of concern for fellow citizens. Her ability to pivot away from her marriage and swiftly invest in her professional life was, undoubtedly, an expression of her family's ability to support her, but also their shared commitment to her vision about care.

Activism in Indonesia has consistently been a young person's field. In 1945 and in 1998, youthful idealism about national futures intersected with a life phase in which ambition and courage could appear as heroic rejections of a corrupt or rigid past. In other words, activists in Indonesia are simultaneously normative and not. They have adopted nonnormative identities as populist, righteous forms of aberrance as the inheritors of a national genealogy of activists as heroes (pemuda, or heroic youth). This is consistent with activist movements elsewhere. As Carole McGranahan has argued, to be an activist is, by definition, to engage in labor that involves care. It calls out injustice even as it is situated in particular historical and political contexts (2020). Activists therefore operate on the edges of the political mainstream yet may be recognizable as attractively aberrant (cf. Ginsburg 1998; Haugerud 2018; Kunreuther 2018).

Activism is also a middle-class person's field. Indonesian activists often embrace an additional identity of *mahasiswa*, or college student, as an overlapping category around which they can frame the state as a bad caregiver or parent to the nation. In some cases, activists have also embraced the aberrant in an attempt to demand equal access to the normative, as Diane Singerman describes of Egyptian youth decrying their endless "waithood" toward marriage, parenthood, and adulthood by virtue of exclusion from the economic mainstream (2013). In others, they have relied on the private backdrop of middle-class respectability to sustain them in their public demands for reform. This has made Indonesian activist experiences amenable to being professionalized as the activists themselves mature. This clearly involves significant access to privileged identities and to elusive forms of globally recognizable social, cultural, and financial capital. As Marina Welker (2014) and Anna Tsing (2004) have separately noted about Indonesian activism, activists often adopt identities that are almost nonsensical outside of the urban core. They use neoliberal concepts like "training" and "NGO," phrases that signify access to the foreign not only because of their English language origins but also because their use reinforces activists' prioritization of abstract ideas like rural uplift or ideas of good governance over the messier needs of those whom they aim to aid.

But in the urban core, activists do not consider themselves privileged so much as radical. For the "generation of 1998" (activists whose shared sense of community came from protesting and resisting the Suharto regime), one of the modes through which they expressed and recognized themselves as activists was in their rejection of New Order norms of domestic life. As Doreen Lee argues, rather than thinking of protest as a public form, and private life as individuated, Indonesia's "youthful culture of democracy . . . bridges public and private domains" (2016, 3), allowing activism to create a form of public intimacy that was not exclusively limited to the familial or the national. In particular, activist base camps were novel forms of shelter that were neither dormitories nor middle-class homes. Porous and high traffic, they were the spatial and emotional opposite of the locked, secured, nuclear families of New Order imagery. Calling this process "domiciliation," Lee argues that activists created interior spaces that were a combination of playing house and camping out (2016, 148), zones where they could socialize without conforming to the particular sleep or surveillance routines that were enforced in student boarding houses. These intense alternative kin communities sacrificed creature comforts for political passion and close relationships, yet also relied on the ability to pop back to natal homes for laundry, showers, and home-cooked (or, more precisely, maid-cooked) meals. Liminal interiors cultivated the unique class of relationships they sheltered: intimate, democratic, and still deeply dependent on middle-class norms. Activist lives therefore never fully threatened heteronormative conceptions of domesticity even as they questioned them.

For Dita, a person committed to analyzing the way that built and lived space facilitates or prevents social justice, her activist life was a potent site of nostalgia.

She remembered how thrilling it had been to organize in 1998, particularly in procuring snacks and drinks for large groups of students politely but defiantly refusing to leave the streets during protests in Yogyakarta. Hanging out in cafes, finding her sociality and her voice, her parents rarely questioned her need to be away from home for days at a time. They knew that she was involved in what they also prioritized: care for the nation. During the years since her divorce and in spite of high-earning professional jobs, she had treated her Jakarta apartment as an activist base camp, and her (and her daughter's) natal home as her escape from it. As her mother, whose four adult, professional children still stay for extended periods at home, said, "I don't manage a home. I manage a boarding house."

Opting In

On September 28, 2018, a 7.8-magnitude earthquake devastated the midsized coastal city of Palu, Sulawesi. Dita began working with the Indonesian Ministry of Housing and Public Works immediately on plans for creating temporary, emergency housing for victims and flew there as soon as the airport reopened. Over the next several months, she spent more time in Palu than anywhere else, experiencing the emotional maelstrom of loss and recovery with fellow experts and activists. Among those new friends and colleagues was Fauzi, a young man whom she had known of but not yet met. Within six months, they were married. How should we interpret Dita's reticence to remarry? And then her apparently sudden willingness to? Was she occupying aberrant adulthood up until her second marriage? Or is there a paucity of terminology to capture what they found in each other?

The simple answer is that she met a man whom she loves deeply. The more complete answer is that Fauzi and Dita consider marriage to be a vessel for emotional attachment to each other and to shared goals. Although not "normal" in terms of dominant Indonesian models, this model's focus on flexibility and intimacy is not as exceptional as it may seem. As Dinah Hannaford has argued, flexibility and intimacy have been in their own close dance as new political and economic cultures demand new domestic configurations (2017). Rather than a cohabitation of two individuals to create a family, Dita and Fauzi's family was closer to what Carla Freeman has described as the kind of "emotional synchrony" (2014, 85) that is central to the 24/7 quality of neoliberal work and personal life. Clearly, this is possible only with their dual incomes. In their family homes, they had female hired help and kin for cooking and cleaning. In their Jakarta convenience apartment, they had occasional maid service for cleaning and ate many meals out. They socialized with friends and worked very long hours. Dita joked that between her three jobs and their three residences, they both pulled all-nighters as if they were still college students.

For professionals like Dita and Fauzi, to marry became, in its own way, a political act of optimism. It could also expand the boundaries of "normal" to include novel forms of family. We might therefore ask how professional women use the category of activist to create relationships, some marital, some not, that prioritize their emotional well-being and their careers, rather than domesticity. Their new communitas now includes natal kin and colleagues, merging work and home, public and private in ways that seemed to, ironically, decrease domestic expectations in spite of three households.

Perhaps Dita's parents were correct in describing Dita as an unlikely candidate for being a normal wife. But it would be a mistake to read their comment as critique. Rather, it was sheer pride that Dita and Fauzi were not expecting to create a normal household. Normal, in this framing, was not the ideal but the potentially pathological. By marrying, Dita was not solving a problem of loneliness but rather enacting a vision for a different future and inverting the idea of aberrance along the way.

When the COVID-19 pandemic arrived in Indonesia in March 2020, Dita happened to be in Palu. Yogyakarta was almost immediately classified as a "red" zone, with high rates of infection, while Palu was relatively unscathed. Its low transmission rates were largely the result of the governor's strict limits on movement in and out of the city. For the first time in her life, Dita's way of being in the world, of being in constant motion, halted. She was effectively stuck at one of her homes. Her parents insisted that she stay there. Like so many professionals, she shifted much of her work, consulting, and activism to remotely working from home. Likewise, she video-chatted with her daughter regularly, helping her with homework at a long distance. In July, when her daughter's school confirmed that the next academic year would be delivered remotely, the family collectively decided that this was the moment to allow her to move to Dita and Fauzi's home in Palu, for "family bonding." With a single plane ride and a few suitcases of clothes, she began a temporary but new life with her mother and stepfather in a new city, with new aunts and uncles, new cousins, and her same friend circle in her classes back home in Yogya.

This entailed profound adjustments for everyone. Dita threw herself into reading about emotional development and blended family parenting. She taught herself to cook by texting the domestic worker who had helped to raise her and her daughter multiple times a day for nostalgic recipes. Fauzi was equally excited about becoming a stepfather. He drove his new teenage stepdaughter to piano lessons and appointments, committed to extending the affection he and Dita shared to her. But perhaps her daughter herself described it best when she expressed surprise for Dita's new enthusiasm for domesticity. She described her mother's new zeal for parenting so intensely as "professional," as if paid, white-collar work was the only concept that could accurately convey the focus that Dita was suddenly applying to perfecting life at home. The exceptional, indeed aberrant, conditions of a pandemic created conditions that Dita and Fauzi treated as a fleeting but exciting opportunity for them to implement a passion for justice and intimacy right at home.

The two decades of Dita's adulthood have witnessed profound political, social, economic, and epidemiological ruptures in Indonesia. Those have also paralleled financial crises, democratic transformations, and the growth of public and private religious intensification. To some in Indonesia, Dita's personal navigation of that history might seem emblematic of a broader social collapse, of proof that men cheat, women suffer, and families are fragile. Yet as the research in this volume evidences, the very rhetoric of crisis can be deceptive. Seen from Dita and her family's perspective, the lives they have created together embrace aberrance. For them, male infidelity is unacceptable, female suffering can be healed, and families can remain a steady source of support, even if those political and professional commitments require time away from home. Rather than inversion, Dita's life might suggest a new normal. As Mary Steedly suggested in 1999, a moment when scholars of Southeast Asia were fascinated with crisis and when Dita herself was just finishing college, rather than focus on crisis, we should attend to the "ordinary routines of everyday life . . . the times when things don't fall apart, when expectations hold, when people get by or get on with their lives" (446). Sometimes the "getting on" might mean opting out of marriage, and sometimes it might just mean opting back in.

Acknowledgments

This essay has benefited from the generous intellectual care of many friends and colleagues, especially Joanna Davidson, Carla Freeman, Dinah Hannaford, and Ann Marie Leshkowich. I am equally grateful for the incisive feedback from the volume's two anonymous reviewers and Sarah Lamb and Kimberly Walters. But most generous of all has been Dita's fearless example of how to flourish.

ACKNOWLEDGMENTS

We are fortunate that the process of bringing this volume into being involved equal measures of intellectual growth, editorial labor, and just plain fun. We knew we were onto something when we first discussed the phenomenon of "opting out" with each other, and our efforts to grapple with and do justice to this topic have been enriched at every turn through conversations with fieldwork interlocutors, colleagues, conference panelists, discussants, and audience members, and most of all, the brilliant group of women anthropologists who have contributed chapters to this book. This was truly an iterative and collective endeavor, and we are grateful to this dream team of authors for the energy and enthusiasm they maintained throughout our experiments with workshopping the initial conference papers, working in small teams to provide feedback and connect themes across the chapters, participating in a Zoom revisions party, and developing a model of feminist collaborative work in process and product.

We thank our three anonymous reviewers who gave us the gift of fresh eyes and thoughtful criticism. We are grateful to those who have given their time and intellectual energy to this project at various stages, including Sarah Pinto, Allison Alexy, Shirin Gerami, Marcia Inhorn, Kimberly Arkin, Ayse Parla, and Rob Weller. We thank Péter Berta for being an early champion of this volume, as well as Jasper Chang and the entire team at Rutgers University Press for shepherding the book through all stages of editing and production in an unprecedented period of global upheaval. Thanks to Emily Williamson Ibrahim for creating such a compelling and beautiful image for our book cover.

Joanna would especially like to thank her *kinderle*, Lyna, Jasper, and Zoly, for being sources of inspiration and joy.

Dinah extends thanks to her beloved tiny person, Charlotte, as well as Kira Deshler, who helped care for her over the course of this project.

Although they are too numerous to name individually, we acknowledge our many family members and friends whose partnership and support are woven into the fabric of this book.

REFERENCES

Abu-Lughod, Lila. 1998. "Introduction: Feminist Longings and Postcolonial Conditions." In *Remaking Women: Feminism and Modernity in the Middle East*, edited by Lila Abu-Lughod, 3–31. Princeton, NJ: Princeton University Press.

Adebayo, Ayobami. 2017. *Stay with Me*. New York: Knopf.

Adjamagbo, A., P. Antoine, and F. B. Dial. 2004. "Le dilemme des Dakaroises: entre travailler et 'bien travailler.'" In *Gouverner le Sénégal: entre ajustement structurel et développement durable*, edited by M. C. Diop, 247–272. Paris: Kathala.

Adorno, Theodor W. 1966/2007. *Negative Dialectics*. Translated by E. B. Ashton. New York: Continuum.

Agarwal, Bina. 1994. *A Field of One's Own: Gender and Land Rights in South Asia*. New York: Cambridge University Press.

Agence Nationale de la Statistique et de la Démographie—ANSD/Sénégal and ICF International. 2015. "Sénégal: Enquête Démographique et de Santé Continue (EDS-Continue 2014)." Rockville, MD: ANSD/Senegal and ICF International.

Agrawal, Anuja. 2015. "Cyber-matchmaking among Indians: Re-arranging Marriage and Doing 'Kin Work.'" *South Asian Popular Culture* 13 (1): 15–30.

Ahearn, Laura. 2001. *Invitations to Love: Literacy, Love Letters, and Social Change in Nepal*. Ann Arbor: University of Michigan Press.

Alexy, Allison. 2010. "The Door My Wife Closed: Houses, Families, and Divorce in Japan." In *Home and Family in Japan: Continuity and Transformation*, edited by Richard Ronald and Allison Alexy, 236–253. London: Routledge.

———. 2020. *Intimate Disconnections: Divorce and the Romance of Independence in Contemporary Japan*. Chicago: University of Chicago Press.

Alharthi, Jokha. 2019. *Celestial Bodies*. Berkeley, CA: Catapult.

Allerton, Catherine. 2007. "What Does It Mean to Be Alone?" In *Questions of Anthropology*, edited by Rita Astuti, Jonathan Parry, and Charles Stafford, 1–28. Oxford: Berg.

———. 2017. What Does It Mean to Be Alone? *Anthropology of This Century* 18 (January).

Allison, Anne. 2013. *Precarious Japan*. Durham, NC: Duke University Press.

Allman, Jean. 1996. "Rounding Up Spinsters: Gender Chaos and Unmarried Women in Colonial Asante." *Journal of African History* 37 (2): 196–214.

Amato, P. R. 1994. "The Impact of Divorce on Women and Men in India and the United States." *Journal of Comparative Family Studies* 25:207–217.

Amit, Roni, and Norma Kriger. 2014. "Making Migrants 'Il-legible': The Policies and Practices of Documentation in Post-apartheid South Africa." *Kronos* 40 (1): 269–290.

Amster, Matthew, and Johan Lindquist. 2005. "Frontiers, Sovereignty, and Marital Tactics: Comparisons from the Borneo Highlands and the Indonesia-Malaysia-Singapore Growth Triangle." *Asia Pacific Journal of Anthropology* 6 (1): 1–17.

Ansell, N. 2001. "'Because It's Our Culture!' (Re)negotiating the Meaning of Lobola in Southern African Secondary Schools." *Journal of Southern African Studies* 27 (4): 697–716.

Ardener, Edwin. 1989a. "Belief and the Problem of Women." In *Edwin Ardener: The Voice of Prophecy and Other Essays*, edited by Malcolm Chapman, 72–85. Oxford: Basil Blackwell.

———. 1989b. "The 'Problem' Revisited." In *Edwin Ardener: The Voice of Prophecy and Other Essays*, edited by Malcolm Chapman, 127–133. Oxford: Basil Blackwell.

Arni, Samhita, and Moyna Chitrakar. 2011. *Sita's Ramayana*. Toronto: Groundwood Books.

Ashforth, Adam. 1999. "Weighing Manhood in Soweto." *Codesria Bulletin* 3 (4): 51–58.

Atkins, Keletso E. 1993. *The Moon Is Dead! Give Us Our Money! The Cultural Origins of an African Work Ethic, Natal, South Africa, 1843–1900*. Portsmouth, NH: James Currey.

Auslander, Mark. 1993. "'Open the Wombs!' Symbolic Politics of Modern Ngoni Witch-Finding." In *Modernity and Its Malcontents: Ritual and Power in Postcolonial Africa*, edited by Jean Comaroff and John L. Comaroff, 167–192. Chicago: University of Chicago Press.

Azevedo, Thales de. 1986. *As Regras do Namoro a Antiga*. São Paulo: Editora Ática.

Bâ, Mariama. 1979. *Une si longue lettre*. Dakar: Nouvelles Editions Africaines.

———. 1981. *So Long a Letter*. Translated by Modupé Bodé-Thomas. London: Heinemann.

Baber, Zaheer. 1996. "After Ayodhya: Politics, Religion and the Emerging Culture of Academic Anti-Secularism in India." *Dialectical Anthropology* 21 (3): 317–343.

Badan Pusat Statistik. 2010a. *Indonesia—Jumlah dan distribusi penduduk*. http://sp2010.bps.go.id/index.php/site/topik?kid=1&kategori=Jumlah-dan-Distribusi-Penduduk.

———. 2010b. *Penduduk Indonesia: Hasil Sensus Penduduk 2010*. https://www.bps.go.id/website/pdf_publikasi/watermark%20_Dokumentasi%20Komprehensif%20SP%202010.pdf.

Bähre, Eric. 2020. "Wealth-in-People and Practical Rationality: Aspirations and Decisions about Money in South Africa." *Economic Anthropology* 7 (2): 267–278.

Bank, Andrew. 2016. *Pioneers of the Field: South Africa's Women Anthropologists*. Cambridge: Cambridge University Press.

Barker, Joshua, Erik Harms, and Johan Lindquist, eds. 2013. *Figures of Southeast Asian Modernity*. Honolulu: University of Hawai'i Press.

Barrow, Christine. 1996. *Family in the Caribbean: Themes and Perspectives*. Kingston, Jamaica: Ian Randle.

———. 1998. "Caribbean Masculinity and Family: Revisiting 'Marginality' and Reputation." In *Caribbean Portraits: Essays on Gender Ideologies and Identities*, 339–358. Kingston, Jamaica: Ian Randle.

———. 2019. "Can There Be Love in the Caribbean?" *Caribbean Review of Gender Studies* 13: 233–266.

Basu, Srimati. 1999. *She Comes to Take Her Rights: Indian Women, Property, and Propriety*. Albany: State University of New York Press.

———. 2020. "The End(s) of Marriage: Feminists, Antifeminists, and Indian Law," *Feminist Anthropology* 1 (2): 184–191.

Beauchemin, C., K. Caarls, and V. Mazzucato. 2013 "Senegalese Migrants between Here and There: An Overview of Family Patterns." MAFE Working Paper 33. http://www.ined.fr/fichier/t_telechargement/60574/telechargement_fichier_fr_wp33_senegal_family.pdf.

Beauvoir, Simone de. 1974. *The Second Sex*. New York: Vintage.

Beguy, Donatien. 2009. "The Impact of Female Employment on Fertility in Dakar (Senegal) and Lomé (Togo)." *Demographic Research* 20:97–128.

Bellot, Gabrielle. 2019. "How Jamaica Kincaid Helped Me Understand My Mother." *Literary Hub*, March 22. https://lithub.com/how-jamaica-kincaid-helped-me-understand-my-mother/.

Berlant, Lauren. 1998. "Intimacy: A Special Issue." *Critical Inquiry* 24 (2): 281–288.

———. 2008. *The Female Complaint: The Unfinished Business of Sentimentality in American Culture*. Durham, NC: Duke University Press.

Bernstein, Elizabeth. 2007. *Temporarily Yours: Intimacy, Authenticity, and the Commerce of Sex*. Chicago: University of Chicago Press.

Bhandare, Namita. 2018. "As Indian Women Leaves Jobs, Single Women Keep Working. Here's Why." *Business Standard*, June 23. https://www.business-standard.com/article/current-affairs/as-indian-women-leave-jobs-single-women-keep-working-here-s-why-118062300375_1.html.

Blackwood, Evelyn. 2004. "Marriage and the Missing Man." *Anthropology News*.

———. 2005. "Wedding Bell Blues: Marriage, Missing Men, and Matrifocal Follies." *American Ethnologist* 32: 3–19.

———. 2010. *Falling into the Lesbi World: Desire and Difference in Indonesia*. Honolulu: University of Hawai'i Press.

Blackwood, Evelyn, and Saskia E. Wieringa. 1999. *Female Desires: Same-Sex Relations and Transgender Practices across Cultures*. New York: Columbia University Press.

Bledsoe, Caroline H. 2002. *Contingent Lives: Fertility, Time, and Aging in West Africa*. Chicago: University of Chicago Press.

Boellstorff, Tom. 1999. "The Perfect Path: Gay Men, Marriage, Indonesia." *GLQ: A Journal of Lesbian and Gay Studies* 5 (4): 475–510.

———. 2005. *The Gay Archipelago: Sexuality and Nation in Indonesia*. Princeton, NJ: Princeton University Press.

Bolick, Kate. 2015. *Spinster: Making a Life of One's Own*. New York: Penguin Random House.

Bop, Codou. 1995. "Les Femmes Chefs de Famille a Dakar." *Africa Development* 20 (4): 51–67.

Bourdieu, Pierre. 1984. *Distinction*. New York: Routledge.

———. 2008. *The Bachelors' Ball: The Crisis of Peasant Society in Béarn*. Cambridge: Polity.

Braun, Lesley. 2014. "Trading Virtue for Virtuosity: The Artistry of Kinshasa's Concert Danseuses." *African Arts* 47 (4): 48–57.

Bremmer, Jan, and Lourens van den Bosch, eds. 1995. *Between Poverty and the Pyre: Moments in the History of Widowhood*. New York: Routledge.

Brenner, Suzanne. 1999. "On the Public Intimacy of the New Order: Images of Women in the Popular Indonesian Print Media." *Indonesia* 67: 13–37.

Brinton, Mary C. 2011. *Lost in Transition: Youth, Work, and Instability in Postindustrial Japan*. New York: Cambridge University Press.

Budlender, D., and C. Fauvelle-Aymar. 2012. "MiWORC Policy Brief 2." In *Migration and Employment in South Africa: Statistical and Econometric Analyses of Internal and International Migrants in Statistics South Africa's Labour Market Data*. Johannesburg: African Centre for Migration & Society, University of the Witwatersrand.

Budlender, D., and F. Lund. 2011. "South Africa: A Legacy of Family Disruption." *Development and Change* 42 (4): 925–946.

Buggenhagen, B. 2012. *Muslim Families in Global Senegal: Money Takes Care of Shame*. Indianapolis: Indiana University Press.

Bunting, Annie, Benjamin Lawrance, and Richard Roberts, eds. 2016. *Marriage by Force? Contestation over Consent and Coercion in Africa*. Athens: Ohio University Press.

Burdick, John. 1998. *Blessed Anastácia: Women, Race, and Popular Christianity in Brazil*. New York: Routledge.

Burrill, Emily. 2015. *States of Marriage: Gender, Justice, and Rights in Colonial Mali*. Athens: Ohio University Press.

Bush, Barbara. 1981. "White 'Ladies,' Coloured 'Favourites' and Black 'Wenches': Some Considerations on Sex, Race and Class Factors in Social Relations in White Creole Society in the British Caribbean." *Slavery and Abolition* 2 (3): 245–262.

Butler, Judith. 1990. *Gender Trouble: Feminism and the Subversion of Identity*. New York: Routledge.

Caldwell, Kia Lilly. 2007. *Negras in Brazil: Re-envisioning Black Women, Citizenship, and the Politics of Identity*. New Brunswick, NJ: Rutgers University Press.

Cannell, Fenella. 1999. *Power and Intimacy in the Christian Philippines*. Cambridge: Cambridge University Press.

Carsten, Janet. 1997. *The Heat of the Hearth: The Process of Kinship in a Malay Fishing Community*. Oxford: Clarendon.

——, ed. 2000. *Cultures of Relatedness: New Approaches to the Study of Kinship*. Cambridge: Cambridge University Press.

——. 2003. *After Kinship*. Cambridge: Cambridge University Press.

Carsten, Janet, Hsiao-Chiao Chui, Siobhan Magee, Eirini Papadaki, and Koreen M. Reece. 2019. "Talking about Kinship." *Anthropology of This Century* 25.

——, eds. 2021. *Marriage in Past, Present and Future Tense*. London: UCL Press.

Cattell, Maria. 2003. "African Widows: Anthropological and Historical Perspectives." *Journal of Women and Aging* 15 (2): 49–66.

Caulfield, Sueann. 2000. *In Defense of Honor: Sexual Morality, Modernity, and Nation in Early Twentieth-Century Brazil*. Durham, NC: Duke University Press.

Cherlin, Andrew. 2010. *The Marriage-Go-Round: The State of Marriage and the Family in America Today*. New York: Penguin Random House.

Chieko. 2009. *Deribarī Hosuto* [Delivery host]. Tokyo: Ōzora Shuppan.

Chimere-Dan, Orieji. 1997. "Non-marital Teenage Childbearing in Southern Africa: The Case of Namibia." *African Population Studies* 12 (2).

Cho, Lee-Jay, Fred Arnold, Tai Hwan Kwon. 1982. *The Determinants of Fertility in the Republic of Korea*. Sejong City: National Research Council, National Academy Press.

Chowdhry, Prem. 2005. "Crisis of Masculinity in Haryana: The Unmarried, the Unemployed and the Aged." *Economic and Political Weekly* 40 (49): 5189–5198.

Claassens, Aninka, and Dee Smythe, eds. 2013. *Marriage, Land and Custom: Essays on Law and Social Change in South Africa*. Claremont: Juta.

Clarke, Edith. 1957. *My Mother Who Fathered Me: A Study of the Family in Three Selected Communities in Jamaica*. London: Allen & Unwin.

Cohen, David W. 1992. *Burying SM: The Politics of Knowledge and the Sociology of Power in Africa*. Portsmouth, NH: Heinemann.

Cole, Jennifer. 2004. "Fresh Contact in Tamatave, Madagascar: Sex, Money and Intergenerational Transformation." *American Ethnologist* 31 (4): 571–586.

——. 2008. "Fashioning Distinction: Youth and Consumerism in Urban Madagascar." In *Figuring the Future: Youth and Temporality in a Global Era*, edited by Jennifer Cole and Deborah Durham, 99–124. Bloomington: Indiana University Press.

——. 2010. *Sex and Salvation: Imagining the Future in Madagascar*. Chicago: University of Chicago Press.

Cole, Jennifer, and Christian Groes, eds. 2016. *Affective Circuits: African Migrations to Europe and the Pursuit of Social Regeneration*. Chicago: University of Chicago Press.

Cole, Jennifer, and Lynn M. Thomas, eds. 2009. *Love in Africa*. Chicago: University of Chicago Press.

Collier, Jane. 1997. *From Duty to Desire: Remaking Families in a Spanish Village*. Princeton, NJ: Princeton University Press.

Comaroff, John L. 1980. *The Meaning of Marriage Payments*. New York: Academic Press.

Comaroff, John L., and Jean Comaroff. 1981. "The Management of Marriage in a Tswana Chiefdom." In *Essays on African Marriage in Southern Africa*, edited by Eileen J. Krige and John L. Comaroff, 29–49. Cape Town: Juta.

Constable, Nicole, ed. 2004. *Cross-Border Marriages: Gender and Mobility in Transnational Asia*. Philadelphia: University of Pennsylvania Press.

Cook, P. A. W. 1931. *Social Organisation and Ceremonial Institutions of the Bomvana*. Cape Town: Juta.

Coontz, Stephanie. 2006. *Marriage, a History: How Love Conquered Marriage*. New York: Penguin Random House.

Cornwall, Andrea. 2002. "Spending Power: Love, Money, and the Reconfiguration of Gender Relations in Ado-Odo, Southwestern Nigeria." *American Ethnologist* 29 (4): 963–980.

Creighton, Millie. 2016. "Through the Korean Wave Looking Glass: Gender, Consumerism, Transnationalism, and Tourism Reflecting Japan-Korea Relations in Global East Asia." *Asia Pacific Journal: Japan Focus* 14: 1–15.

Daffé, G. 2008. "Les Transferts D'argent Des Migrants Sénégalais. Entre Espoir Et Risques De Dependence." In *Le Sénégal Des Migrations*, edited by M.-C. Diop. Paris: Karthala.

Dandona, Rakhi, Lalit Dandona, and G. Anil Kumar. 2006. "Demography and Sex Work Characteristics of Female Sex Workers in India." *BMC International Health and Human Rights* 6 (1): 5.

Dandona, Rakhi, Lalit Dandona, G. Anil Kumar, Juan Pablo Gutierrez, Sam McPherson, Stefano M. Bertozzi, and ASCI FPP Study Team. 2005. "HIV Testing among Female Sex Workers in Andhra Pradesh, India." *AIDS* 19 (17): 2033–2036.

Danely, Jason. 2014. *Aging and Loss: Mourning and Maturity in Contemporary Japan*. New Brunswick, NJ: Rutgers University Press.

Das, Veena. 1979. "Reflections on the Social Construction of Adulthood." In *Identity and Adulthood*, edited by Sudhir Kakar, 89–104. Oxford: Oxford University Press.

———. 2006. *Life and Words: Violence and the Descent into the Ordinary*. Berkeley: University of California Press.

Davidson, Joanna. 2016. *Sacred Rice: An Ethnography of Identity, Environment, and Development in Rural West Africa*. Oxford: Oxford University Press.

———. 2020. "The Problem of Widows." *American Ethnologist* 47 (1): 43–57.

Davis, Deborah S., and Sara L. Friedman. 2014. *Wives, Husbands, and Lovers: Marriage and Sexuality in Hong Kong, Taiwan, and Urban China*. Palo Alto, CA: Stanford University Press.

Davison, Jean. 1996. *Voices from Mutira: Change in the Lives of Gikuyu Women, 1920–1995*. 2nd ed. Boulder, CO: Lynne Rienner.

de Botton, Alain. 1997. *How Proust Can Change Your Life*. New York: Pantheon.

Decoteau, Claire Laurier. 2013. "The Crisis of Liberation: Masculinity, Neoliberalism, and HIV/AIDS in Postapartheid South Africa." *Men and Masculinities* 16 (2): 139–159.

Delius, Peter, and Clive Glaser. 2002. "Sexual Socialisation in South Africa: A Historical Perspective." *African Studies* 61 (1): 27–54.

DePaulo, Bella. 2017. "6 New Things Researchers Learned about Single People in 2017." *The Cut*, December 28. https://www.thecut.com/2017/12/6-new-things-researchers-learned-about-single-people-in-2017.html.

Derks, Annuska. 2008. *Khmer Women on the Move: Exploring Work and Life in Urban Cambodia*. Honolulu: University of Hawai'i Press.

Deuchler, Martina. 1995. *The Confucian Transformation of Korea: A Study of Society and Ideology*. Cambridge, MA: Harvard University Asia Center.

Dhillon, Navtej, and Tarik Yousef, eds. 2009. *Generation in Waiting: The Unfulfilled Promise of Young People in the Middle East*. Washington, DC: Brookings Institution Press.

Dial, F. B. 2008. *Mariage et divorce à Dakar: Itinéraires déminins*. Paris: Karthala.

Dickey, Sara. 2013. "Apprehensions: On Gaining Recognition as Middle-Class in Madurai." *Contributions to Indian Sociology* 47 (2): 217–243.

DiMoia, John P. 2013. *Reconstructing Bodies: Biomedicine, Health, and Nation-Building in South Korea since 1945*. Stanford, CA: Stanford University Press.

Diome, Fatou. 2010. *Celles qui attendent*. Paris: Flammarion.

Diop, Abdoulaye Bara. 1985. *La famille wolof: tradition et changement*. Paris: Karthala.

Douglass, Lisa. 1992. *The Power of Sentiment: Love, Hierarchy, and the Jamaican Family Elite*. Boulder, CO: Westview.

Dupuis-Déri, Francis. 2012. "Le discours de la 'crise de la masculinité' comme refus de l'égalité entre les sexes: histoire d'une rhétorique antiféministe." *Recherches féministes* 25 (1): 89–109.

Durham, Deborah, and Jacqueline Solway, eds. 2017. *Elusive Adulthoods*. Bloomington: Indiana University Press.

Edin, Kathryn, and Maria Kefalas. 2007. *Promises I Can Keep: Why Poor Women Put Motherhood before Marriage*. Berkeley: University of California Press.

Ellece, S. E. 2011. "'Be a Fool Like Me': Gender Construction in the Marriage Advice Ceremony in Botswana—A Critical Discourse Analysis." *Agenda* 87 (25): 43–52.

Elliot, Alice. 2016. 'The Makeup of Destiny: Predestination and the Labor of Hope in a Moroccan Emigrant Town." *American Ethnologist* 43 (3): 488–499.

Engels, Friedrich. 1884. *The Origin of the Family: Private Property and the State*. New York: Pathfinder Press.

Erlank, Natasha. 2004. "'Plain Clean Facts' and Initiation Schools: Christianity, Africans and 'Sex Education' in South Africa, C. 1910–1940." *Agenda* 62:76–83.

Evans-Pritchard, E. E. 1931. "An Alternative Term for 'Bride-Price.'" *Man* 31: 36–39.

Ewelukwa, Uche U. 2002. "Post-colonialism, Gender, Customary Injustice: Widows in African Societies." *Human Rights Quarterly* 24 (2): 424–486.

Fandrych, Ingrid. 2012. "Between Tradition and the Requirements of Modern Life: Hlonipha in South African Bantu Societies, with Special Reference to Lesotho." *Journal of Language and Culture* 3 (4): 67–73.

Ferguson, James. 1990. *The Anti-Politics Machine*. Cambridge: Cambridge University Press.

Fincher, Leta Hong. 2014. *Leftover Women: The Resurgence of Gender Inequality in China*. New York: Zed.

Finkel, Eli. 2017. *The All-or-Nothing Marriage: How the Best Marriages Work*. New York: Dutton.

Finlayson, Rosalie. 2002. "Women's Language of Respect: Isihlonipho Sabafazi." In *Language in South Africa*, edited by Rajend Mesthrie. Cambridge: Cambridge University Press.

Fonseca, Claudia. 2001. "Philanders, Cuckolds, and Wily Women: A Reexamination of Gender Relations in a Brazilian Working-Class Neighborhood." *Men and Masculinities* 3 (3): 261–277.

Foster, Dana Renae. 2013. *A Bird Cannot Fly with One Wing: A Study of Women's Responses to and Attitudes toward Sexual Infidelity in Montego Bay, Jamaica*. Las Vegas: University of Nevada, Las Vegas.

Foucault, Michel. 1988. "Technologies of the Self." In *Technologies of the Self: A Seminar with Michel Foucault*, edited by Luther H. Martin, Huck Gutman and Patrick H. Hutton, 16–49. Amherst: University of Massachusetts Press.

Franklin, Sarah, and Susan McKinnon, eds. 2002. *Relative Values: Reconfiguring Kinship Studies*. Durham, NC: Duke University Press.

Freeman, Carla. 2014. *Entrepreneurial Selves: Neoliberal Respectability and the Making of a Caribbean Middle Class*. Durham, NC: Duke University Press.

———. 2020. "Feeling Neoliberal." *Feminist Anthropology* 1 (1): 71–88.

Freyre, Gilberto. 1933/2003. *Casa Grande e Senzala: Formação da Família Brasileira sob o Regime da Economia Patriarcal*. Rio de Janeiro: José Olympio.

Frosh, Stephen, Ann Phoenix, and Rob Pattman. 2002. *Young Masculinities: Understanding Boys in Contemporary Society*. London: Palgrave.

Fry, Richard. 2016. "For First Time in Modern Era, Living with Parents Edges Out Other Living Arrangements for 18- to 34-Year-Olds." Pew Research Center Social & Demographics

Trends, May 24. https://www.pewsocialtrends.org/2016/05/24/for-first-time-in-modern -era-living-with-parents-edges-out-other-living-arrangements-for-18-to-34-year-olds/.

Gammeltoft, Tine M. 2014. *Haunting Images: A Cultural Account of Selective Reproductive in Vietnam.* Berkeley: University of California Press.

Gassama, A. 2005. "Les marchés du travail domestique au Sénégal." *Innovations* 2 (22): 171–184.

Geertz, Hildred. 1961. *The Javanese Family: A Study of Kinship and Socialization.* Prospect Heights, Illinois: Waveland Press.

Gershon, Ilana. 2011. "Un-friend My Heart: Facebook, Promiscuity and Heartbreak in a Neo-liberal Age." *Anthropological Quarterly* 84 (4): 867–896.

Gibbs, Andrew, Yandisa Sikweyiya, and Rachel Jewkes. 2014. "'Men Value Their Dignity': Securing Respect and Identity Construction in Urban Informal Settlements in South Africa." *Global Health Action* 7: 236–276.

Gilbert, Véronique. 2019. "'A Slut, a Saint, and Everything in Between': Senegalese Women's Mokk Pooj, Interpretive Labor, and Agency." *Signs: Journal of Women in Culture and Society* 44 (2): 379–401.

Ginsburg, Faye. 1987. "Procreation Stories: Reproduction, Nurturance, and Procreation in Life Narratives of Abortion Activists." *American Ethnologist* 14 (4): 623–636.

———. 1998. *Contested Lives: The Abortion Debate in an American Community.* Berkeley: University of California Press.

Gning, Sadio Ba. 2017. "Masculin et féminin, aîné et cadet: recomposition du statut d'aidant et des solidarités intergénérationnelles familiales au Sénégal." *Enfances Familles Générations Revue interdisciplinaire sur la famille contemporaine* 27.

Gockel-Frank, Martina. 2007. "The Gift of God: Reproductive Decisions of Women in Modern Namibia: Case Study of Khorixas, Kunene South" In *Unravelling Taboos. Gender and Sexuality in Namibia*, edited by Suzanne LaFont and Dianne Hubbard, 182–196. Windhoek: Legal Assistance Center.

Goffman, Erving. 1971. *Relations in Public: Microstudies of the Public Order.* London: Penguin.

Goldstein, Donna. 2003. *Laughter Out of Place: Race, Class, Violence, and Sexuality in a Rio Shantytown.* Berkeley: University of California Press.

Gonzalez, Nancie L. 1970. "Toward a Definition of Matrifocality." In *Afro-American Anthropology: Contemporary Perspectives*, edited by Norman E. Whitten and John F. Szwed, 231–244. New York: Free Press.

Gottlieb, Lori. 2010. *Marry Him: The Case for Settling for Mr. Good Enough.* New York: Berkley.

Gray, Catherine. 2018. *The Unexpected Joy of Being Single.* London: Aster.

Green, Cecilia A. 2006. "Between Respectability and Self Respect: Framing Afro-Caribbean Women's Labour History." *Social and Economic Studies* 55 (3): 1–31.

Green, Linda. 1999. *Fear as a Way of Life: Mayan Widows in Rural Guatemala.* New York: Columbia University Press.

Greenfield, Sidney M. 1973. "Dominance, Focality and the Characterization of Domestic Groups: Some Reflections on 'Matrifocality' in the Caribbean." In *The Family in the Caribbean* (Proceedings of the First Conference on the Family in the Caribbean), edited by Gerber Stanford N., 31–49. Río Piedras, Puerto Rico: Institute of Caribbean Studies.

Gregg, Jessica. 2003. *Virtually Virgins: Sexual Strategies and Cervical Cancer in Recife, Brazil.* Palo Alto, CA: Stanford University Press.

Greiner, Clemens. 2011. "Migration, Translocal Networks and Socio-economic Stratification in Namibia." *Africa* 81 (4): 606–627.

Griffiths, A. 1997. *In the Shadow of Marriage.* Chicago: University of Chicago Press.

G'Sell, B. 2016. "The 'Maintenance' of Family: Mediating Relationships in the South African Maintenance Court." *Africa Today* 62 (3): 3–27.

———. 2020. "Multiple Maternities: Performative Motherhood and Support Seeking in South Africa." *Signs: Journal of Women in Culture and Society* 46 (1): 3–29.

Gueye, M. 2004. "Wolof Wedding Songs: Women Negotiating Voice and Space through Verbal Art." PhD diss., State University of New York at Binghamton.

———. 2010. "*Woyyi Céet*: Senegalese Women's Oral Discourses on Marriage and Womanhood." *Research in African Literatures* 41 (4): 65–86.

Gulbrandsen, Ørnulf. 1986. "To Marry—Or Not to Marry: Marital Strategies and Sexual Relations in a Tswana Society." *Ethnos* 51 (1–2): 7–28.

———. 2012. *The State and the Social*. New York: Berghahn Press.

Guyer, Jane I. 1986. "Beti Widow Inheritance and Marriage Law: A Social History." In *Widows in African Societies: Choices and Constraints*, edited by Betty Potash, 193–219. Stanford, CA: Stanford University Press.

———. 1994. "Lineal Identities and Lateral Networks: The Logic of Polyandrous Motherhood." In *Nuptiality in Sub-Saharan Africa: Contemporary Anthropological and Demographic Perspectives*, edited by C. Bledsoe and G. Pison, 231–252. Oxford: Clarendon.

Gwebu, T. 2014. "Urbanization Patterns and Processes and Their Policy Implications in Botswana." In *Population and Housing Census 2011: Analytical Report*, 168–181. Gaborone: Statistics Botswana.

Hall, K., H. Meintjes, and W. Sambu. 2014. "Demography of South Africa's Children." In *South African Child Gauge 2014*, edited by S. Mathews, L. Jamieson, L. Lake, and C. Smith. Cape Town: Children's Institute, University of Cape Town.

Hannaford, D. 2015. "Technologies of the Spouse: Intimate Surveillance in Senegalese Transnational Marriages." *Global Networks* 15 (1): 43–59.

———. 2017. *Marriage without Borders: Transnational Spouses in Neoliberal Senegal*. Philadelphia: University of Pennsylvania Press.

Hannaford, D., and E. E. Foley. 2015. "Negotiating Love and Marriage in Contemporary Senegal: A Good Man Is Hard to Find." *African Studies Review* 58 (2): 205–225.

Haram, Liv. 2001. "'In Sexual Life Women Are Hunters': AIDS and Women Who Drain Men's Bodies: The Case of the Meru of Northern Tanzania." *Society in Transition* 32 (1): 47–55.

Hara Sho. 2018. *Josei Senyō: Kairaku to Iyashi wo 'Fūzoku' de Kau Onnatachi* [For the use of women only: Those who purchase pleasure and healing through the sexual commerce]. Tokyo: Tokuma Shoten.

Harlan, Lindsey. 1995. "Abandoning Shame: Mira and the Margins of Marriage." In *From the Margins of Hindu Marriage: Essays on Gender, Religion, and Culture*, edited by Lindsey Harlan and Paul Courtright, 204–227. Oxford: Oxford University Press.

Hartman, Saidiya. 2019. *Wayward Lives, Beautiful Experiments: Intimate Histories of Riotous Black Girls, Troublesome Women, and Other Radicals*. New York: Norton.

Hasso, Frances S. 2010. *Consuming Desires: Family Crisis and the State in the Middle East*. Stanford, CA: Stanford University Press.

Haugerud, Angelique. 2018. "Activism." In *The Wiley-Blackwell International Encyclopedia of Anthropology*, edited by Hillary Callan. Oxford: John Wiley.

Hautzinger, Sarah. 2007. *Violence in the City of Women: Police and Batterers in Bahia, Brazil*. Berkeley: University of California Press.

Hawley, John Stratton, ed. 1994. *Sati, the Blessing and the Curse: The Burning of Wives in India*. Oxford: Oxford University Press.

Heinrich, Patrick, and Christian Galan, eds. 2018. *Being Young in Super-Aging Japan: Formative Events and Cultural Reactions*. New York: Routledge.

Hellman, Ellen. 1974. "African Townswomen in the Process of Change." *South Africa International* 5 (1): 14–22.

Hetherington, E. Mavis, and John Kelly. 2003. *For Better or Worse: Divorce Reconsidered.* New York: Norton.

Hinote, Brian P., and Gretchen R. Webber. 2012. "Drinking toward Manhood: Masculinity and Alcohol in the Former USSR." *Men and Masculinities* 15 (3): 292–310.

Hirsch, Jennifer S. 2003. *A Courtship after Marriage: Sexuality and Love in Mexican Transnational Families.* Berkeley: University of California Press.

———. 2015. "Desire across Borders: Markets, Migration, and Marital HIV Risk in Rural Mexico." *Culture, Health & Sexuality* 17 (suppl. 1): 20–33.

Hirsch, Jennifer S., and Holly Wardlow, eds. 2006. *Modern Loves: The Anthropology of Romantic Courtship and Companionate Marriage.* Ann Arbor: University of Michigan Press.

Hochschild, Arlie, with Anne Machung. 1989. *The Second Shift: Working Parents and the Revolution at Home.* New York: Penguin.

Hodge, Merle. 2002. "We Kind of Family." In *Gendered Realities: Essays in Caribbean Feminist Thought,* edited by Patricia Mohammed, 474–485. Mona, Jamaica: University of the West Indies Press.

Hodgson, Dorothy L., and Sheryl A. McCurdy, eds. 2001. *"Wicked" Women and the Reconfiguration of Gender in Africa.* Portsmouth, NH: Heinemann.

Hoesterey, James. 2016. *Rebranding Islam: Piety, Prosperity, and a Self-Help Guru.* Palo Alto: Stanford University Press.

Honwana, Alcinda, and Filip De Boeck, eds. 2005. *Makers and Breakers: Children and Youth in Postcolonial Africa.* Oxford: Oxford University Press.

Hordge-Freeman, Elizabeth. 2015. *The Color of Love: Racial Features, Stigma, and Socialization in Black Brazilian Families.* Austin: University of Texas Press.

Hosegood, V., N. McGrath, and T. Moultrie. 2009. "Dispensing with Marriage: Marital and Partnership Trends in Rural KwaZulu-Natal, South Africa, 2000–2006." *Demographic Research* 20: 279–312.

Hota, Pinky. 2020. "Populist Panics: Sex as Excess in Right Wing India." *Anthropological Quarterly* 93 (3): 377–400.

Hulbert, Homer B. 1902. *Korea Review: A Monthly Magazine.* Vol. 2. Seoul: Methodist Publishing.

Hunter, Mark. 2002. "The Materiality of Everyday Sex: Thinking beyond 'Prostitution.'" *African Studies* 61 (1): 99–120.

———. 2006. "Fathers without Amandla: Zulu-Speaking Men and Fatherhood." In *Baba: Men and Fatherhood in South Africa,* edited by Linda Richter and Robert Morrell. Cape Town: Human Science Research Council.

———. 2007. "The Changing Political Economy of Sex in South Africa: The Significance of Unemployment and Inequalities to the Scale of the AIDS Pandemic." *Social Science and Medicine* 64 (3): 689–700.

———. 2009a. "IsiZulu-Speaking Men and Changing Households: From Providers within Marriage to Providers outside Marriage." In *Zulu Identities: Being Zulu, Past and Present,* edited by Benedict Carton, John Laband, and Jabulani Sithole, 566–572. New York: Columbia University Press.

———. 2009b. "Providing Love: Sex and Exchange in Twentieth-Century South Africa." In *Love in Africa,* edited by Jennifer Cole and Lynn M. Thomas, 136–156. Chicago: University of Chicago Press.

———. 2010. *Love in the Time of AIDS: Inequality, Gender, and Rights in South Africa.* Bloomington: Indiana University Press.

———. 2016. "Is It Enough to Talk of Marriage as a Process? Legitimate Co-habitation in Umlazi, South Africa." *Anthropology Southern Africa* 39 (4): 281–296.

Hunter, Monica. 1936/1961. *Reaction to Conquest.* 2nd ed. London: Oxford University Press.

Iken, Adelheid. 1999. *Woman-Headed Households in Southern Namibia: Causes, Patterns and Consequences*. Frankfurt am Main: IKO.

Illaiah, Kancha. 1994. *Why I Am Not a Hindu*. Kolkata: Stree Samya.

Inhorn, Marcia, and Nancy Smith-Hefner. 2020. *Waithood: Gender, Education and Global Delays in Marriage and Child-Bearing*. New York: Berghahn.

Iwobi, Andrew Ubaka. 2008. "No Cause for Merriment: Position of Widows under Nigerian Law." *Canadian Journal of Women and the Law* 20 (1): 37–86.

Jackson, Michael. 2012. *Between Oneself and Another*. Berkeley: University of California Press.

James, Deborah. 2015. *Money from Nothing: Indebtedness and Aspiration in South Africa*. Stanford, CA: Stanford University Press.

———. 2017. "Not Marrying in South Africa: Consumption, Aspiration and the New Middle Class." *Anthropology Southern Africa* 40 (1): 1–14.

Jean-Baptiste, Rachel. 2014. *Conjugal Rights: Marriage, Sexuality, and Urban Life in Colonial Libreville, Gabon*. Athens: Ohio University Press.

Jenkins, Carol L., ed 2003. *Widows and Divorcees in Later Life: On Their Own Again*. New York: Routledge.

Johnson-Hanks, Jennifer. 2005. "When the Future Decides: Uncertainty and Intentional Action in Contemporary Cameroon." *Current Anthropology* 46 (3): 363–385.

———. 2006. *Uncertain Honor: Modern Motherhood in an African Crisis*. Chicago: University of Chicago Press.

Jones, Carla. 2004. "Whose Stress? Emotion Work in Middle-Class Javanese Homes." *Ethnos* 69 (4): 509–528.

———. 2014. "Career Woman" [Wanita Karir]. In *Figures of Southeast Asian Modernity*, edited by Barker Joshua, Erik Harms, and Johan Lindquist, 167–169. Honolulu: University of Hawai'i Press.

Jones, Cecily. 2007. *Engendering Whiteness: White Women and Colonialism in Barbados and North Carolina 1627–1865*. Manchester: Manchester University Press.

Jones, Gavin. 2018. "What Is Driving Marriage and Cohabitation in Low Fertility Countries?" In *Low Fertility Regimes and Demographic and Societal Change*, edited by Dudley Poston Jr., Samsik Lee, and Han Gon Kim, 149–166. Berlin: Springer.

Jordan, Ana, and Amy Chandler. 2019. "Crisis, What Crisis? A Feminist Analysis of Discourse on Masculinities and Suicide." *Journal of Gender Studies* 28 (4): 462–474.

Kamal, Soniah. 2019. *Unmarriageable*. New York: Ballantine Books.

Kanji, S., and F. K. Camara. 2000. *L'union matrimoniale dans la tradition des peuples noirs*. Paris: l'Harmattan.

Kapadia, Karin. 1994. "'Kinship Burns!': Kinship Discourses and Gender in Tamil South India." *Social Anthropology* 2 (3): 281–297.

Karch, Cecilia A. 1981. "The Growth of the Corporate Economy in Barbados: Class/Race Factors 1890–1988." In *Contemporary Caribbean: A Sociological Reader*, 213–241. Maracas, Trinidad and Tobago: College Press.

Karch, Cecilia A., and Henderson Carter. 1997. *The Rise of the Phoenix: The Barbados Mutual Life Assurance Society in Caribbean Economy and Society 1840–1990*. Kingston, Jamaica: Ian Randle.

Kendall, Laurel. 1984. "Wives, Lesser Wives, and Ghosts: Supernatural Conflict in a Korean Village." *Asian Folklore Studies* 43 (2): 215–225.

Kibria, Nazli. 2012. "Transnational Marriage and the Bangladeshi Muslim Diaspora in Britain and the U.S." *Culture and Religion* 13 (2): 277–290.

Kim, Eunjung. 2017. *Curative Violence: Rehabilitating Disability, Gender, and Sexuality in Modern Korea*. Durham, NC: Duke University Press.

Kincaid, Jamaica. 1985. *Annie John*. New York: Plume.

Kirwen, Michael C. 1979. *African Widows: An Empirical Study of the Problems of Adapting Western Christian Teachings on Marriage to the Leviratic Custom for the Care of Widows in Four Rural African Societies*. Maryknoll, NY: Orbis Books.

Kislev, Elyakim. 2019. *Happy Singlehood: The Rising Acceptance and Celebration of Solo Living*. Berkeley: University of California Press.

Klinenberg, Eric. 2012. *Going Solo: The Extraordinary Rise and Surprising Appeal of Living Alone*. New York: Penguin.

Korducki, Kelli María. 2018. *Hard to Do: The Surprising, Feminist History of Breaking Up*. Toronto: Coach House.

Kringelbach, H. 2016. "'Marrying Out' for Love: Women's Narratives of Polygyny and Alternative Marriage Choices in Contemporary Senegal." *African Studies Review* 59 (1): 155–174.

Kubanji, R. 2014. "Nuptiality Patterns and Trends in Botswana." In *Population and Housing Census 2011: Analytical Report*, 224–236. Gaborone: Statistics Botswana.

Kundu, Sreemoyee Piu. 2018. *Status Single: The Truth about Being a Single Woman in India*. New Delhi: Amaryllis.

Kunreuther, Laura. 2018. "Sounds of Democracy: Performance, Protest, and Political Subjectivity." *Cultural Anthropology* 33 (1): 1–31.

Kuper, Adam. 1982. *Wives for Cattle: Bridewealth and Marriage in Southern Africa*. London: Routledge & Kegan Paul.

———. 1987. *South Africa and the Anthropologist*. London: Routledge & Kegan Paul.

Kuriakose, Simi. 2014. "Meet the 5 Kinds of Single Women." *Times of India*, December 24. https://timesofindia.indiatimes.com/life-style/relationships/love-sex/Meet-the-5-kinds -of-single-women/articleshow/18848928.cms.

Lahad, Kinneret. 2012. "Singlehood, Waiting, and the Sociology of Time." *Sociological Forum* 21 (1): 163–186.

Lamb, Sarah. 1999. "Aging, Gender, and Widowhood: Perspectives from Rural West Bengal." *Contributions to Indian Sociology* 33 (3): 541–570.

———. 2000. *White Saris and Sweet Mangoes: Aging, Gender, and Body in North India*. Berkeley: University of California Press.

———. 2001. "Being a Widow and Other Life Stories: Interplay between Lives and Words." *Anthropology and Humanism* 26 (1): 16–34.

———. 2018. "Being Single in India: Gendered Identities, Class Mobilities, and Personhoods in Flux." *Ethos* 46 (1): 49–69.

———. 2020. "Never-Married Women in India: Gendered Life Courses, Desires, and Identities in Flux." In *Waithood: Gender, Education, and Global Delays in Marriage and Childbearing*, edited by Marcia C. Inhorn and Nancy J. Smith-Hefner, 290–314. New York: Berghahn.

Lambek, Michael, and Jacqueline S. Solway. 2001 "Just Anger: Scenarios of Indignation in Botswana and Madagascar." *Ethnos* 66 (1): 49–72.

Landes, Ruth. 1947. *City of Women*. New York: Macmillan.

Lapierre-Adamcyk, Evelyne, and Thomas K. Burch. 1974. "Trends and Differentials in Age at Marriage in Korea." *Studies in Family Planning* 5 (8): 255–260.

Lee, Doreen. 2016. *Activist Archives: Youth Culture and the Political Past in Indonesia*. Durham, NC: Duke University Press.

Lee, Hae-Young. 1980. "Demographic Transition in Korea." *Bulletin of the Population Development and Studies Center* 8/9: 5–18. https://www.jstor.org/stable/43798515.

Lee, R. 2012. "Death in Slow Motion: Funerals, Ritual Practice and Road Danger in South Africa." *African Studies* 71 (2): 195–211.

Lee, Yoonjoo. 2019. "Cohort Differences in Changing Attitudes toward Marriage in South Korea, 1998–2014: An Age-Period-Cohort-Detrended Model." *Asian Population Studies* 15 (3): 266–281.

Leith, J. Clark. 2005. *Why Botswana Prospered*. Montreal: McGill-Queen's University Press.

Leopeng, Bandile Bertrand, and Malose Langa. 2017. "The Fathers of Destiny: Representations of Fatherhood in a Popular South African Magazine." *Journal of Psychology in Africa* 27 (5): 438–442.

Lim, Sungyun. 2019. *Rules of the House: Family Law and Domestic Disputes in Colonial Korea*. Oakland: University of California Press.

Lindsay, Lisa A., and Stephan F. Miescher, eds. 2003. *Men and Masculinities in Modern Africa*. Portsmouth, NH: Heinemann.

Livingston, J. 2009. "Suicide, Risk, and Investment in the Heart of the African Miracle." *Cultural Anthropology* 24 (4): 652–680.

Lopata, Helena Znaniecka. 1987. *Widows*. Vols. 1–2. Durham, NC: Duke University Press.

———. 1996. *Current Widowhood: Myths and Realities*. Thousand Oaks, CA: Sage.

Lukacs, Gabriella. 2019. *Invisibility by Design: Women and Labor in Japan's Digital Economy*. Durham, NC: Duke University Press.

Lynch, Caitrin. 2007. *Juki Girls, Good Girls: Gender and Cultural Politics in Sri Lanka's Global Garment Industry*. Ithaca, NY: ILR/Cornell University Press.

Mahmood, Saba. 2001. "Feminist Theory, Embodiment, and the Docile Agent: Some Reflections on the Egyptian Islamic Revival." *Cultural Anthropology* 16 (2): 202–236.

Mains, Daniel. 2007. "Neoliberal Times: Progress, Boredom, and Shame Among Young Men in Urban Ethiopia." *American Ethnologist* 34: 659–673.

Mani, Lata. 1998. *Contentious Traditions: The Debate on Sati in Colonial India*. Berkeley: University of California Press.

———. 2014. "Sex and the Signal-free Corridor: Towards a New Feminist Imaginary." *Economic and Political Weekly* 49 (6): 26–29.

Manzenreiter, Wolfram, and Barbara Holthus. 2017. "Introduction: Happiness in Japan through the Anthropological Lens." In *Happiness and the Good Life in Japan*, edited by Wolfram Manzenreiter and Barbara Holthus, 1–22. New York: Routledge.

Maqsood, Ammara. 2017. *The New Pakistani Middle Class*. Cambridge, MA: Harvard University Press.

Masquelier, Adeline. 2005. "The Scorpion's Sting: Youth, Marriage and the Struggle for Social Maturity in Niger." *Journal of the Royal Anthropological Institute* 11 (1): 59–83.

Massey, Douglas S., Joaquín Arango, Graeme Hugo, Ali Kouaouci, Adela Pellegrino, and J. Edward Taylor. 1993. "Theories of International Migration: A Review and Appraisal." *Population and Development Review* 19 (3): 431–466.

Massiah, Joycelin. 1983. *Women as Heads of Households in the Caribbean: Family Structure and Feminine Status*. Paris: UNESCO.

Matlon, Jordanna. 2014. "Narratives of Modernity, Masculinity, and Citizenship amid Crisis in Abidjan's Sorbonne." *Antipode* 46 (3): 717–735.

———. 2016. "Racial Capitalism and the Crisis of Black Masculinity." *American Sociological Review* 81 (5): 1014–1038.

Mauss, Marcel. 1950/2002. *The Gift: The Form and Reason for Exchange in Archaic Societies*. London: Routledge.

Mayblin, Maya. 2010. *Gender, Catholicism, and Morality in Brazil: Virtuous Husbands, Powerful Wives*. New York: Palgrave Macmillan.

Mayer, Philip. 1961. *Townsmen or Tribesmen: Conservatism and the Process of Urbanization in a South African City*. Cape Town: Oxford University Press.

———. 1972. *Report on Research on Self-Organisation by Youth among the Xhosa Speaking Peoples of the Ciskei and Transkei. Vol. 1: The Red Xhosa*. Grahamstown, South Africa: Rhodes University.

Mazumdar, Indrani, and N. Neetha. 2011. "Gender Dimensions: Employment Trends in India, 1993–4 to 2009–10." *Economic and Political Weekly* 46 (43): 118–126.

Mbodj-Pouye, Aissatou, and Stefan LeCourant. 2017. "Living Away from Family Is Not Good but Living with It Is Worse: Debating Conjugality across Generations of West African Migrants in France." *Mande Studies* 19:109–130.

McCallum, Cecilia A. 1999. "Restraining Women: Gender, Sexuality and Modernity in Salvador Da Bahia." *Bulletin of Latin American Research* 18 (3): 275–293.

McElaney-Johnson, Ann. 1999. "Epistolary Friendship: La prise de parole in Mariama Bâ's Une si longue letter" *Research in African Literatures* 30 (2): 110–121.

McGranahan, Carole. 2016. "Theorizing Refusal: An Introduction." *Cultural Anthropology* 31 (3): 319–325.

———. 2020. "Activism as Care: Kathmandu, Paris, Toronto, New York City." *kritisk etnografi—Swedish Journal of Anthropology* 3 (1): 43–60.

McKittrick, Meredith. 1997. "Reinventing the Family: Kinship, Marriage and Famine in Northern Namibia, 1948–54." *Social Science History* 23 (3): 265–295.

Medeiros, Melanie A. 2018. *Marriage, Divorce, and Distress in Northeast Brazil: Black Women's Perspectives on Love, Respect, and Kinship.* New Brunswick, NJ: Rutgers University Press.

———. 2022. "Intersectionality and Normative Masculinity in Northeast Brazil." In *Global Perspectives on Gender*, edited by Nadine Fernandez and Katie Nelson. Albany, NY: SUNY Press.

Medeiros, Melanie A., and Tiffany Henriksen. 2019. "Race and Employment Practices in Northeast Brazil's Ecotourism Industry: An Analysis of Cultural Capital, Symbolic Capital and Symbolic Power." *Latin American Research Review* 54 (2): 366–380.

Medie, Peace Adzo. 2020. *His Only Wife.* Chapel Hill, NC: Algonquin.

MEFP. 2017. *Politique Nationale de Migration du Sénégal (PNMS).* Draft version. Dakar: Ministère de l'Economie, des Finances et du Plan.

Mehta, Rama. 1975. *Divorced Hindu Women.* New Delhi, India: Vikas.

Melly, C. M. 2011. "Titanic Tales of Missing Men: Reconfigurations of National Identity and Gendered Presence in Dakar, Senegal." *American Ethnologist* 38:361–376.

Meneley, Anne. 2018. "Consumerism." *Annual Review of Anthropology* 47:117–132.

Mies, Maria. 2012. *The Lace Makers of Narsapur.* North Melbourne: Spinifex Press.

Miller, Errol. 1991. *Men at Risk.* Kingston: Jamaica Pub. House.

Minturn, Leigh. 1993. *Sita's Daughters: Coming Out of Purdah.* New York: Oxford University.

Mkhwanazi, Nolwazi. 2014. "'An African Way of Doing Things': Reproducing Gender and Generation." *Anthropology Southern Africa* 37 (1–2): 107–118.

Mohanty, Chandra T. 1988. "Under Western Eyes: Feminist Scholarship and Colonial Discourses." *Feminist Review* 30:61–88.

———. 2003. *Feminism without Borders: Decolonizing Theory, Practicing Solidarity.* Durham, NC: Duke University Press.

Mohlabane, Neo, Ntombizonke Gumede, and Zitha Mokomane. 2019. "Attitudes towards Marriage in Postapartheid South Africa." In *Family Matters: Family Cohesion, Values and Wellbeing*, edited by Zitha Mokomane, Benjamin J. Roberts, Jarè Struwig, and Stevenson Gordon, 156–181. Cape Town: HSRC Press.

Mojola, Sanyu A. 2014. "Providing Women, Kept Men: Doing Masculinity in the Wake of the African HIV/AIDS Pandemic." *Signs* 39 (2): 341–363.

Mokomane, Zitha. 2005. "Co-habitation in Botswana: An Alternative or a Prelude to Marriage?" *African Population Studies* 20 (1): 19–37.

———. 2006. "The Collection of Marital Status Data in Botswana: A Review of the 'Living Together' Category." *Journal of Population Research* 23 (1): 83–90.

Mollett, Sharlene, and Caroline Faria. 2013. "Messing with Gender in Feminist Political Ecology." *Geoforum* 45: 116–125.

Moodie, T. Dunbar, with Vivienne Ndatshe. 1994. *Going for Gold: Men, Mines, and Migration.* Berkeley: University of California Press.

Moriki, Yoshie. 2017. "Physical Intimacy and Happiness in Japanese Families: Sexless Marriages and Parent-Child Co-sleeping." In *Happiness and the Good Life in Japan*, edited by Wolfram Manzenreiter and Barbara G. Holthus, 41–52. London: Routledge.

Morrell, Robert. 2001. "Corporal Punishment and Masculinity in South African Schools." *Men and Masculinities* 4 (2): 140–157.

Motswapong, Elizabeth, Mmapula Kebaneilwe, Tshenolo Madigele, Musa Dube, Senzokuhle Setume, and Tirelo Moraka-Modie. 2018. "'A Little Baby is on the Way': *Botho/Ubuntu* and Community-Building in Gaborone Baby Showers." *Gender Studies* 16: 50–70.

Mupotsa, Danai. 2015. "The Promise of Happiness: Desire, Attachment and Freedom in Post/apartheid South Africa." *Critical Arts* 29 (2): 183–198.

Mutongi, Kenda. 2007. *Worries of the Heart: Widows, Family, and Community in Kenya.* Chicago: University of Chicago Press.

Myscofski, Carole A. 2013. *Amazons, Wives, Nuns, and Witches: Women and the Catholic Church in Colonial Brazil, 1500–1822.* Austin: University of Texas Press.

Najmabadi, Afsaneh. 2013. *Professing Selves: Transsexuality and Same-Sex Desire in Contemporary Iran.* Durham, NC: Duke University Press.

Nandi, Ashish. 1990. "Sati: A Nineteenth Century Tale of Women, Violence and Protest." In *At the Edge of Psychology: Essays in Politics and Culture*, edited by Ashish Nandy, 1–31. New Delhi: Oxford University Press.

Nanitelamio, J. 1995. "Insertion urbaine et representations des statuts feminins." In *La Ville à Guichets Fermés? Itinéraires, réseaux et insertion urbaine*, edited by A. B. Diop and P. Antoine. Dakar: IFAN.

Narayan, Deepa. 2019. *Chup: Breaking the Silence about India's Women.* New Delhi: Juggernaut.

Ndinda, C., U. O. Okeke Uzodike, C. Chimbwete, R. Pool, and MDP-Microbide Development Programme. 2007. "Gender Relations in the Context of HIV/AIDS in Rural South Africa." *AIDS Care* 19 (7): 844–849.

Nelson, Laura C. 2000. *Measured Excess: Status, Gender, and Consumer Nationalism in South Korea.* New York: Columbia University Press.

Newberry, Janice. 2006. *Back Door Java: State Formation and the Domestic in Working Class Java.* Peterborough, Ontario: Broadview Press.

Niehaus, Isak. 2017. "Marriage, Kinship and Childcare in the Aftermath of AIDS: Rethinking 'Orphanhood' in the South African Lowveld." *Anthropology Southern Africa* 40 (1): 42–55.

Nilsson, F. 2004. *Creating Spaces for Action: ANC-women Politicians' Views on Bridewealth and Gender-Related Power.* Uppsala: Acta Universitatis Upsaliensis.

Nolte, Insa. 2017. "New Histories of Marriage and Politics in Africa." *Gender & History* 29 (3): 742–748.

Nuckolls, Charles W. 1993. *Siblings in South Asia: Brothers and Sisters in Cultural Context.* New York: Guilford.

Nyanzi, Stella, Margaret Emodu-Walakira, and Wilberforce Serwaniko. 2009. "The Widow, the Will, and Widow-Inheritance in Kampala: Revisiting Victimization Arguments." *Canadian Journal of African Studies / Revue canadienne des études africaines* 43 (1): 12–33.

Obbo, Christine. 1986. "Some East African Widows." In *Widows in African Societies: Choices and Constraints*, edited by Betty Potash, 84–106. Stanford, CA: Stanford University Press.

Oboler, Regina Smith. 1985. *Women, Power, and Economic Change: The Nandi of Kenya.* Stanford, CA: Stanford University Press.

OHCHR. 2015. "Le Comité pour l'élimination de la discrimination à l'égard des femmes examine le rapport du Sénégal." https://www.ohchr.org/fr/NewsEvents/Pages/DisplayNews.aspx?NewsID=16212&LangID=F.

Osborn, Emily Lynn. 2011. *Our New Husbands Are Here: Households, Gender, and Politics in a West African State from the Slave Trade to Colonial Rule.* Athens: Ohio University Press.

Othlogile, B. 1994. "Mistress at Law: The Case of the Unprotected Dependent." *PULA: Botswana Journal of African Studies* 8 (2): 1–17.

Owen, Margaret. 1996. *A World of Widows.* London: Zed Books.

Padilla, Mark B., Jennifer S. Hirsch, Miguel Munoz-Laboy, Robert Sember, and Richard G. Parker, eds. 2007. *Love and Globalization: Transformations of Intimacy in the Contemporary World.* Nashville, TN: Vanderbilt University Press.

Papadaki, Eirini. 2021. "Marriage, Time, Affect, and the Politics of Compromise in Athens." In *Marriage in Past, Present and Future Tense,* edited by Janet Carsten, Hsiao-Chaio Chiu, Sioban Magee, Eirini Papadaki, and Koreen M. Reece, 76–94. London: UCL Press.

Park, Hyunjoon, and James M. Raymo. 2013. "Divorce in Korea: Trends and Educational Differentials." *Journal of Marriage and the Family* 75 (1): 110–126.

Parkin, David, and David Nyamwaya. 1987. *Transformations of African Marriage.* Manchester: Manchester University Press.

Patel, Bhaichand, ed. 2006. *Chasing the Good Life: On Being Single.* New Delhi: Viking India.

Pateman, Carole. 1988. *The Sexual Contract.* Stanford, CA: Stanford University Press.

Pauli, Julia. 2010. "Demographic and Anthropological Perspectives on Marriage and Reproduction in Namibia." In *Towards Interdisciplinarity: Experiences of the Long-Term ACACIA Project,* edited by Wilhelm J. G. Möhlig, Olaf Bubenzer, and Gunter Menz, 205–234. Cologne: Heinrich-Barth-Institute.

———. 2011. "Celebrating Distinctions: Common and Conspicuous Weddings in Rural Namibia." *Ethnology* 50 (2): 153–167.

———. 2012. "Creating Illegitimacy: Negotiating Relations and Reproduction within Christian Contexts in Northwest Namibia." *Journal of Religion in Africa* 42 (4): 408–432.

———. 2013. "'Sharing Made Us Sisters': Sisterhood, Migration, and Household Dynamics in Mexico and Namibia." In *The Anthropology of Sibling Relations: Shared Parentage, Experience, and Exchange,* edited by Erdmute Alber, Cati Coe, and Tatjana Theler, 29–50. New York: Palgrave Macmillan.

———. 2017. "The Key to Fertility: Generation, Reproduction and Class Formation in a Namibian Community." In *Fertility, Conjuncture, Difference: Anthropological Approaches to the Heterogeneity of Modern Fertility Declines,* edited by Philip Kreager and Astrid Bochow, 43–71. Oxford: Berghahn.

———. 2019. *The Decline of Marriage in Namibia: Kinship and Social Class in a Rural Community.* Bielefeld: Transcript.

Pauli, Julia, and Rijk van Dijk. 2016. "Marriage as an End or the End of Marriage? Change and Continuity in Southern African Marriages." *Anthropology Southern Africa* 39 (4): 257–266.

Peletz, Michael. 2020. *Sharia Transformations: Cultural Politics and the Rebranding of an Islamic Judiciary.* Berkeley: University of California Press.

Perel, Esther. 2006. *Mating in Captivity: Unlocking Erotic Intelligence.* New York: HarperCollins.

———. 2018. *The State of Affairs: Rethinking Infidelity.* New York: HarperCollins.

Phadke, Shilpa. 2020. "Defending Frivolous Fun: Feminist Acts of Claiming Public Spaces in South Asia." *South Asia: Journal of South Asian Studies* 43 (2): 281–293.

Phadke, Shilpa, Sameera Khan, and Shilpa Ranade. 2011. *Why Loiter? Women and Risk on Mumbai Streets.* New Delhi: Penguin.

Pollock, Sheldon. 1993. "Rāmāyaṇa and Political Imagination in India." *Journal of Asian Studies* 52 (2): 261–297.

Posel, Dorrit. 2005. "The Scandal of Manhood: 'Baby Rape' and the Politicization of Sexual Violence in Post-apartheid South Africa." *Culture, Health & Sexuality* 7 (3): 239–252.

Posel, Dorrit, and Stephanie Rudwick. 2013. "Changing Patterns of Marriage and Cohabitation in South Africa." In *Marriage, Land and Custom: Essays on Law and Social Change in South Africa*, edited by Aninka Claassens and Dee Smythe, 169–180. Claremont: Juta.

———. 2014a. "Marriage and Bridewealth (Ilobolo) in Contemporary Zulu Society." *African Studies Review* 57 (2): 51–72.

———. 2014b. "Ukukipita (Cohabiting): Socio-cultural Constraints in Urban Zulu Society." *Journal of Asian and African Studies* 49 (3): 282–297.

Potash, Betty, ed. 1986a. *Widows in African Societies: Choices and Constraints*. Stanford, CA: Stanford University Press.

———. 1986b. "Wives of the Grave: Widows in a Rural Luo Community." In *Widows in African Societies: Choices and Constraints*, edited by Betty Potash, 44–65. Stanford, CA: Stanford University Press.

Pothen, Sosamma. 1986. *Divorce: Its Causes and Consequences in Hindu Society*. New Delhi: Shakti Books.

Preston-Whyte, Eleanor. 1978. "Families without Marriage: A Zulu Case Study." In *Social System and Tradition in Southern Africa: Essays in Honour of Eileen Jensen Krige*, edited by William J. Argyle and Eleanor Preston-Whyte, 55–85. Cape Town: Oxford University Press.

———. 1981. "Women Migrants and Workers." In *Essays on African Marriage in South Africa*, edited by E. J. Krige and J. L. Comaroff, 158–172. Johannesburg: Juta.

Preston-Whyte, Eleanor, and Maria Zondi. 1989. "To Control Their Own Reproduction: The Agenda of Black Teenage Mothers in Durban." *Agenda* 4:47–68.

Rajagopal, Arvind. 2001. *Politics after Television: Hindu Nationalism and the Reshaping of the Public in India*. Cambridge: Cambridge University Press.

Ramberg, Lucinda. 2014. *Given to the Goddess: South Indian Devadasis and the Sexuality of Religion*. Durham, NC: Duke University Press.

Rebhun, L. A. 2007. "The Strange Marriage of Love and Interest: Economic Change and Emotional Intimacy in Northeast Brazil, Private and Public." In *Love and Globalization: Transformations of Intimacy in the Contemporary World*, edited by Mark Padilla, Jennifer Hirsch, Miguel Muñoz-Laboy, and Richard G. Parker, 107–119. Nashville, TN: Vanderbilt University Press.

Reddock, Rhoda. 1985. "Women and the Slave Plantation Economy in the Caribbean." In *Retrieving Women's History*, edited by Kleinberg S. Jay. Oxford: Berg.

Reece, Koreen M. 2019. "'We are Seeing Things': Recognition, Risk and Reproducing Kinship in Botswana's Time of AIDS." *Africa* 89 (1): 40–60.

Rhine, Kathryn A. 2016. *The Unseen Things: Women, Secrecy, and HIV in Northern Nigeria*. Bloomington: Indiana University Press.

Rice, Kathleen. 2015. "'Most of Them, They Just Want Someone to Under Them': Gender, Generation, and Personhood among the Xhosa." PhD diss., University of Toronto.

———. 2017. "Rights and Responsibilities in Rural South Africa: Implications for Gender, Generation, and Personhood." *Journal of the Royal Anthropological Institute* 23: 28–41.

———. 2020. "Working Women in Rural South Africa: Conflicts and Contradictions." *Anthropological Quarterly* 93 (3): 351–375.

Rinaldo, Rachel. 2019. "Obedience and Authority among Muslim Couples: Negotiating Gendered Religious Scripts in Contemporary Indonesia." *Sociology of Religion: A Quarterly Review* 80 (3): 323–349.

Robertson, Jennifer E. 1998. *Takarazuka: Sexual Politics and Popular Culture in Modern Japan*. Berkeley: University of California Press.

Roitman, Janet. 2017. "Africa Otherwise." In *African Futures: Essays on Crisis, Emergence, and Possibility*, edited by Brian Goldstone and Juan Obarrio, 23–38. Chicago: University of Chicago Press.

Rosaldo, Renato. 1980. *Ilongot Headhunting, 1883–1974: A Study in Society and History*. Stanford, CA: Stanford University Press.

Rosin, Hannah. 2012. *The End of Men: And the Rise of Women*. New York: Riverhead Books.

Rubin, Gayle. 1975. "The Traffic in Women: Notes on the 'Political Economy' of Sex." In *Toward an Anthropology of Women*, edited by Rayna Reiter, 157–210. New York: Monthly Review Press.

———. 1984. "Thinking Sex: Notes for a Radical Theory of the Politics of Sexuality." In *Pleasure and Danger: Exploring Female Sexuality*, edited by Carole S. Vance, 267–319. Boston: Routledge.

Rudwick, Stephanie, and Dorrit Posel. 2014. "Contemporary Functions of Ilobolo (Bridewealth) in Urban South African Zulu Society." *Journal of Contemporary African Studies* 32 (1): 118–136.

———. 2015. "Zulu bridewealth (ilobolo) and Womanhood in South Africa." *Social Dynamics* 41: 289–306.

Rudwick, Stephanie, and Magcino Shange. 2006. "Sociolinguistic Oppression or Expression of 'Zuluness'? 'IsiHlonipho' among isiZulu-Speaking Females." *Southern African Linguistics and Applied Language Studies* 24 (4): 473–482.

SADC. 2015. "Gender Based Violence." *Gender Protocol 2015 Barometer: Botswana*. https://genderlinks.org.za/programme-web-menu/publications/sadc-gender-protocol-2015-barometer-botswana-2015-06-25/.

Safa, Helen. 2005. "The Matrifocal Family and Patriarchal Ideology in Cuba and the Caribbean." *Journal of Latin American and Caribbean Anthropology* 10 (2): 314–338.

Samatar, Abdi. 1999. *An African Miracle*. Portsmouth: Heinemann.

Sarti, Cynthia. 2011. *A Família Como Espelho: Um Estudo Sobre a Moral dos Pobres*. 7th ed. São Paulo: Cortez.

Schapera, I. 1933. "Premarital Pregnancy and Native Opinion: A Note on Social Change." *Africa* 6 (1): 59–89.

———. 1938/1984. *Tswana Law and Custom*. London: Frank Cass.

———. 1940/1971. *Married Life in an African Tribe*. Middlesex: Pelican.

Schnegg, Michael. 2016. "Collective Foods: Situating Food on the Continuum of Private-Common Property Regimes." *Current Anthropology* 57 (5): 683–689.

Schroeder, Richard A. 1996. "'Gone to Their Second Husbands': Marital Metaphors and Conjugal Contracts on the Gambia's Female Garden Sector." *Canadian Journal of African Studies / Revue canadienne des études africaines* 30 (1): 69–87.

Sennott, Christie, Sangeetha Madhavan, and Youngeun Nam. 2021. "Modernizing Marriage: Balancing the Benefits and Liabilities of Bridewealth in Rural South Africa." *Qualitative Sociology* 44 (7): 55–75.

Setume, S. D. 2017. "Cohabitation in Botswana." PhD diss., Leiden University. http://hdl.handle.net/1887/59499.

Sharma, Kalpana, ed. 2019. *Single by Choice: Happily Unmarried Women!* New York: Women Unlimited.

Sheik, Nafisa Essop. 2014. "African Marriage Regulation and the Remaking of Gendered Authority in Colonial Natal, 1843–1875." *African Studies Review* 57 (2): 73–92.

Shemeikka, Riikka, Veijo Notkola, and Harri Siiskonen. 2005. "Fertility Decline in North-Central Namibia: An Assessment of Fertility in the Period 1960–2000 Based on Parish Registers." *Demographic Research* 13 (4): 83–116.

Siegel, James. 1998 *A New Criminal Type in Jakarta: Counter-Revolution Today.* Durham, NC: Duke University Press.

Singerman, Diane. 2007. "The Economic Imperatives of Marriage: Emerging Practices and Identities among Youth in the Middle East." Middle East Youth Initiative Working Paper 6.

———. 2013. "Youth, Gender, and Dignity in the Egyptian Uprising." *Journal of Middle East Women's Studies* 9 (3): 1–27.

Singh, Parul. 2018. "8 Single Moms of TV Who Proved That They Do Not Need a Man to Raise Their Children." Bollywoodshaadis.com, May 13. https://www.bollywoodshaadis.com /articles/single-mothers-of-indian-television-4044.

Singh, Shiv Sahay, and Indrani Dutta. 2017. "Progress, One Girl at a Time." *The Hindu*, August 5. https://www.thehindu.com/society/progress-one-girl-at-a-time/article19433908.ece.

Sinha, Chinki. 2019. "Brave New Woman." *India Today*, October 11. https://www.indiatoday.in /magazine/cover-story/story/20191021-brave-new-woman-1607809-2019-10-11.

Skeggs, Beverley. 1997. *Formations of Class and Gender: Becoming Respectable.* Thousand Oaks, CA: SAGE.

Slater, Mariam K. 1986. "Foreword: Sons and Levirs." In *Widows in African Societies: Choices and Constraints,* edited by Betty Potash, xv–xxii. Stanford, CA: Stanford University Press.

Smith, Daniel Jordan. 2006. "Love and the Risk of HIV: Courtship, Marriage, and Infidelity in Southeastern Nigeria." In *Modern Loves: The Anthropology of Romantic Courtship and Companionate Marriage,* edited by Jennifer S. Hirsch and Holly Wardlow, 135–155. Ann Arbor: University of Michigan Press.

———. 2009. "Managing Men, Marriage, and Modern Love: Women's Perspectives on Intimacy and Male Infidelity in Southeastern Nigeria." In *Love in Africa,* edited by Jennifer Cole and Lynn M. Thomas. Chicago: University of Chicago Press.

———. 2020. "Masculinity, Money, and the Postponement of Parenthood in Nigeria." *Population and Development Review* 46 (1): 101–120.

Smith, Raymond T. 1988. *Kinship and Class in the West Indies: A Genealogical Study of Jamaica and Guyana.* Cambridge: Cambridge University Press.

———. 1996. *The Matrifocal Family: Power, Pluralism, and Politics.* New York: Routledge.

Smith-Hefner, Nancy J. 2005. "The New Muslim Romance: Changing Patterns of Courtship and Marriage among Educated Javanese Youth." *Journal of Southeast Asian Studies* 36 (3): 441–459.

———. 2019. *Islamizing Intimacies: Youth, Sexuality, and Gender in Contemporary Indonesia.* Honolulu: University of Hawai'i Press.

Solway, Jacqueline. 1989. "Review of *Widows in African Societies: Choices and Constraints.*" *American Anthropologist* 91 (3): 803–804.

———. 2016. "'Slow Marriage,' 'Fast Bogadi': Change and Continuity in Marriage in Botswana." *Anthropology Southern Africa* 39 (4): 309–322.

———. 2017. "The Predicament of Adulthood in Botswana." In *Elusive Adulthoods: The Anthropology of New Maturities,* edited by Deborah Durham and Jacqueline Solway: 39–60. Bloomington: Indiana University Press.

Song, Jesook. 2015. *Living on Your Own: Single Women, Rental Housing, and Post-Revolutionary Affect in Contemporary South Korea.* Albany: State University of New York Press.

Sossou, Marie-Antoinette. 2002. "Widowhood Practices in West Africa: Silent Victims." *International Journal of Social Welfare* 11 (3): 201–209.

Sotoudeh, Ramina, Roger Friedland, and Janet Afary. 2017. "Digital Romance: The Sources of Online Love in the Muslim World." *Media, Culture & Society* 39 (3): 429–439.

Spronk, Rachel. 2009. "Media and the Therapeutic Ethos of Romantic Love in Middle-Class Nairobi." In *Love in Africa,* edited by Jennifer Cole and Lynn M. Thomas. Chicago: University of Chicago Press.

Stack, Carol B. 1970. *All Our Kin.* New York: Basic Books.

Stamp, Patricia. 1991. "Burying Otieno: Politics of Gender and Ethnicity in Kenya." *Signs* 16 (4): 808–845.

Statistics Bureau of Japan. 2015. "Heisei 25 (2015) Jinkōdōtai Tōkei (Kakuteisu) no Gaikyō [Heisei 25 (2015)]. Overview of Demographic Statistics (Finalized Numbers)." Ministry of Health, Labor and Welfare. http://www.mhlw.go.jp/toukei/saikin/hw/jinkou/kakutei15 /index.html.

Statistics Korea. 2021. "Marriage and Divorce Statistics in 2020." March 18, 2021. http://kostat .go.kr/portal/eng/pressReleases/8/11/index.board.

Statistics South Africa. 2012. "Documented Immigrants in South Africa, 2011" (D0351-D). Pretoria: Statistics South Africa.

Steedly, Mary Margaret. 1999. "The State of Culture Theory in the Anthropology of Southeast Asia." *Annual Review of Anthropology* 28: 431–454.

Steyn, Anna F., and Colin M. Rip. 1968. "The Changing Urban Bantu Family." *Journal of Marriage and the Family* 30 (3): 499–517.

Stoler, Ann. 2007. "Affective States." In *A Companion to the Anthropology of Politics*, edited by David Nugent and Joan Vincent, 4–20. Malden, MA: Blackwell.

Stout, Noelle M. 2014. *After Love: Queer Intimacy and Erotic Economies in Post-Soviet Cuba.* Durham, NC: Duke University Press.

Strathern, Marilyn. 2020. *Relations: An Anthropological Account.* Durham, NC: Duke University Press.

Suzuki Seiko. 2019. *Otoko wo Kattemita: Iyashi no Mesoddo* [I tried to purchase a man: A method of healing]. Tokyo: Komakusa Shuppan.

Tafira, K. M. 2014. "The South African Woman and the Immigrant Lover: Myths and Dynamics of Cross-Border Love Relationships in a Post-Apartheid South African Community." *Ufahamu: A Journal of African Studies* 38 (1): 155–176.

Takeyama, Akiko. 2005. "Commodified Romance in a Tokyo Host Club." In *Genders, Transgenders and Sexualities in Japan*, edited by Mark J. McLelland and Romit Dasgupta, 200–215. London: Routledge.

———. 2016. *Staged Seduction: Selling Dreams in a Tokyo Host Club.* Stanford, CA: Stanford University Press.

Tallie, T. J. 2019. "'The Myth Is Dead! Give Us Our History!' Reassessing Black Labor in African History." *American Historical Review* 124 (5): 1758–1768.

Telles, Edward E. 2006. *Race in Another America: The Significance of Skin Color in Brazil.* Princeton, NJ: Princeton University Press.

Tersbøl, Britt P. 2002. "How to Make Sense of Lover Relationships: Kwanyama Culture and Reproductive Health." In *Namibia, Society, Sociology*, edited by Volker Winterfeldt, Tom Fox, and Pempelani Mufune, 347–359. Windhoek: University of Namibia Press.

Thomas, Lynn M., and Jennifer Cole. 2009. "Introduction: Thinking through Love in Africa." In *Love in Africa*, edited by Jennifer Cole and Lynn M. Thomas. Chicago: University of Chicago Press.

Times News Network. 2018. "Courts Still Confused about Legal Age of Marriage?" *Times of India.* https://timesofindia.indiatimes.com/life-style/relationships/love-sex/Courts-still -confused-about-legal-age-of-marriage/articleshow/21333081.cms.

Toma, S. 2017. "Engaging with Its Diaspora: The Case of Senegal." In *Africa and Its Global Diaspora*, edited by J. Mangala. Cham: Palgrave Macmillan.

Topley, Marjorie. 1978. "Marriage Resistance in Rural Kwangtung." In *Studies in Chinese Society*, edited by Arthur P. Wolf, 247–268. Stanford, CA: Stanford University Press.

Tovar, Patricia. 1998. "Review of *Current Widowhood: Myths and Realities*, by Helena Znaniecka Lopata." *Signs* 24 (1): 232–236.

Traister, Rebecca. 2016. *All the Single Ladies: Unmarried Women and the Rise of an Independent Nation.* New York: Simon & Schuster.

Trivedi, Ira. 2014. *India in Love: Marriage and Sexuality in the 21st Century.* New Delhi: Aleph.

Tsing, Anna. 2004. *Friction: An Ethnography of Global Connection.* Princeton, NJ: Princeton University Press.

Tsuji, Rika. 2018. "Sexless Marriage in Japan as Women's Political Resistance." *Feminist Encounters: A Journal of Critical Studies in Culture and Politics* 2 (2).

Twamley, Katherine, and Juhi Sidharth. 2019. "Negotiating Respectability: Comparing the Experiences of Poor and Middle-Class Young Urban Women in India." *Modern Asian Studies* 53 (5): 1646–1674.

Ueno Chizuko. 2009. "'Sekusharitī no Kindai' wo Koete" [Beyond sexual modernity]. In *Nihon no Feminizumu Vol 6 Sekusharitī* [Feminism in Japan vol. 6 sexuality], edited by Masako Amano et al., 1–34. Tokyo: Iwanami Shoten.

UN Department of Economic and Social Affairs. 2011. "Population Facts. World Marriage Patterns." https://www.un.org/en/development/desa/population/publications/pdf/popfacts/PopFacts_2011-1.pdf

UNHCR. 2012. "Global Trends 2012—Displacement: The New 20th Century Challenge." Geneva: United Nations High Commissioner for Refugees.

UN Women. 2019. "Families in a Changing World: Progress of the World's Women 2019–2020." https://www.unwomen.org/-/media/headquarters/attachments/sections/library/publications/2019/progress-of-the-worlds-women-2019-2020-en.pdf?la=en&vs=3512.

———. 2020. "Annual Report 2019–2020: Families: Continuity and Change." https://www.unwomen.org/en/digital-library/publications/2020/06/annual-report-2019-2020.

Upton, Rebecca L. 2001. "'Infertility Makes You Invisible': Gender, Health and the Negotiation of Fertility in Northern Botswana." *Journal of Southern African Studies* 27 (2): 349–362.

Utrata, Jennifer. 2019 "Invisible Labor and Women's Double Binds: Collusive Femininity and Masculine Drinking in Russia." *Gender & Society* 33 (6): 911–934.

Uzelac, Ana. 2018. "Their Country's Global Citizens: Political and Economic Agency of Senegalese Diaspora." *Clingendael Spectator* 4 (72).

van der Vliet, Virginia. 1984. "Staying Single: A Strategy against Poverty?" In *Carnegie Conference Papers*, edited by the Carnegie Inquiry into Poverty and Development in Southern Africa, no. 116. Cape Town: Southern African Labour and Development Research Unit, University of Cape Town.

———. 1991. "Traditional Husbands, Modern Wives? Constructing Marriages in a South African Township." In *Tradition and Transition in Southern Africa: Festschrift for Philip and Iona Mayer*, edited by Andrew D. Spiegel and Patrick A. McAllister, 219–242. Johannesburg: Witwatersrand University Press.

Van de Walle, Dominique. 2013. "Lasting Welfare Effects of Widowhood in Mali." *World Development* 51: 1–19.

van Dijk, Rijk. 2012. "A Ritual Connection: Urban Youth Marrying in the Village." In *The Social Life of Connectivity in Africa*, edited by Mirjam de Bruijn and Rijk van Dijk, 141–159. New York: Palgrave Macmillan.

———. 2017. "The Tent versus *Lobola*: Marriage, Monetary Intimacies and the New Face of Responsibility in Botswana." *Anthropology Southern Africa* 40 (1): 29–41.

Veblen, Thorstein. 1924. *The Theory of the Leisure Class.* London: George Allen and Unwin.

Walker, Liz. 2005. "Men behaving differently: South African men since 1994." *Culture, Health & Sexuality* 7 (3): 225–238.

Walters, Kimberly. 2016a. "The Stickiness of Sex Work: Pleasure, Habit, and Intersubstantiality in South India." *Signs: Journal of Women in Culture and Society* 42 (1): 99–121.

————. 2016b. "Humanitarian Trafficking: The Violence of Rescue and the (Mis)calculation of Rehabilitation." *Economic and Political Weekly* 51 (44–45): 55–61.

Walters, Kimberly, Rakhi Dandona, Lawrence C. Walters, Vemu Lakshmi, Lalit Dandona, and John A. Schneider. 2012. "Wives without Husbands: Gendered Vulnerability to Sexually Transmitted Infections among Previously Married Women in India." *AIDS Care* 24 (9): 1103–1110.

Warren, S. 2015. "A New Apartheid: South Africa's Struggle with Immigration." *Huffington Post*, September 1. http://www.huffingtonpost.com/scott-warren/south-africa-immigration apartheid_ b_8068132.html.

Wekker, Gloria. 2006. *The Politics of Passion: Women's Sexual Culture in the Afro-Surinamese Diaspora*. New York: Columbia University Press.

Welker, Marina. 2014. *Enacting the Corporation: An American Mining Firm in Post-Authoritarian Indonesia*. Berkeley: University of California Press.

Werbner, P., and R. Werbner. 2020. "Adultery Redefined: Changing Decisions of Equity in Customary Law as 'Living Law' in Botswana." *Political and Legal Anthropology Review* 43 (1): 136–152.

Whitehouse, Bruce. 2018. "The Exaggerated Demise of Polygyny: Transformations in Marriage and Gender Relations in West Africa." In *International Handbook on Gender and Demographic Processes*, edited by N. Riley and J. Brunson. Dordrecht: Springer.

Whooley, P. 1975. "Marriage in Africa: A Study of the Ciskei." In *Church and Marriage in Modern Africa*, edited by T. D. Verryn. Pretoria: Ecumenical Research Unit.

Whyte, Susan Reynolds. 1990. "The Widow's Dream: Sex and Death in Western Kenya." In *Personhood and Agency: The Experience of Self and Other in African Cultures*, edited by Michael Jackson and Ivan Karp, 95–114. Washington, DC: Smithsonian Institution Press.

————. 1997. *Questioning Misfortune: The Pragmatics of Uncertainty in Eastern Uganda*. Cambridge: Cambridge University Press.

Williams, Beverly Rosa, Patricia Sawyer, and Richard M. Allman. 2012. "Wearing the Garment of Widowhood: Variations in Time since Spousal Loss among Community-Dwelling Older Adults." *Journal of Women and Aging* 24 (2): 126–139.

Williams, Bianca. 2018. *The Pursuit of Happiness: Black Women, Diasporic Dreams, and the Politics of Emotional Transnationalism*. Durham, NC: Duke University Press.

Williams, Erica Lorraine. 2013. *Sex Tourism in Bahia: Ambiguous Entanglements*. Champaign: University of Illinois Press.

Wilson, Peter. 1973. *Crab Antics: The Social Anthropology of English-Speaking Negro Societies of the Caribbean*. New Haven, CT: Yale University Press.

Woortmann, Klaas. 1987. *A Família das Mulheres*. Rio de Janeiro: Edições Tempo Brasileiro.

World Bank. 2017. "Bilateral Remittances Matrix 2017." http://www.worldbank.org/en/topic/m igrationremittancesdiasporaissues/brief/ migration-remittances-data.

————. 2018. "Bilateral Migration Matrix 2018." http://www.worldbank.org/en/topic/migration remittancesdiasporaissues/brief/migration-remittances-data.

Wyrod, Robert. 2016. *AIDS and Masculinity in the African City Privilege, Inequality, and Modern Manhood*. Berkeley: University of California Press.

Yalom, Marilyn. 2001. *A History of the Wife*. New York: HarperCollins.

Yamashita Etsuko. 1996. *Feminizumu wa Doko e Ittanoka: 'Syufu' Kaitairon kara Shufu Bessei made* [Where has the feminism gone? From discussion of deconstructing "housewives" to the system of wives retaining separate family names]. Tokyo: Yamato Shobo.

Yang, Anand A. 1989. "Whose Sati? Widow Burning in Early 19th Century India." *Journal of Women's History* 1 (2): 8–33.

Yang, Hyunah. 2008. "A Journey of Family Law Reform in Korea: Tradition, Equality, and Social Change." *Journal of Korean Law* 8:77–94.

Yarbrough, Michael. 2015. "South African Marriage in Policy and Practice: A Dynamic Story." *South African Review of Sociology* 46 (4): 5–23.

———. 2017. "Very Long Engagements: The Persistent Authority of Bridewealth in a Post-Apartheid South African Community." *Law & Social Inquiry* 43 (3): 1747–4467.

Zelizer, Viviana. 2005. *The Purchase of Intimacy*. Princeton, NJ: Princeton University Press.

Zia, Ather. 2016. "The Spectacle of a Good Half-Widow: Women in Search of Their Disappeared Men in the Kashmir Valley." *Political and Legal Anthropology Review* 39 (2): 164–175.

Zobel, Joseph. 1980. *Black Shack Alley = La Rue Cases-Nègres*. 1st English ed. Washington, DC: Three Continents Press.

NOTES ON CONTRIBUTORS

JOANNA DAVIDSON is associate professor of anthropology at Boston University. She is the author of *Sacred Rice: An Ethnography of Identity, Environment, and Development in Rural West Africa* and various articles in journals such as *American Ethnologist, African Studies Review*, and *Culture, Agriculture, Food & Environment.*

CARLA FREEMAN is the Goodrich C. White Professor of Women's, Gender, and Sexuality Studies and the executive associate dean of Emory College of Arts and Sciences at Emory University. She is the author of *Entrepreneurial Selves: Neoliberal Respectability and the Making of a Caribbean Middle Class* and *High Tech and High Heels in the Global Economy: Women, Work, and Pink Collar Identities in the Caribbean*, and the editor (with Rachel Heiman and March Liechty) of *Global Middle Classes: Theorizing Through Ethnography.* She has published numerous articles on gender, labor, class, affect, and globalization in such journals as *Cultural Anthropology, American Ethnologist, Signs, Critique of Anthropology,* and *Feminist Studies.*

BRADY G'SELL is assistant professor of gender, women's and sexuality studies at University of Iowa. She has authored articles in journals such as *Signs* and *Africa Today* and is finishing her first book manuscript.

DINAH HANNAFORD is associate professor of anthropology at the University of Houston. She is the author of *Marriage without Borders: Transnational Spouses in Neoliberal Senegal* and the forthcoming *Aid and the Help: International Development and the Transnational Extraction of Care*, as well as various articles in journals such as *African Studies Review, Global Networks,* and *Gender, Work & Organization.*

CARLA JONES is associate professor of anthropology at the University of Colorado Boulder. She has written extensively on middle-class respectability in Indonesia in journals such as *American Ethnologist, American Anthropologist, The Journal of Middle East Women's Studies,* and *CyberOrient,* and is the coeditor, with Ann Marie Leshkowich and Sandra Niessen, of *Re-Orienting Fashion: The Globalization of Asian Dress.*

SARAH LAMB is Barbara Mandel Professor of Humanistic Social Sciences and professor of anthropology and women's, gender, and sexuality studies at Brandeis University. She is the author of numerous articles and books, including her most recent book, *Being Single in India: Stories of Gender, Exclusion, and Possibility.* Lamb is the editor of the Rutgers University Press book series *Global Perspectives on Aging* and of the volume *Successful Aging as a Contemporary Obsession: Global Perspectives.*

MELANIE A. MEDEIROS is associate professor of anthropology at the State University of New York at Geneseo. She is the author of *Marriage, Divorce and Distress in Northeast Brazil: Black Women's Perspectives on Love, Respect, and Kinship* (Rutgers University Press) and articles in journals such as *Latin American Research Review, Human Organization, Transforming Anthropology, Culture, Agriculture, Food & Environment,* and *Practicing Anthropology,* as well as the coeditor of the forthcoming volume *Insights on Latin America and the Caribbean.*

LAURA C. NELSON is associate professor of gender and women's studies at the University of California, Berkeley. Her first project in South Korea, *Measured Excess: Gender, Status, and Consumer Nationalism in South Korea,* highlighted the gendered importance of the consumption sector to the South Korean development agenda. Her current projects focus on gender, stress, and breast cancer in South Korea, and on the experiences of South Koreans who slipped past compulsory marriage in the mid-twentieth century.

JULIA PAULI is professor of social and cultural anthropology at the University of Hamburg, Germany. She is author of *The Decline of Marriage in Namibia* and various articles in journals such as *American Ethnologist, Anthropology & Aging, Africa* and *Africa Today.*

JACQUELINE SOLWAY is professor emeritus of the International Development Studies and Anthropology Departments at Trent University and affiliate of African Studies, University of Toronto. She has edited the volumes *The Politics of Egalitarianism* and *Elusive Adulthoods* (with Deborah Durham) and published articles in journals such as *Current Anthropology, Development and Change, Africa, HAU,* and *Journal of Anthropological Research.*

AKIKO TAKEYAMA is associate professor of women, gender, and sexuality studies and director of the Center for East Asian Studies at the University of Kansas. She is president-elect/president of the Association for Feminist Anthropology (2021–2025) and the author of *Staged Seduction: Selling Dreams in a Tokyo Host Club* and *Involuntary Consent: The Illusion of Choice in Japan's Adult Video Industry* (forthcoming).

KIMBERLY WALTERS is associate professor of international studies at California State University, Long Beach. Her work has appeared in *Anthropological Quarterly, Signs, Economic & Political Weekly,* and *AIDS Care* and her book project is entitled *Rescued from Rights: Sex Work, Trafficking, and the Humanitarian State in India.*

INDEX

Page numbers in *italics* represent figures and tables, respectively.

Available titles in The Politics of Marriage and Gender: Global Issues in Local Contexts series: